GCSE
SPANISH

Terry Murray
Head of Modern Languages;
Chief Examiner

Letts
EDUCATIONAL

Letts Educational
Aldine Place
London W12 8AW
Tel: 0208 740 2266
Fax: 0208 743 8451
e-mail: mail@lettsed.co.uk

First published 1995
Revised 1997
Reprinted 1998, 1999 (twice), 2000

British Library Cataloguing in Publication Data
A CIP record for this book is available from the British Library.

ISBN 1 85805 443 5 (Book only)
ISBN 1 85805 442 5 (With CD)

Acknowledgements
The useful IT vocabulary on pages 84–85 is taken from *Modern Languages, Information File No. 1* published in 1990 by the National Council for Educational Technology (NCET) and is reproduced here with the permission of the publishers.

The author would like to thank Edexcel (formerly ULEAC), the Midland Examining Group, the Northern Examinations and Assessment Board, and the Welsh Joint Education Committee for their permission to use questions from past papers.

The answers supplied to Exam Board questions are solely the responsibility of the authors, and are not supplied or approved by the Exam Boards.

The author would like to thank his wife, Rhoda, and children, Catherine, Clare, Michael and Elizabeth for their continuing support and encouragement.

Printed in Great Britain by Bath Press Colourbooks, Glasgow

Letts Educational Ltd, a division of Granada Learning Ltd. Part of the Granada Media Group.

Contents

Examination practice

Introduction

This book has been written to help you revise for the GCSE examination in Spanish. The key to success in these examinations lies in your ability to convince the examiner that you have mastered the four basic skills which all the Examining Groups test in one form or another. The skills are listening and reading comprehension, speaking and writing Spanish.

How to use this book

The first thing you need to find out before you plan your revision programme is exactly what will be expected of you in the examination itself. The analysis of the syllabuses of each of the Examining Groups on pages 6–16 will help you do this. If you are a mature student it can be used to give you guidance on which Group's examination will suit you best. The analysis and summary of the Groups' requirements indicate the emphasis each Group gives to the different skills and how they are tested. You should concentrate on the types of question your Group sets and ensure that you are given the fullest possible information about the grammar and vocabulary which your particular Group expects you to have studied. The syllabus content of each Examining Group is on pages 6–16.

Success at GCSE in Spanish means having a good knowledge of vocabulary and the grammar of the language. This is not a text book or a vocabulary book, but if you use it wisely as an aid to revision and in conjunction with your course books and specimen examination materials, there should not be any difficulty in achieving success in your Examining Group's tests. This book assumes that you have studied Spanish for at least two years. You should work systematically through the grammar sections and follow the advice and hints on how to tackle the tests which you will be expected to take in your examination. Finally, you can practise the types of question which you will have to do. We recommend that you use this book in conjunction with the accompanying audio support. If you do not have a copy of the CD, or have a CD but would prefer a cassette, please complete and return the order form at the back of the book.

Remember, there is a good deal of distilled experience and advice contained in the hints on examination technique. So if you know your vocabulary, you know your grammar and you follow the advice given and improve your examination technique you should find that the reward for your efforts will be the success you are anxious to achieve.

Enjoy your revision and good luck in your Spanish examinations.

About the exam

- You will have to do four exams, Listening, Speaking, Reading and Writing, except in Scotland where there is no Writing exam.
- Each of the four exams carries equal weighting, i.e. 25% per exam. (In Scotland there is 50% for Speaking, 25% for Listening and 25% for Reading. See pages 6–16 for further details.)
- Your teacher will administer your Speaking exam.

- There is a coursework alternative for the Writing exam in most Boards. Check with your teacher: ask if you are doing the coursework or the terminal exam.
- Some Boards offer a coursework alternative for Speaking. Check with your teacher.
- If your Board is SEG you will be doing a modular course and different rules apply. See the Analysis of Syllabuses section for more information.
- Nearly all the questions and rubrics (the instructions at the beginning of the question) will be in Spanish and you will have to answer in Spanish.
- If you are answering a question in Spanish in the Listening or Reading exam and you make a mistake, the mistake will not be penalised unless it makes your meaning unclear.
- About 20% of the questions in the Listening and Reading exams will be in English and you have to answer these in English.
- In the role-play part of your Speaking exam the scene-setting will be in English.
- In some parts of the exams you can use a dictionary. See the Analysis of Syllabuses section to find the rules for your Board, and study the section on 'using a dictionary' on page 5 to help you to make the most of this opportunity. Electronic dictionaries are not permitted.
- In both the Foundation Tier and the Higher Tier for each exam there is what is called *overlapping material.* This means that the questions at the end of the Foundation Tier are *identical* to the questions at the beginning of the Higher Tier.
- In Scotland there are three levels of entry known as Foundation, General and Credit Levels. It is quite normal for you to attempt the papers at two adjacent levels. They will be graded separately and you will be awarded the better of the two sets of grades.
- You need to find out from your teacher whether you are doing the *full course* or the *short course.* If you are doing the full course you will study all five *Areas of Experience.* If you study the short course you will study only two of the five *Areas of Experience* (see page 16). In Scotland there is no short course option.

Grading

You will be graded on the 8-point scale of A★, A, B, C, D, E, F, G.

After your answers are marked, your work will be awarded a number of points depending on how good your work was. There are 8 points available for each skill or component. The points you score for each component are added up and the total number of points decides what grade you get.

This is the scale that all Boards use:

Points per component	Grade	Scale
8	A★	30-32
7	A	26-29
6	B	22-25
5	C	18-21
4	D	14-17
3	E	10-13
2	F	6-9
1	G	2-5
0	U	0-1

- In Scotland there are six grades numbered 1 to 6, with grade 7 being reserved for those who complete the course but fail to meet the grade criteria for any level.

Tiering

- For each skill (listening, speaking, reading and writing) there are two possible levels of entry.
- These levels of entry are called the Foundation Tier and the Higher Tier.
- Foundation Tier will assess Grades C–G.
- Higher Tier will assess Grades A★–D.
- You must enter for all four skills (listening, speaking, reading and writing).
- You may enter either the same tier for all four skills or you may mix your tiers.
- You cannot enter for both Foundation Tier and Higher Tier for the same skill.
- In Scotland there are three entry levels and two grades are assessed at each level.

Foundation Level	(in any of the three areas of assessment) – grades assessed 5 & 6
General Level	(in any of the three areas of assessment) – grades assessed 4 & 3
Credit Level	(in any of the three areas of assessment) – grades assessed 2 & 1

If you are entered for the optional Writing examination in either of the two upper levels the grades assessed are the same as shown above. The following table is a helpful guide to the papers which you are advised to attempt:

Expected External Grade	*Papers/Levels*	*Grades Assessed*
7, 6	Foundation	6, 5
5, 4	Foundation and General	6, 5, 4, 3
3, 2, 1	General and Credit	4, 3, 2, 1

Areas of Experience

These are the topic areas that you will study for your GCSE. These topics have been laid down by the government and all the Exam Boards have to follow them. They are listed below as Areas A–E.

If you do a *full course* you have to cover them all. If you do a *short course* in Years 10 and 11, then you study one of Areas A, B or C and in addition Area D or E, making a total of *two* to be studied for the short course.

A Everyday activities
This should include:
- the language of the classroom
- home life and school
- food, health and fitness

B Personal and social life
This should include:
- self, family and personal relationships
- free time and social activities
- holidays and special occasions

C The world around us
This should include:
- home town and local area
- the natural and made environment
- people, places and customs

D The world of work
This should include:
- further education and training
- careers and employment
- language and communication in the workplace

E The international world
This should include:
- travel at home and abroad
- life in other countries and communities
- world events and issues

Examination rubrics

Rubrics are the instructions at the beginning of a question in any of the papers which tell you what you are expected to do. They will usually be in Spanish.

Ahora...
Now...
Algunas preguntas/frases etc.
Some questions/sentences etc.
Busca las palabras/frases etc.
Find the words/sentences etc.
Contesta a la pregunta de...
Answer ...'s question.
Contesta a las preguntas.
Answer the questions.
Contesta a todas las preguntas.
Answer all the questions.
Contesta en español o *pon* una señal (√) en las casillas
Answer in Spanish or tick the boxes
Da la vuelta
Turn over
Da las gracias...
Thank...
Decide cómo...
Decide how...
Describe...
Describe...
Di...
Say...
Dile lo que has...
Tell him/her what you have...
Ejemplo
Example
Empareja...
Match up...
En cifras
In numbers
En español
In Spanish
En inglés
In English
Entre dos personas
Between two people
Escoge la descripción que corresponde mejor...
Choose the description that best fits...

Escribe...
Write...
...una lista/una postal/una carta/un artículo/un reportaje/las cosas etc.
...a list/a postcard/a letter/an article/a report/the things etc.
Escribe la letra/el número...
Write the letter/number...
Escribe la letra que corresponde...
Write the letter which corresponds/matches...
Escribe las respuestas...
Write the answers...
Escribe unas ... palabras.
Write about ... words.
Escucha atentamente...
Listen carefully ...
Está hablando con ...
She is talking to ...
Estás enviando...
You are sending...
Estás oyendo ...
You are listening to ...
Explica...
Explain...
Falso
False
Habla/escribe sobre/de...
He/She is talking/writing about...
Habrá dos pausas durante el anuncio/extracto.
There will be two pauses during the advert/extract.
Haz unos apuntes
Make notes
He aquí
Here is
... una lista/alguna información/una postal/una carta/unos anuncios/un texto/un extracto
... a list/some information/a postcard/a letter/some adverts/a text/an extract
de un periódico/una revista etc.
from a newspaper/magazine etc.
He aquí lo que tienes que pedir o decir y lo que tienes que preguntar.
This is what you must ask for or say and what you must ask.
Incluye la siguiente información.
Include the following information.
Indica sí o no
Indicate yes or no
Las respuestas siguientes
The following answers
Lee atentamente...
Read carefully...
Lee las preguntas/la lista etc.
Read the questions/the list etc.
Mira los apuntes/los dibujos etc.
Look at the notes/drawings etc.
No necesitarás todas las letras
You will not need all the letters
Para cada pregunta/persona/cliente etc.
For each question/person/customer etc.
Pon un señal (√) en la casilla correcta
Tick the appropriate box
Pon una señal (√) al lado de sólo 5 letras/casillas
Tick only 5 letters/boxes
Pregúntale lo que...
Ask what...
Preséntate.
Introduce yourself.
Primero...
First...
Rellena el formulario.
Fill in the form.
Rellena los blancos.
Fill in the blanks.
Saluda...
Greet...
Si la frase/afirmación es verdad, pon una señal (√) en la casilla Verdadero
If the sentence/statement is correct, tick the true box
Vas a oír ...
You are going to hear ...
... un mensaje/una conversación/un diálogo/un programa/un reportaje en la radio/un interviú en la televisión etc.
...a message/conversation/dialogue/programme/report/account on the radio/interview on television etc.
Vas a oír la conversación dos veces.
You are going to hear the conversation twice.
Verdadero
True

Question types

For the Listening and Responding and the Reading and Responding, there are a number of question types that you need to understand.
There may be:

1 Multiple-choice questions. An example is question 3 on page 136.
2 True/false questions. An example is question 7 on page 140.
3 Grid completion. An example is question 22 on page 154.
4 Matching (you have to tick correct box or write appropriate letter). An example is question 20 on page 152.
5 Note completion. An example is question 19 on page 152.

Using a dictionary

In some parts of the exam you will be allowed to use a dictionary. (To find out which parts, look at the Analysis of syllabuses section in this book.) In theory this should make the exams easier. In practice, as many candidates will lose marks through mis-use of the dictionary as candidates who gain marks through proper use of the dictionary.

- Mis-use of the dictionary can lead to mistakes.
- Over-use of the dictionary can lead to a serious loss of time.

Six rules for the use of a dictionary

1. Get familiar with your dictionary.
   - You will see that one half is target language to English and the other half is English to target language.
   - Use a marker pen on the edge of the pages to mark off the first half. Then you won't waste time looking in the wrong half.
   - Use the words in bold at the top of the page to find an entry.
   - Spend time looking at how each entry is laid out so that you understand that words have different meanings and that each meaning is dealt with in turn.
2. Do not bother looking up words which you do not need to answer the question. Stick to the *key* words.
3. Work out how long it takes you on average in seconds to find a word. Then work out for each of your exams how many words you will have time *realistically* to look up in the exam without spoiling your chances of getting the answers down.
4. Do your exam with little or no help from the dictionary and *then* at the end of the exam use the dictionary with the time left.
5. In the Speaking and Writing exams use language that you know to be correct rather than trying to create something new with the help of the dictionary. You won't have time.
6. Learn the list of abbreviations in your dictionary.

Below is an example of what entries on a page in a dictionary might look like.

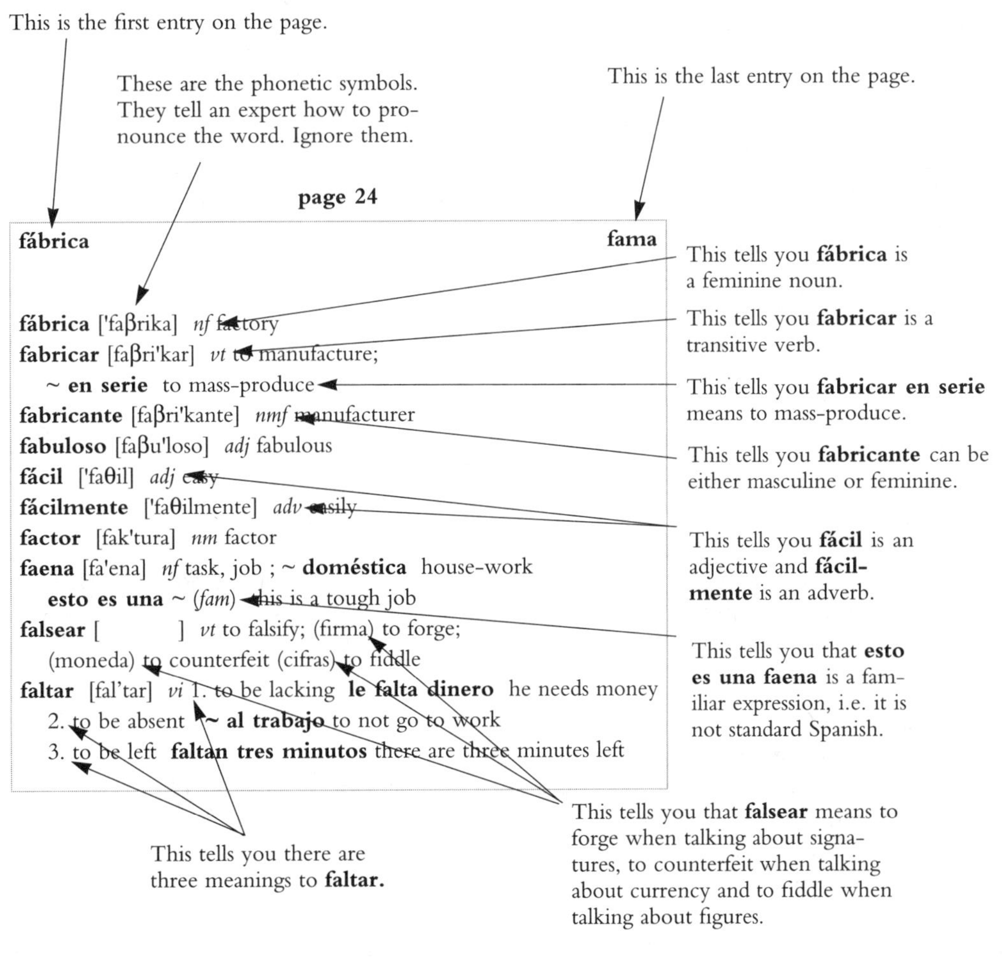

Syllabus analysis

The following table lists all of the topics you will need to revise for your Spanish GCSE course, no matter which syllabus you are studying. It has spaces for you to write notes in and fill in work dates, and it has a tick column for indicating finished topics so that you can easily see what you still have to do.

Topic	Covered in Unit No	Target finish date	Notes	✔
Foundation Tier				
Grammar	1.1–3.26			
Vocabulary	4.1–4.8			
Listening	5.1–5.6			
Speaking	6.1–6.7, 6.9			
Reading	7.1–7.5			
Writing	8.1–8.6			
Higher Tier				
Grammar	1.1–3.26			
Vocabulary	4.1–4.8			
Listening	5.7–5.11			
Speaking	6.1–6.8, 6.10–6.11			
Reading	7.1–7.3, 7.6–7.7			
Writing	8.1–8.2, 8.7–8.14			

Specific details for each syllabus are given on the following pages.

Edexcel Foundation (incorporating London Examinations)

Address: Stewart House, 32 Russell Square, London, WC1B 5DN Tel: 0171 331 4000

Listening and responding

- Dictionaries are *not* allowed.
- You have to listen to a cassette recorded by native speakers. You will hear everything at least *twice*.
- Your teacher will stop the cassette to allow you time to write your answers.
- The questions will require non-verbal responses (i.e. ticking boxes), target-language answers or answers in English.
- About 20% of the questions will be answered in English. These will usually be at the end of the tests.

Foundation Tier

The test will last approximately 25 minutes.

- You will have to understand instructions, announcements, telephone messages, short narratives, advertisements, news items.
- For Grades E, F and G you will have to identify main points and extract specific details.
- For Grades C and D you will have to identify points of view and understand references to the past, present and future.

Higher Tier

The test will last approximately 35 minutes.

- You will have to do some of the harder Foundation Tier questions.
- You will hear radio broadcasts, discussions, presentations and interviews.
- You will have to identify points of view, understand references to the past, present and future, recognise attitudes and emotions and be able to draw conclusions.

Speaking

You must choose between the Coursework Option and the Terminal Exam Option.

Terminal Exam Option

The test will be recorded by your teacher.

- You may use a dictionary during the preparation time.
- Whether you do Foundation or Higher Tier, you do two role-plays and two conversations.
- The role-plays will either be in the form of instructions in English with pictures to guide you, or prompts in the target language.
- The two conversations will be chosen from this list. You choose the first one; your teacher chooses the second one: shopping; school/college and future plans; friends; food and meals; leisure and entertainment; the world of work; holidays; local area; home and family; daily routine at home, school and work; special occasions; pocket money.

Foundation Tier

The test will last 8–9 minutes

- Role-play A will be simple. Role-play B will have some unpredictability.
- In the conversations, if you want to get Grades C or D you will have to be able to refer to the past, present and the future and be able to express personal opinions.

Higher Tier

The test will last 11–12 minutes

- Role-play B will have some unpredictability. Role-play C will have even more unpredictability. It will be marked for communication *and* quality of language.
- In the conversations you will have to produce longer sequences of speech and use a variety of structures and vocabulary in order to express ideas and justify points of view.

Coursework Option

Your teacher has details of what you must do.

- You must submit three units of work.
- Each unit must have a transaction and a conversation element.
- One of the units must be from Areas of Experience D or E.
- The work must be completed by the end of the first week in May of Year 11.
- Your work will be marked by the teacher and moderated by the Board.

Reading and Responding

- You may use a dictionary.
- 20% of the questions will be in English and require an answer in English.
- The English questions will usually come at the end of the tests.

Foundation Tier

The test will last 30 minutes

- The materials will be signs, notices, adverts, messages, letters, leaflets, newspaper and magazine extracts.
- You will have to identify main points and extract specific detail.
- For Grades C and D you will have to identify points of view, understand unfamiliar language and understand references to past, present and future events.

Higher Tier

The test will last 50 minutes

- You will do the harder questions from the Foundation Tier.
- The texts will be longer than in the Foundation Tier.
- You will have to identify points of view, understand unfamiliar language, understand references to past, present and future events, recognise attitudes and emotions, and be able to draw inferences and conclusions.

Writing

You must choose between the Coursework Option and the Terminal Exam Option.

Terminal Exam Option

You will have the use of a dictionary throughout.

Foundation Tier

The test will last 30 minutes. You have to do *three* tasks:

1 Write a list, e.g. a shopping list.
2 Write a message or a postcard of about 30 words.
3 Write about 70 words, e.g. a letter.

Higher Tier

The test will last 50 minutes. You have to do *two* tasks:

1 Task 3 from the Foundation Tier
2 Write about 150 words, e.g. a narrative or a letter.

Coursework Option

You have to submit three pieces of work. Your teacher has full details of how to approach these.

- They must be from three different Areas of Experience – one must be from Areas of Experience C or D.
- They can be a collection of short pieces or a single piece of writing.
- For Grades D–G submit at least 250–350 words in total.
- For Grades A*–C submit at least 500–600 words.
- Your teacher may guide you but cannot correct your work in detail before it is submitted.
- Coursework must be submitted by the end of the first week in May of Year 11.
- Your teacher will mark your work and it will be moderated by the Board.

Midland Examining Group (MEG)

Address: 1 Hills Road, Cambridge, CB1 2EU Tel: 01223 553311

Listening and Responding

The test will last approximately 40 minutes.

- Dictionaries are *not* allowed.
- You will listen to a cassette recorded by native speakers. You will hear everything at least twice.
- The questions will require non-verbal responses (i.e. ticking boxes), target-language answers or answers in English.
- About 20% of the questions will be answered in English. These will be the first one in the Foundation Tier and one of the last ones in the Higher Tier.

Foundation Tier

- You attempt Sections 1 and 2 of the paper.
- You will have to understand instructions, announcements, telephone messages, short narratives, advertisements, news items.
- For Grades E, F and G you will have to identify main points and extract specific details.
- For Grades C and D you will have to identify points of view and understand references to the past, present and future.

Higher Tier

- You will have to do some of the harder Foundation Tier questions, i.e. you attempt Sections 2 and 3 of the paper.
- You will hear radio broadcasts, discussions, presentations and interviews.
- You will have to identify points of view, understand references to the past, present and future, recognise attitudes and emotions and be able to draw conclusions.

Speaking

The test will last 10–12 minutes. It will be recorded by your teacher.

- You may use a dictionary during the preparation period.
- Whether you do Foundation or Higher Tier, you have to do two role-plays, make a presentation and take part in a conversation.

- The role-plays will either be in the form of instructions in English with pictures to guide you, or prompts in the target language.
- The Presentation means that you have to prepare a topic of your choice chosen from the Areas of Experience. In the exam you talk for one minute on your topic and then you discuss your topic more freely with the teacher. You may bring a cue-card with up to five short headings into the exam to help you remember what to say. You may use illustrative materials for your presentation. You must not use written notes.
- General Conversation means that the examiner (your teacher) will lead you into a conversation on *three* topics, drawn from the Areas of Experience, such as life at home and at school, holidays, friends, opinions. You will not know the titles of the topics before the exam. You cannot use the same topic for your presentation and your conversation. Your teacher will ensure that this does not happen. The more you say, the more accurate your language is, the more complex your language is, the higher your score.
- Your exam will be recorded on cassette. Either your teacher will mark it and send it away to the Board for moderation or he/she will send it off for external marking.

Foundation Tier

- Role-play A will be simple. Role-play B will have some unpredictability.
- In the Presentation and Conversation, if you want to get Grade C you will have to be able to refer to the past, present and the future and to be able to express personal opinions.

Higher Tier

- Role-play B will have some unpredictability. Role-play C will require you to act as a story-teller, relating an incident that happened in the past. You must develop the incident in your own way. It will be marked for communication *and* quality of language.
- In the Presentation and Conversation you will have to produce longer sequences of speech and use a greater variety of structures and vocabulary in order to express ideas and justify points of view.

Reading and Responding

The test will last 50 minutes.

- You may use a dictionary.
- 20% of the questions will be in English and require an answer in English. These will be at the beginning of the Foundation Tier and near the end of the Higher Tier.

Foundation Tier

- The materials will be signs, adverts, messages, letters, leaflets, newspaper and magazine extracts.
- You will have to identify main points and extract specific detail.
- For Grades C and D you will have to identify points of view, understand unfamiliar language and understand references to past, present and future events.

Higher Tier

- You will do the harder questions from the Foundation Tier.
- The texts will be longer than at Foundation Tier.
- You will have to identify points of view, understand unfamiliar language, understand references to past, present and future events, recognise attitudes and emotions, and be able to draw inferences and conclusions.

Writing

You must choose between the Coursework Option and the Terminal Exam Option.

Terminal Exam Option

The test will last 50 minutes. You will have the use of a dictionary throughout.

Foundation Tier

You have to do *four* tasks:

1–2 Single-word tasks, e.g. form-filling, writing a list.

3 A message or postcard of about 40 words.

4 A text of about 100 words, e.g. a letter. You will have a choice of two.

Higher Tier

You have to do *two* tasks:

1 Task 4 from the Foundation Tier.

2 Write a composition of about 150 words. It could be a report on something you have experienced. You will have a choice of two.

Coursework Option

You have to submit three pieces of work. Your teacher has full details of how to approach these.

- For Grades E, F and G the pieces should be about 40 words, e.g. design a poster, complete a booking form.
- For Grades C and D the pieces should be about 100 words, e.g. an article or a letter.
- For Grades A* to C the pieces should be about 150 words, e.g. tell the story of a film, an account of an adventure or an experience.

Northern Examinations and Assessment Board (NEAB)

Address: 12 Harter Street, Manchester, M1 6HL Tel: 0161 953 1180

Listening and Responding

- Dictionaries are only allowed during the five-minute reading time at the beginning and the five-minute checking time at the end.
- You have to listen to a cassette recorded by native speakers. You will hear everything twice.
- Your teacher will stop the cassette to allow you time to write your answers.
- The questions will require non-verbal responses (i.e. ticking boxes), target-language answers or answers in English.
- About 20% of the questions will be answered in English.

Foundation Tier

The test will last approximately 30 minutes

- You will have to understand instructions, announcements, telephone messages, short narratives, advertisements, news items.
- For Grades E, F and G you will have to identify main points and extract specific details.
- For Grades C and D you will have to identify points of view and understand references to the past, present and future.

Higher Tier

The test will last approximately 40 minutes

- You will have to do some of the harder Foundation Tier questions.
- You will hear radio broadcasts, discussions, presentations and interviews.
- You will have to identify points of view, understand references to the past, present and future, recognise attitudes and emotions and be able to draw conclusions.

Speaking

The test will be recorded by your teacher.

- You will be given ten minutes preparation time during which you can use a dictionary. You can also make notes. You can take the notes with you into the exam but not the dictionary.
- Whether you do Foundation or Higher Tier, you do two role-plays, a presentation followed by a discussion, and then a general conversation.
- The role plays will either be in the form of instructions in English with pictures to guide you, or prompts in the target language
- You prepare your presentation before the exam. You have to provide a stimulus, e.g. a book, an article, a poster. Then you talk about your stimulus and your teacher will ask you questions.
- You will have a conversation on at least two, or at most three of the following topics: education and career; self and others; home and abroad; home and daily routine; leisure; holidays and travel.

You will not know which of the topics you will have to talk about until the day of the exam.

Foundation Tier

The test will last 8–10 minutes.

- Role-play A will be simple. Role-play B will have some unpredictability.
- In the conversations, if you want to get Grades C or D you will have to be able to refer to the past, present and the future and to be able to express personal opinions.

Higher Tier

The test will last 10–12 minutes.

- Role-play B will have some unpredictability. Role-play C will have even more unpredictability. It will be marked for communication *and* quality of language

- In the conversations you will have to produce longer sequences of speech and use a variety of structures and vocabulary in order to express ideas and justify points of view.

Reading and Responding

- You may use a dictionary.
- 20% of the questions will be in English and require an answer in English. These will be at the beginning of the Foundation Tier and near the end of the Higher Tier.

Foundation Tier

The test will last 30 minutes.

- The materials will be signs, notices, advertisements, messages, letters, leaflets, newspaper and magazine extracts.
- You will have to identify main points and extract specific detail.
- For Grades C and D you will have to identify points of view, understand unfamiliar language and understand references to past, present and future events.

Higher Tier

The test will last 50 minutes.

- You will do the harder questions from the Foundation Tier.
- The texts will be longer than at Foundation Tier.
- You will have to identify points of view, understand unfamiliar language, understand references to past, present and future events, recognise attitudes and emotions, and be able to draw inferences and conclusions.

Writing

You must choose between the Coursework Option and the Terminal Exam Option.

Terminal Exam Option

- You can use a dictionary throughout.
- Provided the tasks are completed the number of words is not important. The Board, however, does suggest numbers of words for the more difficult questions.

Foundation Tier

The test will last 40 minutes. You have to do *three* tasks:

1. A short list or a form to be completed.
2. A message or postcard or text for a poster. (**1** and **2** should require a total of about 40 words.)
3. A letter (approximately 90 words) in which you must use different tenses if you want to get a Grade C.

Higher Tier

The test will last 60 minutes. You have to do *two* tasks:

1. Task 3 from the Foundation Tier.
2. A text of about 120 words, e.g. an article, a letter, publicity material.

Coursework Option

- You must submit three assignments drawn from a list of about 60: your teacher has a copy of the list.
- Your assignments must cover at least three of the Areas of Experience.
- If you are a Foundation Tier candidate your assignments should total 200–300 words.
- If you are a Higher Tier candidate your assignments should total 300–500 words.
- To get a C or above you must use past, present and future tenses and express personal opinions.

Northern Ireland Council for the Curriculum Examinations and Assessment (NICCEA)

Address: Clarendon Dock, 29 Clarendon Road, Belfast, BT1 3BG Tel: 01232 261200

Listening and Responding

The test will last 30 minutes.

- Dictionaries are *not* allowed.

- You have to listen to a cassette recorded by native speakers. You will hear everything twice.
- The questions will require non-verbal responses (i.e. ticking boxes), target-language answers or answers in English.
- About 20% of the questions will be answered in English.

Foundation Tier

- You will have to understand instructions, announcements, telephone messages, short narratives, advertisements, news items.
- For Grades E, F and G you will have to identify main points and extract specific details.
- For Grades C and D you will have to identify points of view and understand references to the past, present and future.

Higher Tier

- You will have to do some of the harder Foundation Tier questions.
- You will hear radio broadcasts, discussions, presentations and interviews.
- You will have to identify points of view, understand references to the past, present and future, recognise attitudes and emotions and be able to draw conclusions.

Speaking

The test will last 30 minutes. It will be recorded by your teacher.

- You can use a dictionary only in the ten-minute preparation time.
- Whether you do Foundation or Higher Tier, you will do role-plays and a general conversation.
- The role-plays will either be in the form of instructions in English with pictures to guide you, or prompts in the target language.

Foundation Tier

- Role-play A will be simple. Role-play B will have some unpredictability.
- In the conversations, if you want to get Grades C or D you will have to be able to refer to the past, present and the future and to be able to express personal opinions.

Higher Tier

- Role-play B will have some unpredictability. Role-play C will have even more unpredictability. It will be marked for communication *and* quality of language.
- In the conversations you will have to produce longer sequences of speech and use a variety of structures and vocabulary in order to express ideas and justify points of view.

Reading and Responding

The test will last 40 minutes.

- You may use a dictionary.
- 20% of the questions will be in English and require an answer in English. These will be at the beginning of the Foundation Tier and near the end of the Higher Tier.

Foundation Tier

- The materials will be signs, notices, advertisements, messages, letters, leaflets, newspaper and magazine extracts.
- You will have to identify main points and extract specific detail.
- For Grades C and D you will have to identify points of view, understand unfamiliar language and understand references to past, present and future events.

Higher Tier

- You will do the harder questions from the Foundation Tier.
- The texts will be longer than at Foundation Tier.
- You will have to identify points of view, understand unfamiliar language, understand references to past, present and future events, recognise attitudes and emotions, and be able to draw inferences and conclusions.

Writing

The test will last 45 minutes.

- You can use a dictionary throughout.
- Provided the tasks are completed the number of words is not important. The Board however does suggest numbers of words for the more difficult questions.

Foundation Tier

- You may have to complete forms, produce lists, write notes or cards.
- You will have to write a text, such as a letter.
- There will be about 120 words in total.

Higher Tier
You have to do two tasks:
- The text or letter from the Foundation Tier.
- A longer text, e.g. a letter, report or account.

Scottish Qualifications Authority (formerly SEB)

Address: Ironmills Road, Dalkeith, Midlothian, EH22 1LE Tel: 0131 663 6601

In Scotland the exam is called Standard Grade. In England there are two Tiers; in Scotland there are three Levels: Foundation, General and Credit. Candidates may attempt Listening and Reading papers in two adjacent levels: Foundation and General or General and Credit.

Listening

This counts for 25% of your mark.
- Dictionaries are not allowed.
- There will be three separate papers, one at each level.
- Material will be presented on tape and heard twice.
- Questions will be set in English, to be answered in English.
- There will be a progression in difficulty across the three levels.
- The items in each paper will be connected thematically, the theme will be stated in English.
- Responses expected from candidates will vary from a few words to a detailed answer. No long answers will be expected at Foundation Level.

Speaking

This counts for 50% of your mark.
- Dictionaries are not allowed.
- There will be no end of course examination – assessments will be made throughout your course and recorded on tape.
- These assessments will be made by your teacher, but in March each year a Moderator will visit the school to assess the candidates' performance based on a Speaking activity set by the Board.
- Speaking activities can be wide ranging – a sample will be used for moderation purposes and these will involve a face-to-face conversation with your teacher lasting ten minutes.

Reading

This counts for 25% of your mark.
- You may use a dictionary in all three levels.
- Questions will be set in English to be answered in English at all three levels.
- Questions will require general or detailed responses and there will be a progression in difficulty and in length from Foundation to Credit Level.
- Responses expected will vary from a few words to a detailed answer across the levels.
- Items within each paper will be connected by a thematic development which will be stated in English.

Writing

- This is an optional paper and can only be taken at General or Credit Level. Success in this paper will be recorded on the certificate but will not contribute to the overall grade awarded.
- Dictionaries are allowed at both levels.
- At General Level you will be asked to write a number of short simple messages in Spanish.
- At Credit Level you will be required to respond to a passage, or passages in Spanish by writing an answer of about 200 words in Spanish, expressing your views coherently.

Southern Examining Group (SEG) Modular

Address: Stag Hill House, Guildford, GU2 5XJ Tel: 01483506506

This course is divided into four modules. Each module will last about 15 weeks.

Module 1

Title: Contact with a Spanish-speaking country.
When assessed: February of Year 10.
The three tests: Listening, Speaking and Reading. Each counts for 5% of your final mark.
Listening: You listen to a cassette recorded by native speakers. You will hear the material up to three times. You answer questions mostly in the target language, but some of the questions will be non-verbal (e.g. box-ticking) or in English. Dictionaries are not allowed.
Speaking: You must produce a short tape-recorded monologue. Your teacher will help you with choosing a title. You can use a dictionary when preparing it, but not when actually recording it. You can use prompts, but you cannot read aloud from a prepared script.
Reading: You have to do a variety of reading tests and you may use a dictionary.

Module 2

Title: Organising a visit to a Spanish-speaking country.
When assessed: June of Year 10.
The two tests: Listening and Reading. Each counts for 10% of your final mark.
Listening: You listen to a cassette recorded by native speakers and answer the questions in an examination booklet. You may not use a dictionary. You will hear each item twice.
Reading: You have to do a variety of reading tests and you may use a dictionary.

Module 3

Title: Holidays and travel.
When assessed: Through coursework during the autumn term of Year 11.
There are two skills tested: Speaking (5%) and Writing (10%).
Speaking: As for Module 1.
Writing: You have to produce two pieces of written work as coursework. It is not a test. You are allowed to draft and re-draft. Use IT if you want.
Foundation Tier
(a) One piece of writing of about 30 words, for example a postcard, message or form.
(b) One piece of writing of 100–120 words, for example a letter or a response to a questionnaire.
Higher Tier
Two pieces of writing, of different types, of 100–120 words. They may be for example formal or informal letters, articles or reports.

Module 4: External exam

This takes place in the normal summer examination period of Year 11. There are four exams:
Speaking (15%)
One role-play and one conversation. You have five minutes (*Foundation*) or eight minutes (*Higher*) preparation time during which you can use a dictionary, but you may not make notes.
Listening (10%)
As for Module 2.
Reading (10%)
As for Module 2.
Writing (15%)
You have to produce one piece of written work. You may use a dictionary.
Foundation Tier
One piece of writing of about 80 words, e.g. a response to a questionnaire or a letter.
Higher Tier
One piece of writing of about 120 words, e.g. a response to a letter, an article or a report.

Welsh Joint Education Committee (WJEC)

Address: 245 Western Avenue, Cardiff, CF5 2YX Tel: 01222 265000

Listening and Responding

The test will last 45 minutes.

- Dictionaries are only allowed during the ten-minute reading time at the beginning and the ten-minute checking time at the end.
- You have to listen to a cassette recorded by native speakers. You will hear everything three times.
- The questions will require non-verbal responses (i.e. ticking boxes), target-language answers or answers in English/Welsh.
- About 20% of the questions will be answered in English/Welsh.

Foundation Tier

- You will have to understand instructions, announcements, telephone messages, short narratives, advertisements, news items.
- For Grades E, F and G you will have to identify main points and extract specific details
- For Grades C and D you will have to identify points of view and understand references to the past, present and future.

Higher Tier

- You will have to do some of the harder Foundation Tier questions.
- You will hear radio broadcasts, discussions, presentations and interviews.
- You will have to identify points of view, understand references to the past, present and future, recognise attitudes and emotions and be able to draw conclusions.

Speaking

The test will be recorded by your teacher.

- You can use a dictionary only during the preparation time.
- Whether you do Foundation or Higher Tier, you do two role-plays and a conversation.
- The role-plays will either be in the form of instructions in English/Welsh with pictures to guide you, or prompts in the target language.

Foundation Tier

The test will last 10 minutes.

- Role-play A will be simple. Role-play B will have some unpredictability.
- In the conversation, if you want to get Grades C or D you will have to be able to refer to the past, present and the future and to be able to express personal opinions.

Higher Tier

The test will last 12 minutes.

- Role-play B will have some unpredictability. Role-play C will have even more unpredictability. It will be marked for communication and quality of language.
- In the conversation you will have to produce longer sequences of speech and use a variety of structures, tenses and vocabulary in order to express ideas and justify points of view.

Reading and Responding

The test will last 40 minutes.

- You may use a dictionary.
- 20% of the questions will be in English/Welsh and require an answer in English/Welsh.

Foundation Tier

- The materials will be signs, notices, advertisements, messages, letters, leaflets, newspaper and magazine extracts.
- You will have to identify main points and extract specific detail.
- For Grades C and D you will have to identify points of view, understand unfamiliar language and understand references to past, present and future events.

Higher Tier

- You will do the harder questions from the Foundation Tier.
- The texts will be longer than at Foundation Tier.
- You will have to identify points of view, understand unfamiliar language, understand references to past, present and future events, recognise attitudes and emotions, and be able to draw inferences and conclusions.

Writing

You must choose between the Coursework Option and the Terminal Exam Option.

Terminal Exam Option

You may use a dictionary throughout.
Foundation Tier
The exam lasts 45 minutes. You will be expected to:
- elicit and provide information
- describe events in the past, present and future
- express opinions, emotions and ideas

Higher Tier
The exam lasts 60 minutes. You will be expected to:
- write in different ways to suit the audience and the context
- justify any ideas and points of view expressed
- write with increased accuracy and an increasingly wide range of language

Coursework Option

Five pieces of work may be submitted in the coursework option. These will be pieces of work done in class under teacher supervision. A dictionary may be used. Further details are given in the WJEC syllabus.

Short course

This is what you need to know if you are taking a short course.
- The exam boards do not mark your papers more leniently because you are taking a short course. The same level of competence is expected for, say, a grade A* in the short course as for a grade A* in the full course.
- The main difference between a full course and a short course is that the full course tests knowledge of all five Areas of Experience (see page 3), whereas the short course tests only two.
- In theory you could be studying one Area from either A, B or C and one Area from D and E. In practice you are likely to be doing Areas B and D – but do check with your teacher.
- When learning vocabulary concentrate on the words that deal with Areas of Experience B and D (see pages 68–76 and 83–85). However, you should also learn as much vocabulary as you can from the other Areas of Experience.

Speaking

Make sure that you can talk about family, free time, holidays and your future career.

Listening

Again the topics of family, free time, holidays and your future career will be tested. Make sure you know the vocabulary.

Reading

You may well have a lot of questions set on texts to do with the world of work. Make sure you know the words for unemployment, salary, working times, boss, lunch break, training, tax, etc. See the Area D vocabulary section on pages 83–86.

Writing

It is absolutely essential that you know how to write a letter applying for a job. It could be a temporary summer job or a permanent post. Study the letters in Chapter 8.

Devising a revision programme

Organising your revision

You cannot expect to remember all the grammar and vocabulary that you have learned over a period of three or four years unless you are prepared to revise. You need to be able to recall the vocabulary and rules of grammar from your memory during any part of the examination.

Organise your revision by making a timetable. Choose a time when you are at your most receptive. It might be best to revise in the early evening before you get too tired, or early in the morning after a good night's sleep. Having decided when to revise, put the times on to your revision timetable.

You also need a suitable place to revise. Find a quiet, or fairly quiet room away from distractions like TV or loud music. You need a table, a chair, adequate light (a table lamp will often help you to concentrate) and a comfortable temperature. It is better to revise when sitting at a table than when lying down. It is more effective to revise inside the house rather than basking in the sun.

How to revise for Spanish

When revising vocabulary do not just keep reading the words and their meanings through aimlessly. Try to learn the words in context. Remember you need to know the gender and the plural of all nouns.

Learn lists of words in short spells at a time and always give yourself a written test. In other words you must review the words you have learned. Without this review you will forget what you have learned very quickly.

When revising grammar points you should make notes on a postcard, which will then help you to do some light revision on the night before the exam. Look for the important key facts about Spanish grammar and make notes on them as you revise. Use the test yourself section of this book to test what you have revised. If you have not understood and are still getting it wrong then go back to the relevant grammar section and look at it again.

The reviewing of what you have revised is very important. You should try to carry out this testing and retesting of what you have learned during a revision session after 24 hours, then after a week and maybe again after a month. You should keep your summary notes for use just before the exam.

Plan all your revision in short bursts, depending on your span of concentration.

1. You learn most by studying for 20–40 minutes and then testing yourself to see how much you remember.
2. Take regular breaks. On your timetable you could split a two-hour session into four shorter periods, like this: revise for 25 minutes; break for 10 minutes; work another 25 minutes; then stop, have a longer break (20–30 minutes) and then work for another 35–40 minutes. Give yourself a reward at the end of the revision period, e.g. watch TV, read a book, listen to a record or the radio, or go and see a friend.
3. Have a definite start time and finish time. Learning efficiency tends to fall at the beginning of a revision session but rises towards the end.
4. Allow two hours each day for revision at the beginning of your programme and build up to three hours a day or more during the last three or so weeks of revision before the examinations start. Make sure Spanish has a weekly session in your revision programme.

Some other tips:

Don't waste revision time

(a) Recognise when your mind begins to wander.
(b) If you have things on your mind deal with them first; or make a list of the 'things you need to do' then go back to your revision.
(c) Get up and move about – do something different, make a cup of tea, etc.
(d) Think with your daydream – it will probably go away.
(e) Change your revision subject – move to another subject, then come back to Spanish revision.

Work in pairs

(a) Learning vocabulary is easy this way; you can test one another.
(b) Practise talking Spanish with a friend.
(c) Listen to Spanish radio broadcasts together.

Understand the work

Learning grammar 'parrot fashion' can lower recall. Remember: *work, test, rest, reward.*

Do not give up

You may feel irritable and depressed, but recognise that this is a common problem. Do not give up.

Here is the 'Ladder to Success' which can help you understand how to prepare properly not only for your Spanish examinations but other examinations as well.

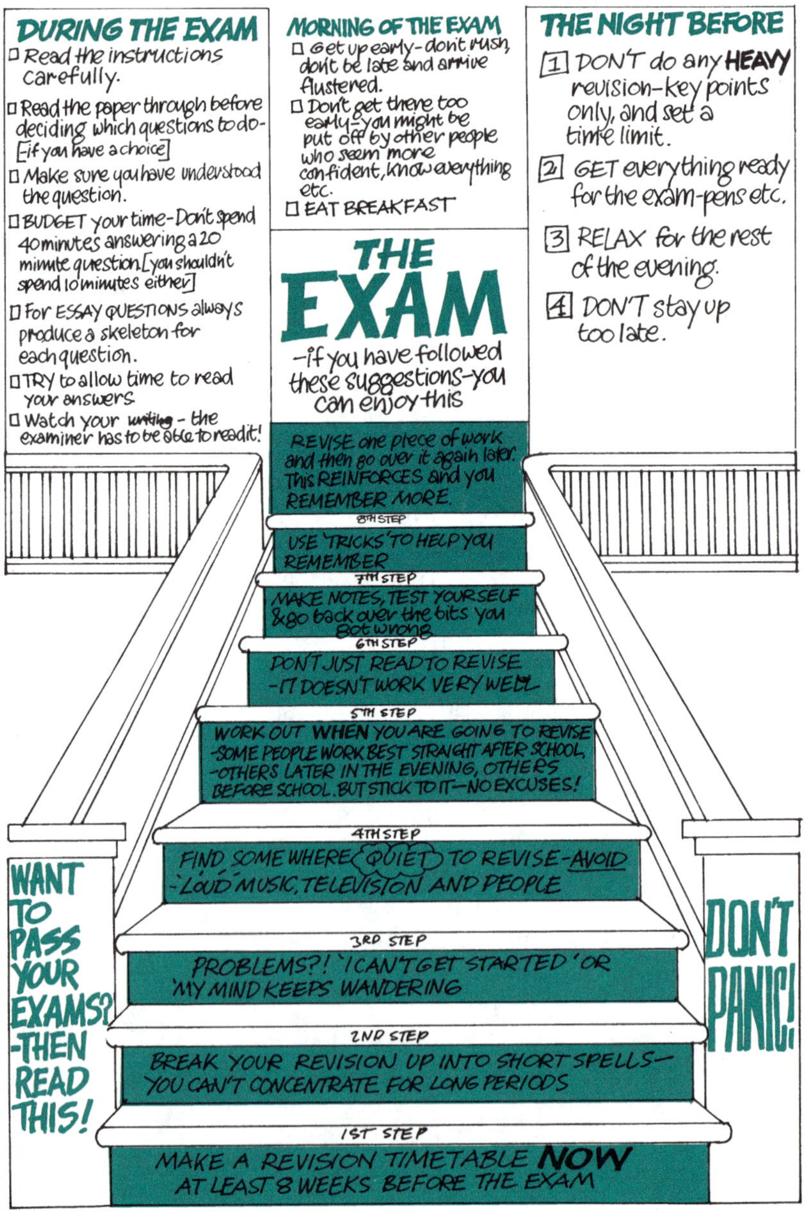

Chapter 1
Grammar revision

This section provides a comprehensive guide to all the grammar required for the GCSE examinations for all the UK examination boards.

- If you are to communicate accurately in Spanish, an understanding of Spanish grammar is essential no matter how extensive your vocabulary may be.
- You will also find that as your knowledge of grammar increases, so will your confidence and this will improve your competence in all four skill areas.
- You need to plan your revision programme so that you have enough time to work through the following sections. Allow yourself a minimum of eight weeks before the exam.

1.1 Grammatical terms

Before you start your grammar revision, you need to familiarise yourself with some grammatical terms. Look at this sentence:

The boy eats a delicious dinner slowly in the kitchen.

The	definite article
boy	noun (subject)
eats	verb
a	indefinite article
delicious	adjective
dinner	noun (object)
slowly	adverb
in	preposition
the	definite article
kitchen.	noun

The *definite article* is the grammatical name given to the word 'the'.

The *indefinite article* is the name given to the word 'a' or 'an'.

A *noun* is a person, place, thing or animal.

A *verb* is a word that describes an action (e.g. eats).

An *adjective* is a word that describes a noun (e.g. delicious).

An *adverb* is a word that describes a verb. It tells you how an action is done (e.g. slowly). Many adverbs in English end in '-ly'.

A *preposition* is a word placed before a noun or a pronoun to indicate time, place or condition (e.g. *in* the kitchen).

A *conjunction* is a word that links two parts of a sentence e.g. he was eating *and* drinking. The most common conjunctions in English are 'and' and 'but'.

A *pronoun* is a word that stands in place of a noun. In the sentence above, we could replace the noun 'the boy' by the pronoun 'he'. Similarly, 'a dinner' could be replaced by 'it'.

A *negative* is a word like 'not' or 'never' that indicates an action is not being done.

Gender refers to whether a word is masculine or feminine.

The *subject* is the name given to the person or thing doing the action. In the sentence above, the subject is 'the boy'.

The *object* is the name given to the person or thing that has the action done to it. In the sentence above, 'a dinner' is the object.

1.2 Definite and indefinite articles

	Definite article (the)		***Indefinite article (a, an, some)***	
	masculine	*feminine*	*masculine*	*feminine*
singular	el	la	un	una
plural	los	las	unos	unas

(a) Note that **de** + **el** becomes **del**
a + **el** becomes **al**
e.g. el libro **del** niño *the boy's book*
Fui **al** supermercado. *I went to the supermarket.*

(b) **el** and **un** are used before feminine nouns that begin with a stressed **a-** or **ha-** (but not when separated by an adjective).
e.g. el agua *the water*
el arma *the weapon*
la vieja arma *the old weapon*
But la alfombra *the carpet* (the **a-** is not stressed)
However the noun stays feminine:
El agua está fría. *The water is cold.*
The plural is always **las** or **unas.**
e.g. las aguas *the waters*
las armas *the weapons*
unas armas *some weapons*

(c) The definite article is used

1. when referring to nouns in a general sense:
   El vino es importante en España. *Wine is important in Spain.*
2. with the name of a language except when it comes directly after **aprender, hablar** or **saber**:
   El español es fácil. *Spanish is easy.*
   Hablo español. *I speak Spanish.*
3. before titles:
   la reina Isabel *Queen Elizabeth*
   el señor García *Mr. García*
   However, leave out the article when talking directly to the person:
   Buenos días, señor García. *Good morning, Mr. García.*
4. when saying 'on Saturday', 'on Friday':
   el sábado *on Saturday*
   el viernes *on Friday*
5. in certain expressions when it is not used in English:
   en la cama *in bed* — en el hospital *in hospital*
   en la iglesia *in church* — en la televisión *on television*
   en la cárcel *in prison* — en el colegio *in school*

(d) The definite article is omitted with the numbers of monarchs:
Felipe segundo *Philip the Second*

(e) The indefinite article is omitted

1. before occupations and nationality:
   Ella es profesora. *She is a teacher.*
   El es inglés. *He is an Englishman.*
2. before **medio, mil, ¡qué ... !, tal**:
   medio litro *half a litre*
   mil pesetas *a thousand pesetas*
   ¡qué día! *what a day!*
   tal cosa *such a thing*

1.3 Nouns

(a) All nouns are either masculine or feminine. When you learn a new noun, you must learn which it is.

(b) Usually nouns that end in **-o** are masculine and nouns that end in **-a** are feminine. Note the following words which end in **-a** but are *masculine*:

el crucigrama *crossword*	el problema *problem*
el futbolista *footballer*	el programa *programme*
el clima *climate*	el síntoma *symptom*
el día *day*	el sistema *system*
el idioma *language*	el telegrama *telegram*
el mapa *map*	el tema *theme*
el pijama *pyjamas*	el tranvía *tram*
el planeta *planet*	

The following words end in **-o** but are *feminine:*

la foto *photograph*	la moto *motorcycle*
la mano *hand*	la radio *radio*

(c) Compound nouns are masculine

e.g. el abrelatas *tin-opener*
el sacacorchos *corkscrew*
el parabrisas *windscreen*

(d) Countries that end in **-a** are feminine

e.g. (la) España *Spain*
(la) Gran Bretaña *Great Britain*
(la) Francia *France*

Otherwise they are masculine

e.g. (el) Perú *Peru*
(el) Paraguay *Paraguay*

(e) Some words change their meaning according to their gender

e.g. el capital *capital* (money)	la capital *capital* (city)
el coma *coma*	la coma *comma*
el cura *priest*	la cura *cure*
el frente *front* (e.g. military)	la frente *forehead*
el orden *order* (i.e. sequence)	la orden *order* (i.e. command)
el parte *report*	la parte *part*
el pendiente *earring*	la pendiente *slope*
el policía *policeman*	la policía *police*

(f) Fruits are often feminine and their fruit-trees masculine

e.g. el cerezo *cherry tree*	la cereza *cherry*
el ciruelo *plum tree*	la ciruela *plum*
el manzano *apple tree*	la manzana *apple*
el naranjo *orange tree*	la naranja *orange*

(g) Words ending in **-eza, -ión, -dad, -tad, -umbre, -ie, -nza** are nearly always feminine

e.g. la belleza *beauty*	la dirección *address, direction*
la verdad *truth*	la libertad *freedom*
la costumbre *custom*	la serie *series*
la enseñanza *education*	

(h) To form the plural of nouns add **-s** to an unstressed vowel and **-es** to a consonant

e.g. el chico *the boy*	el dolor *pain*
los chicos *the boys*	los dolores *pains*
la silla *the chair*	la flor *flower*
las sillas *the chairs*	las flores *flowers*

However

Words ending in **-z** change the **-z** to **-ces** in the plural

e.g. el lápiz *pencil*	la vez *time*
los lápices *pencils*	las veces *times*

Words ending in a stressed **-ión, -ón** or **-és** lose their accents in the plural

e.g.	la canción *song*	el francés *Frenchman*
	las canciones *songs*	los franceses *the French*
	el montón *pile*	
	los montones *piles*	

(i) Surnames are not normally made plural
e.g. los García *the Garcías, the García family*

(j) Note that the following usually denote a mixture of sexes:
los abuelos *grandparents*
los hermanos *brothers and sisters*
los hijos *children* (i.e. boys and girls)

1.4 Adjectives

Notice how the following adjectives agree in number and gender.

(a) Adjectives ending in **-o**:

	masculine	*feminine*
singular	blanco	blanca
plural	blancos	blancas

(b) Adjectives ending in **-e** or in a consonant do not change when feminine:

	masculine	*feminine*
singular	verde	verde
plural	verdes	verdes

	masculine	*feminine*
singular	azul	azul
plural	azules	azules

(c) Adjectives of nationality do not follow the above rule:

	masculine	*feminine*
singular	español	española
plural	españoles	españolas

(d) Adjectives that end in **-án** and **-or** like **holgazán** (lazy) and **hablador** (talkative) do not follow the rule (b):

	masculine	*feminine*
singular	holgazán	holgazana
plural	holgazanes	holgazanas

	masculine	*feminine*
singular	hablador	habladora
plural	habladores	habladoras

(e) Some adjectives (**bueno, malo, alguno, ninguno, primero, tercero**) drop the letter **-o** before a masculine singular noun, and **algún** and **ningún** require an accent:
un buen/mal hombre *a good/bad man*
algún/ningún dinero *some/no money*
el primer/tercer ejemplo *the first/third example*

Also **santo** becomes **san** before the name of a saint:
Felipe es un santo *Philip is a saint*
San Felipe *Saint Philip*

However, **Santo Domingo** and **Santo Tomás** keep the **-to** to help pronunciation.

(f) **grande** becomes **gran** before a masculine singular and a feminine singular noun:
un gran hombre *a great man*
una gran mujer *a great woman*

(g) Some adjectives change their meaning according to their position:
su **antiguo** amigo *his former friend*
el edificio **antiguo** *the ancient building*
el **pobre** chico *the poor boy* (i.e. unfortunate)
el chico **pobre** *the poor boy* (i.e. without any money)

por **pura** curiosidad *from sheer curiosity*
el agua **pura** *pure water*
la **misma** cosa *the same thing*
el rey **mismo** *the king himself*

(h) cada (each) never changes:
cada niño *each boy*
cada niña *each girl*

(i) -ísimo, -ísima, -ísimos, -ísimas can be added to adjectives after the final vowel is removed to give the meaning 'extremely':
un chico guapo *a handsome boy*
un chico guapísimo *an extremely handsome boy*

1.5 Adverbs

In English most adverbs end in '-ly': slowly, quickly, carefully, briefly.

To form an adverb in Spanish, take the feminine form of the adjective and add **-mente**:

lento *slow* | cuidadoso *careful*
lentamente *slowly* | cuidadosamente *carefully*

rápido *fast*
rápidamente *quickly*

Notice how to make an adverb from an adjective that ends in **-e** or a consonant:

breve *brief* | normal *normal*
brevemente *briefly* | normalmente *normally*

If two adverbs come together, **-mente** is added to the second one only:
lenta y cuidadosamente *slowly and carefully*

Some adverbs do not end in **-mente**:
bien *well*
mal *badly*
despacio *slowly*

Some useful adverbs

abajo downstairs
La cocina está abajo. *The kitchen is downstairs.*
ahora now
Ahora son las seis. *It is six o'clock now.*
allí, allá there
¡El libro está allí! *The book is there!*
a menudo often
¿Vas a menudo al cine? *Do you often go to the cinema?*
apenas (si) scarcely
Apenas (si) pude verle. *I could scarcely see him.*
aquí here
¡Aquí está! *Here he is!*
arriba upstairs
Mi hermano está arriba. *My brother is upstairs.*
aún/todavía still
Duerme aún/todavía. *He is still asleep.*
bastante enough, quite
No tengo bastante dinero. *I haven't got enough money.*
Es bastante alto. *He is quite tall.*
casi almost
El equipo casi ganó. *The team almost won.*
de repente suddenly
El coche frenó de repente. *The car braked suddenly.*
desgraciadamente/por desgracia unfortunately
Desgraciadamente/por desgracia murió. *Unfortunately he died.*

en seguida immediately
Se fue en seguida. *He left immediately.*
hasta until, even
No vino hasta las seis. *He did not come till six.*
Hasta Pedro fue a la fiesta. *Even Pedro went to the party.*
luego then
Comió un bocadillo; luego salió. *He ate a sandwich, then went out.*
mucho a lot
La chica come mucho. *The girl eats a lot.*
por tanto/por consiguiente so (therefore)
Llovía y por tanto (por consiguiente) no salí. *It was raining and so I didn't go out.*
pronto soon
Pronto se va de vacaciones. *He is soon going on holidays.*
quizá perhaps
Quizá lo hizo. *Perhaps he did it.*
siempre always
Siempre llega tarde. *He always arrives late.*
sólo, solamente only
Sólo los franceses saben cocinar. *Only the French can cook.*
Tenemos solamente cinco. *We only have five.*
también also
Él fue y yo fui también. *He went and I went as well (too/also).*
ya now, already
Ya ha llegado. *He has already arrived.*
Ya es hora de irnos. *It is time for us to go now.*

1.6 Comparative and superlative of adjectives and adverbs

(a) Normally **más ... que**, **menos ... que** are used to form the comparative:
Él es más rico que ella. *He is richer than she is.*
Él es menos inteligente que ella. *He is less intelligent than she is.*
Notice these irregular forms:
mejor *better*
peor *worse*
mayor *bigger/older*
menor *smaller/younger*
más grande (bigger) and **más pequeño** (smaller) can also be used.
Notice also:
la calle mayor *the main street*
la plaza mayor *the main square*

(b) más is used to form the superlative:
el libro **más** interesante que tengo *the most interesting book that I have*
la chica **más** guapa *the prettiest girl*
Notice the following:
el/la mejor, los/las mejores *the best*
el/la peor, los/las peores *the worst*
el/la mayor, los/las mayores *the biggest/the oldest*
el/la menor, los menores/las menores *the smallest/the youngest*
When using a superlative, 'in' is translated by **de**:
el mejor jugador del equipo *the best player in the team*
las peores casas de la ciudad *the worst houses in the city*

(c) tan ... como *as (so) ... as*
tanto como *as (so) much as*
El chico es **tan** alto **como** la chica. *The boy is as tall as the girl.*
La chica no es **tan** alta **como** el chico. *The girl is not as tall as the boy.*

Tengo **tanto** dinero **como** mi hermano. *I have as much money as my brother.*
No tengo **tantos** amigos **como** él. *I do not have as many friends as he does.*

(d) Adverbs also form the comparison with **más**:
Tú hablas **más** claramente que él. *You speak more clearly than he does.*

1.7 Numerals

Cardinal numbers

0	cero	31	treinta y uno
1	uno(un), una	32	treinta y dos
2	dos	40	cuarenta
3	tres	41	cuarenta y uno
4	cuatro	50	cincuenta
5	cinco	51	cincuenta y uno
6	seis	60	sesenta
7	siete	61	sesenta y uno
8	ocho	70	setenta
9	nueve	71	setenta y uno
10	diez	80	ochenta
11	once	81	ochenta y uno
12	doce	90	noventa
13	trece	91	noventa y uno
14	catorce	100	ciento (cien)
15	quince	101	ciento uno
16	dieciséis	102	ciento dos
17	diecisiete	200	doscientos/as
18	dieciocho	300	trescientos/as
19	diecinueve	400	cuatrocientos/as
20	veinte	500	quinientos/as
21	veintiuno	600	seiscientos/as
22	veintidós	700	setecientos/as
23	veintitrés	800	ochocientos/as
24	veinticuatro	900	novecientos/as
25	veinticinco	1000	mil
26	veintiséis	2000	dos mil
27	veintisiete	10,000	diez mil
28	veintiocho	100,000	cien mil
29	veintinueve	1,000,000	un millón
30	treinta	2,000,000	dos millones

(a) uno loses its **-o** when in front of a masculine singular noun:
Dame uno. *Give me one.*
Dame un caramelo. *Give me a sweet.*

(b) The hundreds have a separate feminine form:
doscientos libros *200 books*
doscientas pesetas *200 pesetas*

(c) cien is used for exactly 100:
Tengo cien libras. *I have £100.*
ciento is used for numbers 101–199:
ciento cuarenta *140*

(d) mil does not change and does not have **un** or **una** in front of it:
mil pesetas *a thousand pesetas*
dos mil pesetas *two thousand pesetas*

(e) un millón (plural **millones**) requires **de** before a noun:
un millón de pájaros *a million birds*
dos millones de pájaros *two million birds*

(f) **ciento** is not followed by **y**; **y** is only used between tens and units:
ciento cuatro *104*
ciento treinta y cinco *135*
(g) You cannot say 'nineteen hundred' in Spanish; **mil** must be used:
mil novecientos *1900*

Ordinal numbers

primero	*first*	sexto	*sixth*
segundo	*second*	séptimo	*seventh*
tercero	*third*	octavo	*eighth*
cuarto	*fourth*	noveno	*ninth*
quinto	*fifth*	décimo	*tenth*

(a) Ordinal numbers agree like other adjectives ending in **-o**:
la tercera calle *the third street*
(b) Do not confuse **cuatro** (four) with **cuarto** (fourth).
(c) **primero** and **tercero** lose their **-o** before a masculine single noun:
el primer ejemplo *the first example*
el tercer gol *the third goal*
(d) Although the ordinal numbers exist after **décimo,** they are rarely used. Use the cardinal number after the noun:
el piso quince *the fifteenth floor*
el siglo veinte *the twentieth century*
(e) With kings and queens, leave out 'the':
Carlos quinto *Charles the Fifth*

1.8 Time

(a) ¿Qué hora es? *What time is it?*
¿A qué hora? *At what time?*
Es la una. *It is 01.00.*
Son las dos. *It is 02.00.*
Son las tres. *It is 03.00.*
Son las cuatro y cuarto. *It is 04.15.*
Son las cinco y media. *It is 05.30.*
Son las seis menos cuarto. *It is 05.45.*
Son las siete y cinco. *It is 07.05.*
Son las ocho menos diez. It is 07.50.
Es (el) mediodía. *It is 12.00 noon.*
Es (la) medianoche. *It is 12.00 midnight.*
a las tres de la madrugada *at three in the (early) morning*
a las siete de la mañana *at seven in the morning*
a las dos de la tarde *at two in the afternoon*
a las once de la noche *at eleven at night*
a eso de las tres *at about three o'clock*
a las cuatro en punto *at four o'clock exactly*
(b) Before dark, the Spaniards say **de la tarde**:
a las cuatro de la tarde *at four in the afternoon*
After dark, use **de la noche**:
a las siete de la noche *at seven in the evening*
(c) Use **por la mañana**, **por la tarde**, **por la noche** when no time is given:
Fue de compras por la mañana. *He went shopping in the morning.*
Fue de compras a las diez de la mañana. *He went shopping at ten in the morning.*

1.9 Negatives

(a) nadie *nobody*
nada *nothing*
nunca/jamás *never*
ninguno,-a, *no*
ni … ni … *neither … nor …*
tampoco *(n)either*
No hay **nadie** en la calle. *There is nobody in the street.*
No hay **nada** en la calle. *There is nothing in the street.*
No voy **nunca/**no voy **jamás**. *I never go.*
No hay **ningún** trabajo allí. *There is no work there.*
Ni mi amigo **ni** yo lo vimos. *Neither my friend nor I saw it.*
No fui y ella no fue **tampoco.** *I did not go and she did not go either.*

(b) When the negative word comes after the verb, **no** must be placed before the verb:
Nunca voy a la iglesia. *I never go to church.*
No voy nunca al colegio. *I never go to school.*

(c) When **nadie** is the direct object it requires a personal **a**:
No veo **a** nadie. *I see nobody.*

(d) **ninguno** loses its **-o** before a masculine singular noun and requires an accent:
ningún trabajo *no work*

1.10 Pronouns

Subject pronouns

(a) A Spanish verb can be used with or without the subject pronoun:
yo miro *or* miro *I look*
tú miras *or* miras *you look* (sing. fam.)
él mira *or* mira *he looks*
ella mira *or* mira *she looks*
usted (abbreviated to 'Vd.') mira *or* mira *you look* (sing. polite)
nosotros/as miramos *or* miramos *we look*
vosotros miráis *or* miráis *you look* (pl. fam.)
ellos miran *or* miran *they look* (m.)
ellas miran *or* miran *they look* (f.)
ustedes (abbreviated to 'Vds.') miran *or* miran *you look* (pl. polite)

(b) It is normal to omit the subject pronoun except when its omission would cause confusion:
Él es de aquí pero **ella** es belga. *He is from here but she is Belgian.*

(c) Note that there are five subject pronouns meaning 'you'. **Tú** is used to address a friend, a relative or a child. **Vosotros** (fem. **vosotras**) is used to address more than one of such people. **Usted** (**Vd.**) and **ustedes** (**Vds.**) are the singular and plural forms used to address people with whom you are not familiar.

(d) The use of **usted** and **ustedes** is becoming less and less frequent; however if in doubt you are always safe to use the polite form.

Direct object pronouns

(a) me *me*
te *you* (fam. sing.)
le, lo *him*
la *her*
le, lo *you* (polite, sing. m.)
la *you* (polite, sing. f.)
lo *it* (m.)
la *it* (f.)

nos *us*
os *you* (fam. pl.)
les, los *them* (m.)
las *them* (f.)
los, les *you* (polite, pl. m.)
las *you* (polite, pl. f.)

él **me** ve *he sees me*
él **te** ve *he sees you*
él **le/lo** ve *he sees him/it/you*
él **la** ve *he sees her/it/you*
él **nos** ve *he sees us*
él **os** ve *he sees you*
él **les/los** ve *he sees them/you*
él **las** ve *he sees them/you*

(b) Pronouns normally come before the verb. When there are two parts to the verb, they normally come before the first part:

Me ha visto. *He has seen me.*

(c) Pronouns are attached to the end of the verb:

1. when it is an infinitive (i.e. it ends in **-ar, -er** or **-ir**):
   Voy a hacerlo. *I am going to do it.*
2. when it is a present participle (i.e. it ends in **-ando** or **-iendo**):
   Estoy haciéndolo. *I am doing it.* (notice the accent)
3. when it is a positive command:
   ¡Escúchame! *Listen to me!*

but *not* with negative commands:

¡No le escuches! *Do not listen to him!*

(d) To avoid confusion with **lo**, **le**, **la**, **los**, **les**, **las**, the following words are often inserted after the verb:

a él, a ella, a Vd., a ellos, a ellas, a Vds.
Lo miro a él. *I am looking at him.*
Lo miro a Vd. *I am looking at you.*

Indirect object pronouns

(a)
me *to me*
te *to you* (fam. sing.)
le *to him, to her, to it, to you* (polite sing.)
nos *to us*
os *to you* (fam. pl.)
les *to them, to you* (polite pl.)
me da el dinero *he gives the money to me*
te da el dinero *he gives the money to you*
le da el dinero *he gives the money to him, to her, to you*
nos da el dinero *he gives the money to us*
os da el dinero *he gives the money to you*
les da el dinero *he gives the money to them, to you*

(b) When there is a direct and an indirect object pronoun together, the indirect one always comes first:

Me lo ha vendido. *He has sold it to me.*
Dámelo. *Give it to me.*

(c) When two pronouns beginning with **l-** come together, the first one becomes **se**:

Se lo ha vendido. *He has sold it to him.*
Dáselo. *Give it to them.*

It is often necessary to add **a él**, **a ella**, **a Vd.**, **a ellos**, **a ellas**, **a Vds.** to make the meaning clear as **se** can mean 'to him', 'to her', 'to you', 'to them':

Se lo ha vendido **a él**. *He has sold it to him.*
Se lo ha vendido **a ella**. *He has sold it to her.*

(d) When a pronoun is added to a present participle, the participle requires an accent:

dando *giving*
d**á**ndole *giving him*

(e) When two pronouns are added to an infinitive, the infinitive requires an accent:

No voy a dar el dinero al niño. *I am not going to give the money to the child.*
No voy a d**á**rselo. *I am not going to give it to him.*

Prepositional pronouns

(a) These pronouns are used after a preposition:

mí *me*	nosotros, nosotras *us*
ti *you*	vosotros, vosotras *you*
él, sí *him, it*	ellos, sí *them*
ella, sí *her, it*	ellas, sí *them*
Vd., sí *you*	Vds., sí *you*

(b) El regalo es para mí. *The present is for me.*
Ella está detrás de ti. *She is behind you.*
¡Sus gafas están delante de Vd.! *Your glasses are in front of you!*

(c) Note that **sí** is used instead of **él**, **ella**, **Vd.**, **ellos**, **ellas**, **Vds.** when the person referred to after the preposition is the same as the subject of the sentence:
Lo quiere para sí. *He wants it for him* (i.e. himself).
Lo quiere para él. *He wants it for him* (i.e. for someone else).

(d) Note that **con mí** becomes **conmigo** *with me*
con ti becomes **contigo** *with you*
con sí becomes **consigo** *with him (her, you, it, them)*

(e) Prepositional pronouns are often used with the verb **gustar** to give emphasis:
¡A mí me gusta pero a ti no te gusta! *I like it but you do not!*

(f) Note that **mí** and **sí** have an accent but **ti** does not.

1.11 Personal 'a'

(a) When the direct object of a sentence is a person, **a** is placed before the person:
Visité **a** Juan. *I visited Juan.*
Visité la catedral. *I visited the cathedral.*

(b) It is sometimes used with regard to a pet when the speaker wishes to show affection for the animal:
¿Has visto **al** perro? *Have you seen the dog?*

(c) It is not used after **tener**:
Tengo un amigo. *I have a friend.*
But
Encontré a un amigo. *I met a friend.*

(d) It is not used when the person is not specified:
Busco un mecánico. *I am looking for a mechanic.*

1.12 Demonstrative adjectives and pronouns (this, that, these, those)

Demonstrative adjectives:

(a)

este chico *this boy*	aquel chico *that boy*
esta chica *this girl*	aquella chica *that girl*
estos chicos *these boys*	aquellos chicos *those boys*
estas chicas *these girls*	aquellas chicas *those girls*

ese chico *that boy*
esa chica *that girl*
esos chicos *those boys*
esas chicas *those girls*

(b) In the above examples, 'this', 'that', 'these' and 'those' are adjectives and they are immediately followed by a noun.

(c) Notice there are two ways of saying 'that' and 'those'. People or things which are referred to by **aquel** etc are further away than people or things referred to by **ese** etc:

Me gusta ese libro pero no me gusta aquel libro.
I like that book but I don't like that book (i.e. over there).

Demonstrative pronouns:

(d)

no me gusta éste *I don't like this one*
no me gusta ésta *I don't like this one*
no me gustan éstos *I don't like these*
no me gustan éstas *I don't like these*

no me gusta ése *I don't like that one*
no me gusta ésa *I don't like that one*
no me gustan ésos *I don't like those*
no me gustan ésas *I don't like those*

no me gusta aquél *I don't like that one*
no me gusta aquélla *I don't like that one*
no me gustan aquéllos *I don't like those*
no me gustan aquéllas *I don't like those*

(e) Notice that the above words **éste** etc are pronouns: they are not immediately followed by a noun.

(f) Opinions vary about whether an accent is required on the above pronouns. You are safer if you put the accent.

(g) **esto** (this); **eso** (that); **aquello** (that)

These three pronouns cannot refer to a particular verb. They refer to a whole idea or sentence.

¿Qué es esto? *What's this?*
No tengo dinero y eso no me gusta.
I have no money and I don't like that. (it is not the money that the speaker does not like but rather the idea of not having any money)

1.13 Possessive adjectives

(a)

mi libro *my book*
mis libros *my books*

tu libro *your book* (fam. sing.)
tus libros *your books* (fam. sing.)

su libro *his book*
su libro *her book*
sus libros *his/her books*
su libro *your book* (polite sing.)
sus libros *your books* (polite sing.)

nuestro hermano *our brother*
nuestra hermana *our sister*
nuestros hermanos *our brothers*
nuestras hermanas *our sisters*

vuestro hermano *your brother* (fam. pl.)
vuestra hermana *your sister* (fam. pl.)
vuestros hermanos *your brothers* (fam. pl.)
vuestras hermanas *your sisters* (fam. pl.)

sus libros *their books*
su libro *your book* (polite pl.)
sus libros *your books* (polite pl.)

(b) **nuestro** and **vuestro** are the only possessive adjectives to have a feminine form.

(c) When saying 'your' in Spanish, first you must decide whether to use the familiar singular (**tu** or **tus**), the familiar plural (**vuestro**, **vuestra**, **vuestros**, **vuestras**), or the polite form (**su** or **sus**).

(d) Notice that these adjectives agree in number and gender with the noun that follows them and not with the possessor. For instance a common mistake is to think that **su** means 'his' or 'her' and that **'sus'** means 'their'. Both **su** and **sus** can mean 'his', 'her' or 'their'. The correct form depends on whether the thing possessed is singular (**su**) or plural (**sus**).

(e) **su** and **sus** can mean 'his', 'her', 'your' or 'their'. Confusion can be avoided as follows:

su libro de él *his book*
su libro de ella *her book*
su libro de Vd. *your book*
sus libros de ellos *their books*
sus libros de ellas *their books* (feminine possessors)
sus libros de Vds. *your books* (plural possessors)

(f) The definite article and not the possessive adjective is normally used with parts of the body and with clothing:

Lo tengo en la mano. *I have it in my hand.*
Voy a quitarme el abrigo. *I am going to take off my coat.*

1.14 Possessive pronouns

(a)

singular		***plural***		
masculine	*feminine*	*masculine*	*feminine*	
el mío	la mía	los míos	las mías	*mine*
el tuyo	la tuya	los tuyos	las tuyas	*yours* (sing. fam.)
el suyo	la suya	los suyos	las suyas	*his, hers, yours* (sing. polite)
el nuestro	la nuestra	los nuestros	las nuestras	*ours*
el vuestro	la vuestra	los vuestros	las vuestras	*yours* (pl. fam.)
el suyo	la suya	los suyos	las suyas	*theirs, yours* (pl. polite)

(b) Here are some examples of the above:

Tengo mi libro y **el tuyo**. *I have my book and yours.*
Tienes tu libro y **el mío**. *You have your book and mine.*
He vendido mi coche y **el vuestro**. *I have sold my car and yours.*

(c) When the verb **ser** is used, omit the article:

Éste es mío y ése es tuyo. *This one is mine and that one is yours.*

(d) Notice the following:

Es amigo mío. *He is a friend of mine.*
Son amigos nuestros. *They are friends of ours.*

(e) As **suyo** can mean 'his', 'hers', 'yours' or 'theirs', confusion is often avoided as follows:

es de él *it's his*
es de ella *it's hers*
es de Vd. *it's yours* (sing. polite)
es de ellos *it's theirs* (m.)
es de ellas *it's theirs* (f.)
es de Vds. *it's yours* (pl. polite)

1.15 Relative pronouns

(a) In English the relative pronouns are 'who', 'whom', 'which' and 'that'.

(b) In the following sentences, it is correct to use **que** when referring to people or things, whether subject or object:

el hombre que está esperando *the man who is waiting*
el hombre que vi *the man that I saw*
(*or* el hombre a quien vi)
la casa que me gusta *the house that I like*
la casa que vendí *the house that I sold*

(c) Notice that in English the relative pronoun is often omitted but it must always be inserted in Spanish:

el libro que leí anoche *the book I read last night*

(d) After prepositions, use **el que**, **la que**, **los que** or **las que**. **Quien** (plural **quienes**) may be used for people:

la playa por la que anduvo *the beach that he walked along*
la chica con la que/con quien salí *the girl with whom I went out/the girl I went out with*
el pueblo cerca del que vivo *the town near which I live*

(e) Instead of **el que**, **la que**, **los que** or **las que**, **el cual**, **la cual**, **los cuales**, **las cuales** may be used. However, **el que** etc is far more common.

(f) **lo que** means 'what' in the sense of 'that which' when no question is being asked:

Describe lo que vas a hacer. *Describe what you are going to do.*
Dime lo que hiciste. *Tell me what you did.*

(g) **todo lo que** means 'everything that':

Todo lo que hace sale bien. *Everything that he does turns out well.*

(h) **cuyo, cuya, cuyos, cuyas** mean 'whose' or 'of which':

Notice that **cuyo** etc agrees with the noun that follows it and not with the possessor:

el hombre cuya hija es actriz *the man whose daughter is an actress*
la casas cuyas ventanas estaban rotas *the house, the windows of which were broken*

1.16 Interrogatives

(a)

¿adónde? *where to?*
¿a qué hora? *what time?*
¿cómo? *how?*
¿cuándo? *when?*
¿cuál? (pl. ¿cuáles?) *which?*
¿cuánto? (f. ¿cuánta?) *how much?*
¿cuántos? (f. ¿cuántas?) *how many?*
¿cuánto tiempo? *how long?*
¿desde cuándo? *since when?*
¿dónde? *where?*
¿para qué? *what for?*
¿por qué? *why?*
¿qué? *what?*
¿quién? (pl. ¿quiénes?) *who?*

(b) Note that all interrogatives have an accent. An accent is still required when the question is indirect:

No sé d**ó**nde está. *I don't know where he is.*
Le pregunté qui**é**n era. *I asked him who he was.*

(c) **qué** can be used in exclamations:

¡Qué día! *What a day!*
¡Qué desastre! *What a disaster!*

If an adjective is used, **más** or **tan** is inserted:

¡Qué día más hermoso! *What a beautiful day!*
¡Qué desastre tan horroroso! *What a horrible disaster!*

(d) **cuál** is used to differentiate between a choice of two or more:

¿Cuál es su hermano? *Which one is his brother?*

(e) ¿Cómo está? *How is he?*

But ¿Cómo es? *What is he like?*

1.17 'Ser' and 'estar'

Both these verbs mean 'to be'. To work out which to use, the following formula is useful:

(a) In a 'who' situation, use **ser**:

¿Quién es? Es nuestro profesor. *Who is he? He is our teacher.*
Él es francés y ella es belga. *He is French and she is Belgian.*

(b) In a 'what' situation, use **ser**:

¿Qué es eso? Es una mesa. *What is that? It's a table.*

(c) In a 'when' situation, use **ser**:

¿Qué hora es? Son las dos. *What time is it? It is two o'clock.*
¿Qué fecha es? Es el dos de mayo. *What's the date? It's the second of May.*
Es verano. *It's summer.*

(d) In a 'where' situation, use **estar**:

¿Dónde está la estación? Está allí. *Where is the station? It's there.*

(e) In a 'what like' situation, you must work out whether the description refers to a temporary characterisic or a permanent characteristic. If the characteristic is temporary use **estar;** if permanent use **ser**:

El cielo está azul. *The sky is blue* (but it may well change colour soon).
La puerta es azul. *The door is blue* (although it may be repainted, the colour is a fairly permanent feature of the door).

Note also that with continuous tenses, **estar** is used:

Estoy corriendo. *I am running.*
Estaba lloviendo. *It was raining.*
Estaremos trabajando. *We will be working.*

1.18 'Conocer' and 'saber'

Both of these verbs mean 'to know'. **Conocer** is to know a person or a place, and **saber** is to know a fact or how to do something:

Conozco Madrid muy bien. *I know Madrid very well.*
¿No conoces a María? *Don't you know María?*
Sé la hora pero no sé la fecha. *I know the time but not the date.*
Ella sabe nadar y él sabe cocinar. *She can swim and he can cook.*

1.19 'Deber' and 'tener que'

Both of these verbs mean 'to have to'. **Deber** implies a moral responsibility whereas **tener que** implies a physical necessity:

Debo visitar a mi abuela esta semana. *I must visit my grandmother this week.*
Tengo que tomar el autobús. No tengo coche. *I have to get the bus. I have no car.*

1.20 'Tener'

Note these expressions which use **tener**:

tengo quince años *I am fifteen*
tengo calor *I am hot*
tengo éxito *I am successful*
tengo frío *I am cold*
tengo ganas de ir al cine *I want to go to the cinema*
tengo hambre *I am hungry*
el partido tiene lugar mañana *the match takes place tomorrow*
tengo miedo *I am frightened*
tengo prisa *I am in a hurry*
tengo que ir *I have to go*
tengo razón *I am right*
tengo sed *I am thirsty*
tengo sueño *I am sleepy*
tengo suerte *I am lucky*

With these expressions, to say 'very' use **mucho** or **mucha**:

tengo mucho calor *I am vey hot*
tengo mucha prisa *I am in a great hurry*
tengo mucho miedo *I am very frightened*

1.21 Prepositions

Prepositions are words that come before a noun and link the noun with the rest of the sentence.

a, en to, into (**a** does *not* mean 'at' which is usually **en**).
Fui al campo. *I went to the countryside.*
Estoy en el campo. *I am in the countryside.*

a lo largo de/por along	Anduvimos a lo largo de/por la playa. *We walked along the beach.*
a pesar de in spite of	Salimos a pesar del tiempo. *We went out in spite of the weather.*
al lado de beside	Vive al lado de la iglesia. *He lives beside the church.*
alrededor de around	Corrió alrededor de la mesa. *He ran round the table.*
antes de before	Llegué antes de las seis. *I arrived before six.* Antes de salir, me duché. *Before going out, I had a shower.*
cerca de near	La ciudad está cerca del mar. *The city is near the sea.*
con with	Le vi con su hermana. *I saw him with his sister.*
contra against	Jugó contra un equipo francés. *He played against a French team.*
debajo de/bajo under	El banco está debajo del/bajo el árbol. *The bench is under the tree.*
delante de in front of	Se paró delante de la casa. *He stopped in front of the house.*
desde from	Desde la casa, se ve la calle. *From the house, you can see the street.*
después de after	Después de llegar, se acostó. *After arriving, he went to bed.*
detrás de behind	Se escondió detrás de la puerta. *He hid behind the door.*
durante during	Durante el viaje, durmió. *He slept during the journey*
en in	Está en casa. *He is in the house.*
en vez de instead of	Yo fui en vez de él. *I went instead of him.*
encima de above	La luz está encima de la mesa. *The light is above the table.*
enfrente de opposite	Se encontraron enfrente del cine. *They met opposite the cinema.*
entre between, among	Está entre los dos puntos. *It is between the two points.* Lo distribuyó entre sus amigos. *He gave it out among his friends.*
hacia towards	Viajó hacia el norte. *He travelled towards the north.*
hasta until, as far as, up to	Trabajó hasta las seis. *He worked up to six o'clock.*
lejos de far from	Vive lejos de aquí. *He lives far from here.*
más que, más de	Tengo más que él. *I have more than he has.*
(with a number) more than	Tengo más de tres. *I have more than three.*
salvo/menos except	Todos fuimos salvo ella. *We all went except her.*
según according to	Según el periódico, está muerto. *According to the paper, he is dead.*
sin without	Sin perder un momento, se fue. *Without wasting a moment, he went.*
sobre on, about (with time), concerning	Está sobre la mesa. *It is on the table.* Vino sobre las seis. *He came about six.* Hablamos sobre el tiempo. *We spoke about the weather.*

1.22 Verbs

Verbs are the most important part of any sentence and your command or otherwise of verbs will be one of the major factors that influence the grade you get. In English we have few changes in the ending of our verbs:

I eat, you eat, he eats, we eat, you eat, they eat.

The verb-ending changes once for the 'he' part of the present tense. In Spanish there are six different endings to be learnt for the verb **comer** in the present tense.

Also the meaning of a verb often changes depending on where the stress lies:

llego *I arrive* llegó *he arrived*

so accents are very important.

You will be expected to know the following tenses: the *present,* the *imperfect,* the *perfect,* the *preterite,* the *pluperfect,* the *future* and the *conditional.* Your board's syllabus mentions the subjunctive but the board will not expect you to *produce* a subjunctive: in the exam there may be a verb in the subjunctive that you have to recognise. You will not have to recognize that the verb is in the subjunctive: you will just have to recognise what the verb means. So the subjunctive need not concern you overmuch until you start A level! The one exception to the above is the use of the subjunctive as a command. But there are ways of making a command in Spanish without a detailed knowledge of the subjunctive. So make sure you know all the other tenses before you start worrying about the subjunctive.

Another peculiarity of Spanish verbs is the radical-changing verb. It is worth remembering that there are no radical changes in the imperfect, the perfect, the pluperfect, the future or the conditional. There are no radical changes in **-ar** and **-er** verbs in the preterite. So you need only be concerned with radical changes in the present tense and some **-ir** verbs in the preterite.

When you read a verb table, you will usually see a Spanish verb in a list of six.

e.g.	miro	miramos
	miras	miráis
	mira	miran

It is important to know the significance of each of these six.

The first is for 'I' so **miro** means 'I look'.

The second is for 'you' (singular familiar), so **miras** means 'you look'.

The third is for 'he', 'she', 'it' or 'you' (polite singular), so **mira** means either 'he looks' or 'she looks' or 'it looks' or 'you look'.

The fourth is for 'we' so **miramos** means 'we look'.

The fifth is for 'you' (familiar plural) so **miráis** means 'you look'.

The sixth is for 'they' or 'you' (polite plural) so **miran** means either 'they look' or 'you look'.

1.23 Present tense

The infinitives of all verbs end in either **-ar, -er** or **-ir**.

Regular verbs

-ar verbs	**-er verbs**	**-ir verbs**
miro *I look*	como *I eat*	vivo *I live*
miras *you look*	comes *you eat*	vives *you live*
mira *he, she looks, you look*	come *he, she eats, you eat*	vive *he, she lives, you live*
miramos *we look*	comemos *we eat*	vivimos *we live*
miráis *you look*	coméis *you eat*	vivís *you live*
miran *they look, you look*	comen *they eat, you eat*	viven *they live, you live*

Radical-changing verbs

Radical-changing means that the stem of the verb changes in numbers 1, 2, 3 and 6.

If there are two vowels in the stem of the infinitive e.g. **entender, preferir,** it is the last vowel of the stem that changes:

entiendo *I understand*
prefiero *I prefer*

There are three groups:

Group 1
Verbs that change **-e** to **-ie; -ar** verbs, **-er** verbs and **-ir** verbs fall into this group.
Examples of Group 1 **-ar** verbs:

cerrar *to close*	**cie**rro *I close*
despertar *to awaken*	**cie**rras *you close*
empezar *to begin*	**cie**rra *he, she closes, you close*
pensar *to think*	cerramos *we close*
sentarse *to sit down*	cerráis *you close*
nevar *to snow*	**cie**rran *they close, you close*

Examples of Group 1 **-er** verbs:

encender *to light*
entender *to understand*
perder *to lose*
querer *to want, to like, to love*

p**ie**rdo *I lose*	perdemos *we lose*
p**ie**rdes *you lose*	perdéis *you lose*
p**ie**rde *he, she loses, you lose*	p**ie**rden *they lose, you lose*

Examples of Group 1 **-ir** verbs:

divertirse *to amuse oneself*
preferir *to prefer*
sentir *to feel*

pref**ie**ro *I prefer*	preferimos *we prefer*
pref**ie**res *you prefer*	preferís *you prefer*
pref**ie**re *he, she prefers, you prefer*	pref**ie**ren *they prefer, you prefer*

Group 2

Verbs that change **-o** or **-u** to **-ue**; these can be either **-ar, -er** or **-ir** verbs.

Examples of Group 2 **-ar** verbs:

acordarse *to remember*
contar *to tell*
costar *to cost*
encontrar *to find*
jugar *to play*
volar *to fly*

enc**ue**ntro *I meet*	encontramos *we meet*
enc**ue**ntras *you meet*	encontráis *you meet*
enc**ue**ntra *he, she meets, you meet*	enc**ue**ntran *they meet, you meet*

Examples of Group 2 **-er** verbs:

doler *to hurt*
poder *to be able*
llover *to rain*
volver *to return*

v**ue**lvo *I return*	volvemos *we return*
v**ue**lves *you return*	volvéis *you return*
v**ue**lve *he, she returns, you return*	v**ue**lven *they return, you return*

Examples of Group 2 **-ir** verbs:

dormir *to sleep*
morir *to die*

d**ue**rmo *I sleep*	dormimos *we sleep*
d**ue**rmes *you sleep*	dormís *you sleep*
d**ue**rme *he, she sleeps, you sleep*	d**ue**rmen *they sleep, you sleep*

Group 3

Examples of verbs that change **-e** to **-i**:

despedirse de *to say goodbye to*
pedir *to ask for*
reír *to laugh*
repetir *to repeat*
seguir *to follow*
vestirse *to dress oneself*

p**i**do *I ask*	pedimos *we ask*
p**i**des *you ask*	pedís *you ask*
p**i**de *he, she asks, you ask*	p**i**den *they ask, you ask*

Verbs that are irregular in the present tense

Many verbs that are irregular in the present tense are only irregular in the first person singular. After that they are regular:

hacer	**hago** *I do, make*
	haces *you do, make*
	hace *he does, makes, you do*
	hacemos *we make*
	hacéis *you make*
	hacen *they make, you make*

Other verbs that are irregular in the first person only are:

caber *to be room for*	**quepo**, cabes, etc
caer *to fall*	**caigo**, caes, etc
conducir *to drive*	**conduzco**, conduces, etc
conocer *to know*	**conozco**, conoces, etc
dar *to give*	**doy**, das, etc
ofrecer *to offer*	**ofrezco**, ofreces, etc
poner *to put*	**pongo**, pones, etc
saber *to know*	**sé**, sabes, etc
salir *to go out*	**salgo**, sales, etc
traer *to bring*	**traigo**, traes, etc
ver *to see*	**veo**, ves, etc

Other irregular verbs

decir *to say*	**huir** *to flee*	**ser** *to be*
digo	huyo	soy
dices	huyes	eres
dice	huye	es
decimos	huimos	somos
decís	huís	sois
dicen	huyen	son
estar *to be*	**ir** *to go*	**tener** *to have*
estoy	voy	tengo
estás	vas	tienes
está	va	tiene
estamos	vamos	tenemos
estáis	vais	tenéis
están	van	tienen
haber *to have*	**oír** *to hear*	**venir** *to come*
he	oigo	vengo
has	oyes	vienes
ha	oye	viene
hemos	oímos	venimos
habéis	oís	venís
han	oyen	vienen

1.24 The present continuous

To form the present continuous, you need to know how to form the present participle.

To form the present participle of an **-ar** verb, remove the **-ar** and add **-ando.**
e.g. habl**ar** *to speak*, habl**ando** *speaking*

To form the present participle of an **-er** verb, remove the **-er** and add **-iendo.**
e.g. com**er** *to eat*, com**iendo** *eating*

To form the present participle of an **-ir** verb, remove the **-ir** and add **-iendo.**
e.g. viv**ir** *to live*, viv**iendo** *living*

To form the present continuous, take the present tense of **estar** and add the present participle. Here are examples of regular verbs in the present continuous tense:

hablar estoy hablando *I am talking*
estás hablando *you are talking*
está hablando *he, she is talking, you are talking*
estamos hablando *we are talking*
estáis hablando *you are talking*
están hablando *they, you are talking*

comer estoy comiendo *I am eating*
estás comiendo *you are eating*
está comiendo *he, she is eating, you are eating*
estamos comiendo *we are eating*
estáis comiendo *you are eating*
están comiendo *they, you are eating*

vivir estoy viviendo *I am living*
estás viviendo *you are living*
está viviendo *he, she is living, you are living*
estamos viviendo *we are living*
estáis viviendo *you are living*
están viviendo *they, you are living*

1.25 Perfect tense

The perfect tense in English always has 'has' or 'have' in it.
e.g. I have gone, they have run, he has seen

The perfect tense in Spanish is formed by taking the present tense of **haber** and adding the past particple. So you need to know about **haber** and you need to know about past participles.

Present tense of 'haber'

he *I have* hemos *we have*
has *you have* habéis *you have*
ha *he has, she has, you have* han *they have, you have*

Past participles

To find a past participle of a verb in English, just imagine that the words 'I have' are in front of it. So in English if you want to find the past participle of the verb 'to write', put 'I have' in front of it. We would say 'I have written' so 'written' is the past participle of 'to write'. In the same way, 'gone' is the past participle of 'to go' and so on.

In Spanish, to form the past participle of an **-ar** verb, take off the **-ar** and add **-ado.** So the past participle of **hablar** is **hablado.**

To form the past participle of an **-er** verb or an **-ir** verb, take off the **-er** or **-ir** and add **-ido.** So the past participle of **comer** is **comido** and the past participle of **vivir** is **vivido.**

Here is the perfect tense of three regular verbs:

hablar he hablado *I have spoken*
has hablado *you have spoken*
ha hablado *he, she has spoken, you have spoken*
hemos hablado *we have spoken*
habéis hablado *you have spoken*
han hablado *they have, you have spoken*

comer he comido *I have eaten*
has comido *you have eaten*
ha comido *he, she has eaten, you have eaten*
hemos comido *we have eaten*
habéis comido *you have eaten*
han comido *they have, you have eaten*

vivir he vivido *I have lived*
has vivido *you have lived*
ha vivido *he, she has lived, you have lived*
hemos vivido *we have lived*
habéis vivido *you have lived*
han vivido *they have, you have lived*

Irregular past participles

Some past participles do not obey the rules and must be learnt separately:

abrir *to open*	he **abierto** *I have opened*
cubrir *to cover*	he **cubierto** *I have covered*
decir *to say*	he **dicho** *I have said*
descubrir *to discover*	he **descubierto** *I have discovered*
escribir *to write*	he **escrito** *I have written*
hacer *to do, to make*	he **hecho** *I have done/made*
morir *to die*	ha **muerto** *he has died*
poner *to put*	he **puesto** *I have put*
romper *to break*	he **roto** *I have broken*
ver *to see*	he **visto** *I have seen*
volver *to return*	he **vuelto** *I have returned*

1.26 Preterite tense

The preterite is sometimes known as the simple past. It is used to tell about events in the past – e.g. I went, you ran, they bought.

Here is the preterite of three regular verbs. Note that there are two sets of endings, one for **-ar** verbs and one for **-er** and **-ir** verbs.

hablar hablé *I spoke*
hablaste *you spoke*
habló *he, she, you spoke*
hablamos *we spoke*
hablasteis *you spoke*
hablaron *they, you spoke*

comer comí *I ate*
comiste *you ate*
comió *he, she, you ate*
comimos *we ate*
comisteis *you ate*
comieron *they, you ate*

vivir viví *I lived*
viviste *you lived*
vivió *he, she, you lived*
vivimos *we lived*
vivisteis *you lived*
vivieron *they, you lived*

Note the role played in English by 'did' in the negative and question forms of the preterite:

hablé *I spoke*
no hablé *I did not speak*
¿hablé? *did I speak?*

Radical-changing verbs in the preterite

There are no **-ar** or **-er** radical-changing verbs in the preterite.

Some **-ir** verbs change to an **i** in numbers 3 and 6, i.e. in the third persons singular and plural. Some such verbs are:

pedir *to ask for*	preferir *to prefer*	reír *to laugh*
seguir *to follow*	sentir *to feel*	servir *to serve*
sonreír *to smile*	vestirse *to get dressed*	

pedir	pedí	pedimos
	pediste	pedisteis
	pidió	pidieron

Note what happens to the first person singular of verbs that end in **-zar, -gar** and **-car**.

empezar *to start*	empe**cé** *I started*
jugar *to play*	ju**gué** *I played*
buscar *to look for*	bus**qué** *I looked for*

Note the preterite of **caer** and the spelling changes that take place in the third persons singular and plural:

caí	caímos
caíste	caísteis
cayó	cayeron

Irregular preterites

dar *to give*	di	dimos
	diste	disteis
	dio	dieron

ser (to be) and **ir** (to go) have the same preterite:

fui	fuimos
fuiste	fuisteis
fue	fueron

Preteritos graves

These are irregular and are called **grave** because the stress in the first and third persons singular does not fall as it usually does on the last syllable but on the second to last.

andar *to walk*	**haber** *to have*	**querer** *to want*	**traer** *to bring*
anduve	hube	quise	traje
anduviste	hubiste	quisiste	trajiste
anduvo	hubo	quiso	trajo
anduvimos	hubimos	quisimos	trajimos
anduvisteis	hubisteis	quisisteis	trajisteis
anduvieron	hubieron	quisieron	trajeron (note there is no **i** here)
decir *to say*	**hacer** *to do, make*	**saber** *to know*	**venir** *to come*
dije	hice	supe	vine
dijiste	hiciste	supiste	viniste
dijo	hizo	supo	vino
dijimos	hicimos	supimos	vinimos
dijisteis	hicisteis	supisteis	vinisteis
dijeron (note there is no **i** here)	hicieron	supieron	vinieron
estar *to be*	**poder** *to be able*	**tener** *to have*	
estuve	pude	tuve	
estuviste	pudiste	tuviste	
estuvo	pudo	tuvo	
estuvimos	pudimos	tuvimos	
estuvisteis	pudisteis	tuvisteis	
estuvieron	pudieron	tuvieron	

1.27 Imperfect tense

The imperfect tense is used for things that 'used to happen' or 'were happening' – e.g. I used to play football, I was going to the cinema etc. It is often used to describe situations in the past – e.g. it was raining, she was wearing a coat.

To form the imperfect, add one of two sets of endings to the stem of the verb as follows (the **-aba** endings are for **-ar** verbs and the **-ía** endings are for **-er** and **-ir** verbs):

hablar
hablaba *I was speaking, I used to speak*
hablabas *you were speaking, you used to speak*
hablaba *he, she, was speaking, you were speaking, he, she, you used to speak*
hablábamos *we were speaking, we used to speak*
hablabais *you were speaking, you used to speak*
hablaban *they, you were speaking, they, you used to speak*

comer
comía *I was eating, I used to eat*
comías *you were eating, you used to eat*
comía *he, she, was eating, you were eating, he, she, you used to eat*
comíamos *we were eating, we used to eat*
comíais *you were eating, you used to eat*
comían *they, you were eating, they, you used to eat*

vivir
vivía *I was living, I used to live*
vivías *you were living, you used to live*
vivía *he, she was living, you were living, he, she, you used to live*
vivíamos *we were living, we used to live*
vivíais *you were living, you used to live*
vivían *they, you were living, they, you used to live*

Irregular imperfects

ir *to go*	**ser** *to be*	**ver** *to see*
iba	era	veía
ibas	eras	veías
iba	era	veía
íbamos	éramos	veíamos
ibais	erais	veíais
iban	eran	veían

1.28 Pluperfect tense

The pluperfect is used for things that had happened. This tense is identified in English by the word 'had' – e.g. he had seen, they had gone.

To form the pluperfect in Spanish, take the imperfect of **haber** and add the past participle:

hablar
había hablado *I had spoken*
habías hablado *you had spoken*
había hablado *he, she, you had spoken*
habíamos hablado *we had spoken*
habíais hablado *you had spoken*
habían hablado *they had spoken, you had spoken*

comer
había comido *I had eaten*
habías comido *you had eaten*
había comido *he, she, you had eaten*
habíamos comido *we had eaten*
habíais comido *you had eaten*
habían comido *they had eaten, you had eaten*

vivir

había vivido *I had lived*
habías vivido *you had lived*
había vivido *he, she, you had lived*
habíamos vivido *we had lived*
habíais vivido *you had lived*
habían vivido *they had lived, you had lived*

1.29 Future tense

The future tense is used to describe future events and in English the words 'will' and 'shall' are used to convey the future tense – e.g. I shall see, they will go.

To form the future tense in Spanish, you add endings to the infinitive. There is only one set of endings for the future:

-é, -ás, -á, -emos, -éis, -án

hablar	**comer**	**vivir**
hablaré *I will speak*	comeré *I will eat*	viviré *I will live*
hablarás *you will speak*	comerás *you will eat*	vivirás *you will live*
hablará *he, she, you will speak*	comerá *he, she, you will eat*	vivirá *he, she, you will live*
hablaremos *we will speak*	comeremos *we will eat*	viviremos *we will live*
hablaréis *you will speak*	comeréis *you will eat*	viviréis *you will live*
hablarán *they, you will speak*	comerán *they, you will eat*	vivirán *they, you will live*

Irregular futures

Note that all have the same ending.

decir *to say*	**hacer** *to do, make*	**poner** *to put*	**saber** *to know*	**tener** *to have*
diré	haré	pondré	sabré	tendré
dirás	harás	pondrás	sabrás	tendrás
dirá	hará	pondrá	sabrá	tendrá
diremos	haremos	pondremos	sabremos	tendremos
diréis	haréis	pondréis	sabréis	tendréis
dirán	harán	pondrán	sabrán	tendrán
haber *to have*	**poder** *to be able*	**querer** *to want*	**salir** *to go out*	**venir** *to come*
habré	podré	querré	saldré	vendré
habrás	podrás	querrás	saldrás	vendrás
habrá	podrá	querrá	saldrá	vendrá
habremos	podremos	querremos	saldremos	vendremos
habréis	podréis	querréis	saldréis	vendréis
habrán	podrán	querrán	saldrán	vendrán

'Ir a' + infinitive

Another way of expressing the future is to say that you are 'going to do something'. This is done in Spanish by **ir a** + the infinitive:

voy a comer *I am going to eat*
vas a trabajar *you are going to work*

1.30 Conditional tense

This is recognised in English by the use of the word 'would' or sometimes 'should' – e.g. I would go, I should like etc.

In Spanish you form the conditional by adding the endings used for the imperfect of **-er** and **-ir** verbs to the infinitive.

hablar	**comer**	**vivir**
hablaría *I would speak*	comería *I would eat*	viviría *I would live*
hablarías *you would speak*	comerías *you would eat*	vivirías *you would live*
hablaría *he, she, you would speak*	comería *he, she, you would eat*	viviría *he, she, you would live*
hablaríamos *we would speak*	comeríamos *we would eat*	viviríamos *we would live*
hablaríais *you would speak*	comeríais *you would eat*	viviríais *you would live*
hablarían *they, you would speak*	comerían *they, you would eat*	vivirían *they, you would live*

Irregular conditionals

The same verbs that are irregular in the future are irregular in the conditional. The irregular conditionals use the same stems as the irregular futures.

decir *to say*	**hacer** *to do, make*	**poner** *to put*	**saber** *to know*	**tener** *to have*
diría	haría	pondría	sabría	tendría
dirías	harías	pondrías	sabrías	tendrías
diría	haría	pondría	sabría	tendría
diríamos	haríamos	pondríamos	sabríamos	tendríamos
diríais	haríais	pondríais	sabríais	tendríais
dirían	harían	pondrían	sabrían	tendrían
haber *to have*	**poder** *to be able*	**querer** *to want*	**salir** *to go out*	**venir** *to come*
habría	podría	querría	saldría	vendría
habrías	podrías	querrías	saldrías	vendrías
habría	podría	querría	saldría	vendría
habríamos	podríamos	querríamos	saldríamos	vendríamos
habríais	podríais	querríais	saldríais	vendríais
habrían	podrían	querrían	saldrían	vendrían

Chapter 2
Test yourself on grammar

2.1 Articles

Revise the Grammar section and then before you look at the answers give the Spanish for:

1 The teacher's chair.
2 I went to the market.
3 The new carpet.
4 The dirty water.
5 The water is dirty.
6 I like cats.
7 English is easy.
8 I learn English.
9 I speak English.
10 I know English.
11 King Charles.
12 Good evening, Mr. Gómez.
13 I know Mr. Gómez.
14 I went there on Saturday.
15 King Charles the Third.
16 He is a lawyer and his wife is a Spaniard.
17 The crossword, the climate, the map, the problem, the programme, the tram.
18 The photo, the hand, the radio, the corkscrew, the windscreen.
19 The priest found a cure.
20 The captain gave an order.
21 He found an earring.
22 The apples on the appletree.
23 The address, the series, the customs.
24 He lost his pencils twice.
25 The French like the songs.
26 I like the Suárez family.

2.2 Adjectives

Revise the Grammar section and then before you look at the answers give the Spanish for:

1 The white chair and the green table.
2 Spanish cooking, talkative people.
3 We have had a good day.
4 The first book, the third table.
5 Saint Thomas was a great man.

6 His former job was in an ancient building.
7 The poor man asked for money.
8 The teacher himself made the same error.
9 Each book is extremely expensive.

2.3 Adverbs

Revise the Grammar section and then before you look at the answers give the Spanish for:

1 Carefully, simply, quietly.
2 Carefully and quietly.
3 He did it slowly and badly.
4 I am upstairs, he is downstairs.
5 I am here, he is there.
6 I often go there when I have enough money.
7 He did not come till seven, then he ate a lot and also drank a lot.
8 He has already arrived.
9 He is taller than him and a better player.
10 The main square is the most interesting place in the town.
11 She is as tall as her mother.
12 I do not have as much money as my brother.
13 Speak more slowly.

2.4 Numbers

Revise the Grammar section and then before you look at the answers write the Spanish words for:

1 16
2 23
3 34
4 101
5 506
6 702
7 950
8 200 books
9 190
10 100,000
11 1000 pounds
12 a million pounds
13 He was born in 1946.
14 The four people stayed on the fourth floor.

2.5 Time

Revise the Grammar section and then before you look at the answers give the Spanish for:

1 It is four in the morning.
2 It is eleven at night.
3 It is ten to seven in the morning.
4 It is a quarter past six in the evening.
5 At a quarter to four in the afternoon.

2.6 Negatives

Revise the Grammar section and then before you look at the answers give the Spanish for:

1 Nobody visits him.
2 He never goes to church.

3 He has no money.
4 Neither his brother nor his sister helped him.
5 I did not go and he did not go either.

2.7 Pronouns

Revise the Grammar section and then before you look at the answers give the Spanish for:

1 I saw him but he did not see me.
2 We saw her but she did not see us.
3 I visited them, they visited you, he visited us.
4 I am watching you. I am going to visit you.
5 Give it to me.
6 Do not give it to them.
7 I sent it to him.
8 I sent them to them.
9 The present is for him.
10 He wants it for himself.
11 She is with me.

2.8 Personal 'a'

Revise the Grammar section and then before you look at the answers give the Spanish for:

1 I saw my mother.
2 I saw the match.
3 I have a friend.
4 I am looking for a doctor.
5 I saw the dog in the kitchen.

2.9 Demonstrative adjectives and pronouns

Revise the Grammar section and then before you look at the answers give the Spanish for:

1 I saw this book in this room.
2 I saw that book in that room.
3 I saw these books in these rooms.
4 I saw those books in those rooms.

2.10 Possessive adjectives

Revise the Grammar section and then before you look at the answers give the Spanish for:

My chair, my chairs, your sister, your sisters, his dog, her dog, his dogs, her dogs, our house, our friends, your book, your books, their friend, their friends.

2.11 Possessive pronouns

Revise the Grammar section and then before you look at the answers give the Spanish for:

Your friend and mine, my friend and yours, your friend and ours, my friend and theirs.

2.12 Relative pronouns

1 The book that I bought.
2 The town near which I live.
3 Tell me what is happening.
4 I want to know everything that is happening.
5 The man whose wife works here.

2.13 Interrogatives

Revise the Grammar section and then before you look at the answers give the Spanish for:

1 Where are you going?
2 What time will you be back?
3 When will he arrive?
4 How many friends has he?
5 Why did he do it?
6 Who is with him?
7 Which is your favourite?

2.14 'Ser' and 'estar'

Revise the Grammar section and then before you look at the answers give the Spanish for:

1 He is a teacher.
2 It is a chair.
3 It is late.
4 It is near here.
5 The traffic lights are red.
6 The car is red.
7 I am listening.

2.15 'Conocer' and 'saber'

Revise the Grammar section and then before you look at the answers give the Spanish for:

1 I know London.
2 I know his friend.
3 I know the time.
4 I can ride a bicycle.

2.16 'Deber' and 'tener que'

Revise the Grammar section and then before you look at the answers give the Spanish for:

1 I must not keep him waiting.
2 I must work in order to live.

2.17 'Tener'

Revise the Grammar section and then before you look at the answers give the Spanish for:

1 I am hot.
2 I am cold.
3 I am hungry.
4 I am thirsty.
5 I am successful.
6 I want to go out.
7 The match takes place on Sunday.
8 I am in a great hurry.

2.18 Prepositions

Revise the Grammar section and then before you look at the answers give the Spanish for:

1 I walked along the river in spite of the weather.
2 The apple-tree is beside the house. The flowers are around the house.
3 Before arriving, I stopped near his house.
4 It is under the window against the wall.
5 From the house, you can see it in front of you.
6 After arriving, he put his coat behind the door.
7 During the exam he smoked instead of writing.
8 The flat is opposite the cinema, between two shops and is over a Post Office.
9 He is travelling towards Valencia and will not arrive until eight.
10 He earns more than me: he earns more than two thousand pounds a month.
11 According to his friends, he left without his money … everything except his credit card.
12 We arrived at about six and talked about the weather.

2.19 Present tense

Revise the Grammar section and then before you look at the answers give the Spanish for:

1 I eat fish.
2 I watch the film while he looks for his book.
3 They live in a city but I live in the country.
4 I close the door.
5 He awakens me at six.
6 They begin to study at seven.
7 We think that it is silly.
8 They sit down to eat.
9 It never snows in Spain.
10 I light the candle at nine.
11 We understand what he says.
12 They lose every game.
13 I want to go home.
14 I always have a good time in Spain.
15 He prefers France.
16 I feel tired.
17 Do you remember that day?
18 I tell the story to the child.
19 We find things under his bed.
20 They play tennis on Saturdays.
21 I fly to Spain tomorrow.
22 My arm hurts.
23 I can do it.
24 It rains in the winter.
25 We return tomorrow.

26 Do you sleep till six?
27 I am dying of hunger.
28 He says goodbye to his friends.
29 You ask for the bill.
30 They laugh when he repeats the question.
31 I continue to get dressed.
32 I do, I fall, I drive, I know, I give, I offer, I put, I know, I go out, I bring, I see.
33 I say that I am in the dining room.
34 She flees the danger.
35 We go when we hear the noise.
36 I am a member and I have a card.
37 They come from Barcelona.
38 I am eating the meal while she is talking.

2.20 Perfect tense

Revise the Grammar section and then before you look at the answers give the Spanish for:

1 I have spoken, he has eaten, they have lived.
2 I have opened the box.
3 We have covered the food.
4 They have said what they think.
5 You have discovered the truth.
6 She has written a letter.
7 I have done the same.
8 He has died.
9 I have put it on the table.
10 He has broken the chair.
11 We have seen the beach.
12 I have returned.

2.21 Preterite tense

Revise the Grammar section and then before you look at the answers give the Spanish for:

1 I spoke, he ate, she spoke, we lived, they lived, you ate (sing. fam.), you ate (pl. fam.).
2 He asked for wine though he preferred beer.
3 She laughed and followed him.
4 They felt cold as he opened the door.
5 He served the meal.
6 She smiled as she dressed.
7 I started, I played, I looked for an opportunity.
8 When he fell, they fell.
9 I gave her a kiss.
10 I went to the party. It was marvellous.
11 I walked towards him.
12 I said 'hello'.
13 He was there.
14 There was an accident.
15 I did it.
16 He could not do it.
17 We did not want to go.
18 They knew what to do.
19 I had to do it.
20 He brought me a beer.
21 He came at six.

2.22 Imperfect tense

Revise the Grammar section and then before you look at the answers give the Spanish for:

1 I was looking through the window.
2 She was eating paella.
3 We were living in Valencia.
4 I was going to visit Spain.
5 He was my friend.
6 From the balcony, one could see the city.

2.23 Pluperfect tense

Revise the Grammar section and then before you look at the answers give the Spanish for:

1 Someone had stolen my bicycle!
2 I had visited her already.
3 She had never eaten paella.
4 They had never seen Valencia.

2.24 Future tense

Revise the Grammar section and then before you look at the answers give the Spanish for:

1 I will find the book.
2 He will eat in a restaurant.
3 They will not see the film.
4 She will not say who did it.
5 There will be an accident.
6 I will do it.
7 I will be able to go.
8 He will put it on the table.
9 We will not want to go.
10 He will know the address.
11 We will go out this evening.
12 The match will not take place.
13 They will come at six.

2.25 'Ir a' + infinitive

Revise the Grammar section and then before you look at the answers give the Spanish for:

1 I am going to study this evening.
2 We are going to eat at six.
3 They are going to visit his friends.

2.26 Conditional tense

Revise the Grammar section and then before you look at the answers give the Spanish for:

1 He said that he would speak to her.
2 He said that he would not eat it.
3 He said that he would live there all his life.
4 He said that he would tell the truth.
5 He said that there would be an accident.
6 He said that he would do his homework.
7 He said that he would not be able to do it.
8 He said that he would put the book on the table.
9 He said that he would like to see me.
10 He said that he would know the result.
11 He said that he would go out with her.
12 He said that he would have to go.
13 He said that he would come to the party.

Chapter 3
Test yourself suggested answers

Here are suggested answers to the *Test yourself* section. It should be noted that these suggestions are not the only way to translate the sentences. If in doubt you should ask your teacher.

3.1 Articles

1 La silla del profesor.
2 Fui al mercado.
3 La alfombra nueva.
4 El agua sucia.
5 El agua es sucia.
6 Me gustan los gatos.
7 El inglés es fácil.
8 Aprendo inglés.
9 Hablo inglés.
10 Sé inglés.
11 El rey Carlos.
12 Buenas tardes, señor Gómez.
13 Conozco al señor Gómez.
14 Fui allí el sábado.
15 El rey Carlos tercero.
16 Él es abogado y su esposa es española.
17 El crucigrama, el clima, el mapa, el problema, el programa, el tranvía.
18 La foto, la mano, la radio, el sacacorchos, el parabrisas.
19 El cura encontró una cura.
20 El capitán dio una órden.
21 Encontró un pendiente.
22 Las manzanas en el manzano.
23 La dirección, la serie, la aduana.
24 Perdió sus lápices dos veces.
25 A los franceses les gustan las canciones.
26 Me gusta la familia Suárez.

3.2 Adjectives

1 La silla blanca y la mesa verde.
2 La cocina española, la gente habladora.
3 Hemos tenido un buen día.
4 El primer libro, la tercera mesa.
5 Santo Tomás era un gran hombre.
6 Su trabajo anterior estaba en un edificio antiguo.

7 El hombre pobre pidió dinero.
8 El profesor mismo hizo el mismo error.
9 Cada uno de los libros es carísimo.

3.3 Adverbs

1 Cuidadosamente, sencillamente, silenciosamente.
2 Cuidadosa y silenciosamente.
3 Lo hizo lentamente y mal.
4 Estoy arriba, él está abajo.
5 Estoy aquí, él está allí.
6 Voy allí a menudo cuando tengo suficiente dinero.
7 No vino hasta las siete; luego comió mucho y también bebió mucho.
8 Ya ha llegado.
9 Él es más alto que él y mejor jugador.
10 La plaza mayor es el sitio más interesante del pueblo.
11 Ella es tan alta como su madre.
12 No tengo tanto dinero como mi hermano.
13 Habla más despacio.

3.4 Numbers

1 dieciséis
2 veintitrés
3 treinta y cuatro
4 ciento uno
5 quinientos seis
6 setecientos dos
7 novecientos cincuenta
8 doscientos libros
9 ciento noventa
10 cien mil
11 mil libras
12 un millón de libras
13 Nació en mil novecientos cuarenta y seis.
14 Las cuatro personas se quedaron en el cuarto piso.

3.5 Time

1 Son las cuatro de la madrugada.
2 Son las once de la noche.
3 Son las siete menos diez de la mañana.
4 Son las seis y cuarto de la tarde.
5 A las cuatro menos cuarto de la tarde.

3.6 Negatives

1 Nadie le visita.
2 Nunca va a la iglesia.

3 No tiene ningún dinero.
4 Ni su hermano ni su hermana le ayudaron.
5 No fui y él no fue tampoco.

3.7 Pronouns

1 Le vi pero él no me vio.
2 La vimos pero ella no nos vio.
3 Les visité, te visitaron, nos visitó.
4 Estoy mirándote. Voy a visitarte.
5 Dámelo.
6 No se lo dé.
7 Se lo mandé.
8 Se los mandé.
9 El regalo es para él.
10 Lo quiere para sí.
11 Está conmigo.

3.8 Personal 'a'

1 Vi a mi madre.
2 Vi el partido.
3 Tengo un amigo.
4 Busco un médico.
5 Vi al perro en la cocina.

3.9 Demonstrative adjectives and pronouns

1 Vi este libro en esta sala.
2 Vi ese libro en esa sala.
3 Vi estos libros en estas salas.
4 Vi esos libros en esas salas.

3.10 Possessive adjectives

Mi silla, mis sillas, tu hermana, tus hermanas, su perro, su perro, sus perros, sus perros, nuestra casa, nuestros amigos, vuestro libro, vuestros libros, su amigo, sus amigos.

3.11 Possessive pronouns

Tu amigo y el mío, mi amigo y el tuyo, vuestro amigo y el nuestro, mi amigo y el suyo.

3.12 Relative pronouns

1 El libro que compré.
2 El pueblo cerca del que vivo.
3 Dime lo que pasa.
4 Quiero saber todo lo que pasa.
5 El hombre cuya esposa trabaja aquí.

3.13 Interrogatives

1 ¿Adónde vas?
2 ¿A qué hora vuelves?
3 ¿Cuándo llegará?
4 ¿Cuántos amigos tiene?
5 ¿Por qué lo hizo?
6 ¿Quién está con él?
7 ¿Cuál es tu favorito?

3.14 'Ser' and 'estar'

1 Él es profesor.
2 Es una silla.
3 Es tarde.
4 Está cerca de aquí.
5 Los semáforos están rojos.
6 El coche es rojo.
7 Estoy escuchando.

3.15 'Conocer' and 'saber'

1 Conozco Londres.
2 Conozco a su amigo.
3 Sé la hora.
4 Sé montar en bicicleta.

3.16 'Deber' and 'tener que'

1 No debo hacerle esperar.
2 Tengo que trabajar para vivir.

3.17 'Tener'

1 Tengo calor.
2 Tengo frío.
3 Tengo hambre.
4 Tengo sed.
5 Tengo éxito.
6 Tengo ganas de salir.
7 El partido tiene lugar el domingo.
8 Tengo mucha prisa.

3.18 Prepositions

1 Fui de pie a lo largo del río a pesar del tiempo.
2 El manzano está al lado de la casa. Las flores están alrededor de la casa.
3 Antes de llegar, me paré cerca de su casa.
4 Está debajo de la ventana contra la pared.
5 Desde la casa, puedes verlo delante de ti.
6 Después de llegar, puso el abrigo detrás de la puerta.
7 Durante el examen fumó en vez de escribir.
8 El piso está enfrente del cine, entre dos tiendas y está encima de una oficina de correos.

9 Viaja hacia Valencia y no llegará hasta las ocho.
10 Gana más que yo: gana más de dos mil libras al mes.
11 Según sus amigos, se fue sin su dinero ... todo salvo su tarjeta de crédito.
12 Llegamos sobre las seis y hablamos sobre el tiempo.

3.19 Present tense

1 Como pescado.
2 Veo la película mientras él busca su libro.
3 Viven en la ciudad pero yo vivo en el campo.
4 Cierro la puerta.
5 Me despierta a las seis.
6 Empiezan a estudiar a las siete.
7 Pensamos que es una tontería.
8 Se sientan para comer.
9 Nunca nieva en España.
10 Enciendo la vela a las nueve.
11 Entendemos lo que dice.
12 Pierden todos los partidos.
13 Quiero ir a casa.
14 Siempre me divierto en España.
15 Prefiere Francia.
16 Me siento cansado.
17 ¿Te acuerdas de aquel día?
18 Cuento la historia al niño.
19 Encontramos cosas debajo de su cama.
20 Juegan al tenis los sábados.
21 Vuelo a España mañana.
22 Me duele el brazo.
23 Sé hacerlo.
24 Llueve en invierno.
25 Volvemos mañana.
26 ¿Duermes hasta las seis?
27 Me muero de hambre.
28 Se despide de sus amigos.
29 Pides la cuenta.
30 Se ríen cuando repite la pregunta.
31 Sigo vistiéndome.
32 Hago, me caigo, conduzco, sé, doy, ofrezco, pongo, conozco, salgo, traigo, veo.
33 Digo que estoy en el comedor.
34 Huye del peligro.
35 Nos vamos cuando oímos el ruido.
36 Soy socio y tengo una tarjeta.
37 Vienen de Barcelona.
38 Estoy comiendo la comida mientras ella está hablando.

3.20 Perfect tense

1 He hablado, él ha comido, han vivido.
2 He abierto la caja.
3 Hemos cubierto la comida.
4 Han dicho lo que piensan.
5 Has descubierto la verdad.
6 Ella ha escrito una carta.
7 He hecho lo mismo.
8 Se ha muerto.
9 Lo he puesto en la mesa.
10 Ha roto la silla.
11 Hemos visto la playa.
12 He vuelto.

3.21 Preterite tense

1 Hablé, comió, habló, vivimos, vivieron, comiste, comisteis.
2 Pidió vino aunque prefería cerveza.
3 Se rió y le siguió.
4 Sintieron frío cuando abrió la puerta.
5 Sirvió la comida.
6 Sonrió mientras se vestía.
7 Empecé, jugué, busqué una oportunidad.
8 Cuando se cayó él, se cayeron ellos.
9 Le di un beso.
10 Fui a la fiesta. Fue maravillosa.
11 Anduve hacia él.
12 Dije 'hola'.
13 Estuvo allí.
14 Hubo un accidente.
15 Lo hice.
16 No pudo hacerlo.
17 No quisimos marcharnos.
18 Supieron qué hacer.
19 Tuve que hacerlo.
20 Me trajo una cerveza.
21 Vino a las seis.

3.22 Imperfect tense

1. Miraba por la ventana.
2. Comía paella.
3. Vivíamos en Valencia.
4. Iba a visitar España.
5. Era mi amigo.
6. Desde el balcón, se veía la ciudad.

3.23 Pluperfect tense

1. Alguien había robado mi bicicleta.
2. Ya la había visitado.
3. Nunca había comido paella.
4. Nunca habían visto Valencia.

3.24 Future tense

1. Encontraré el libro.
2. Comerá en un restaurante.
3. No verán la película.
4. No dirá quién lo hizo.
5. Habrá un accidente.
6. Lo haré.
7. Podré ir.
8. Lo pondrá en la mesa.
9. No querremos ir.
10. Sabrá la dirección.
11. Saldremos esta tarde.
12. El partido no tendrá lugar.
13. Vendrán a las seis.

3.25 'Ir a' + infinitive

1. Voy a estudiar esta tarde.
2. Vamos a comer a las seis.
3. Van a visitar a sus amigos.

3.26 Conditional tense

1. Dijo que hablaría con ella.
2. Dijo que no lo comería.
3. Dijo que viviría allí toda su vida.
4. Dijo que diría la verdad.
5. Dijo que habría un accidente.
6. Dijo que haría sus deberes.
7. Dijo que no podría hacerlo.
8. Dijo que pondría el libro en la mesa.
9. Dijo que querría verme.
10. Dijo que sabría el resultado.
11. Dijo que saldría con ella.
12. Dijo que tendría que ir.
13. Dijo que vendría a la fiesta.

Chapter 4
Vocabulary

4.1 Introduction

- This vocabulary chapter contains the words you need to know for GCSE.
- In their GCSE syllabuses all the Exam Boards have a list of about 1500 words: this list is called the Minimum Core Vocabulary.
- The exams are based on these lists.
- This chapter covers the minimum core vocabulary for six major exam boards (MEG, NEAB, Edexcel (formerly ULEAC), SEG, WJEC, NICCEA).
- The first section of words, Days, Months, etc, is a section common to all Boards.
- Each Exam Board will use words outside its list for the more difficult questions – so you should try to learn all the words in this chapter.
- All the Exam Boards have the same topic areas: these areas are called the Areas of Experience.
- The words in this chapter have been categorised into the Areas of Experience which are the topic categories that all Boards use.
- There is also a section on IT vocabulary. These words are not on the Exam Boards' lists.

4.2 Important words

Words common to all Boards

Days

los días de la semana the days of the week
lunes Monday
martes Tuesday
miércoles Wednesday
jueves Thursday
viernes Friday
sábado Saturday
domingo Sunday

Months

los meses del año the months of the year
enero January
febrero February
marzo March
abril April
mayo May
junio June
julio July
agosto August
setiembre September
octubre October
noviembre November
diciembre December

Numbers

los números cardinales cardinal numbers
cero 0
uno 1
dos 2
tres 3

cuatro 4
cinco 5
seis 6
siete 7
ocho 8
nueve 9
diez 10
once 11
doce 12
trece 13
catorce 14
quince 15
dieciséis 16
diecisiete 17
dieciocho 18
diecinueve 19
veinte 20
veintiuno 21
veintidós 22
veintitrés 23
veinticuatro 24
veinticinco 25
veintiséis 26
veintisiete 27
veintiocho 28
veintinueve 29
treinta 30
treinta y uno 31
treinta y dos 32
cuarenta 40
cincuenta 50
sesenta 60
setenta 70
ochenta 80
noventa 90
cien 100
ciento uno 101
ciento noventa 190
doscientos 200
doscientos once 211
mil 1000
dos mil 2000
un millón 1 000 000
dos millones 2 000 000

los números ordinales ordinal numbers
primero first
segundo second
tercero third
cuarto fourth
quinto fifth
sexto sixth
séptimo seventh
octavo eighth
noveno ninth
décimo tenth

Time

la hora the time
¿Qué hora es? What's the time?
Son las siete It's seven o'clock
Son las dos y cinco It's five past two
Son las nueve y cuarto It's a quarter past nine
Son las cuatro y media It's half past four
Son las seis menos veinte It's twenty to six
Es la una menos cuarto It's a quarter to one
Son las doce It's twelve o'clock noon/midnight
Son las doce y media It's half past twelve
A las cuatro y veinticinco de la tarde At 16.25
A las tres menos cuarto de la tarde At 14.45
A las seis de la tarde At 18.00
de la mañana a.m.
de la tarde p.m. until dark
de la noche p.m. after dark
A las cuatro de la mañana At 4 o'clock in the morning

Date

¿Qué fecha es hoy? What's the date today?
Hoy es lunes trece de enero de mil novecientos noventa y seis It's Monday the thirteenth of January 1996
El domingo primero de mayo Sunday the first of May

Seasons

las estaciones del año the seasons
la primavera spring
el verano summer
el otoño autumn
el invierno winter
en primavera in spring
en verano, en otoño, en invierno in summer/autumn/winter
durante el verano during the summer

Question words

los interrogativos question words
¿a qué hora? what time?
¿de quién? ¿de quiénes? whose?
¿con quién? ¿con quiénes? with whom?
¿cuántas veces? how often?
¿cuánto tiempo? how long?
¿cuántos? ¿cuántas? how many?
¿cómo? how?
¿dónde? where?
¿por qué? why?
¿qué? what?
¿cuándo? when?
¿quién? ¿quiénes? who?

4.3 Useful words

Quantities

la cantidad quantity
el centímetro centimetre
la cucharada spoonful
la decena de about ten
la docena dozen
el gramo gramme
el kilo kilo
el kilogramo kilogramme
el kilómetro kilometre
el litro litre
media docena half dozen
medio kilo half a kilo
la milla mile
la mitad half
el montón pile
el par pair
el pedazo piece
la pieza piece
por ciento per cent
el resto remains
el trozo piece

Negatives

no … jamás never
no … nada nothing
no … nadie nobody
no … ni … ni neither … nor
no … ninguno no
no … nunca never
no … tampoco neither

Prepositions

a lo largo de along
a mediados de half way through
acerca de concerning
además de in addition to
alrededor de around
bajo under
a causa de because of
cerca de near
con with
contra against
debajo de under
delante de in front of
desde since
después de after
detrás de behind
durante during
en medio de in the middle of
encima de above
enfrente de opposite
entre between, among
al final de at the end of
fuera de outside
hacia towards
hasta until
junto a next to
al lado de beside
lejos de far from
a orillas de on the banks of
para for
por for, through, by
según according to
sin without
sobre on
tras behind
a través de across

'Tener' expressions

tener calor to be hot
tener dieciséis años to be sixteen
tener dolor de … to have a sore …
tener éxito to be successful
tener fiebre to have a temperature
tener frío to be cold
tener ganas de to want to
tener hambre to be hungry
tener lugar to take place
tener miedo to be frightened
tener prisa to be in a hurry
tener que to have to
tener razón to be right
tener sed to be thirsty
tener sueño to be sleepy
tener suerte to be lucky

Other words and expressions

a propósito by the way
algo something
alguien somebody
alguno some
aquel that
así so
aun even
aunque although
como as
con respecto a regarding
conmigo, contigo with me, with you
al contrario on the contrary
entretanto meanwhile
incluso even
mientras while
pero but
por lo tanto therefore
porque because
pues then
puesto que since
quizá(s) perhaps

si if
sin embargo however
sobre todo especially
tal such
tal vez perhaps
tan so
unos some
ya que since

4.4 Area of Experience A – Everyday activities

Home life

At home

el aire climatizado air conditioning
el aire acondicionado air conditioning
el balcón balcony
la bombilla light-bulb
la calefacción central central heating
la casa house
la cerradura lock
la chimenea fireplace/chimney
la cortina curtain
el cristal pane of glass
el cuadro picture
el cubo de la basura rubbish bin
la electricidad electricity
el electrodoméstico electrical appliances
el interruptor switch
la lámpara lamp
la luz light
el magnetofón tape recorder
los muebles furniture
el objeto object
la papelera waste-paper basket
la pared wall
la persiana blinds
la pintura painting
el primer piso first floor
la puerta door
la puerta principal front door
el radiador radiator
el reloj clock
el rincón corner (inside)
el suelo floor
la tabla plank, board
el techo ceiling
el tejado roof
la valla fence
la ventana window

The rooms

la bodega wine cellar
el comedor dining room
el cuarto de baño bathroom
el cuarto de estar lounge
el desván attic
el dormitorio bedroom
la entrada entrance
la escalera stairs
el estudio study
el garaje garage
la habitación room
el hogar home
el pasillo corridor
el patio patio, yard
el piso floor
la planta baja ground floor
la sala de estar lounge
el salón lounge
el sótano basement
el vestíbulo hall

Materials

el acero steel
el algodón cotton
el cuero leather
el hierro iron
la lana wool
la madera wood
el mármol marble
el nylon nylon
el oro gold
la piel leather
la plata silver
el plomo lead
la seda silk
el vidrio/cristal glass

Adjectives

amueblado furnished
anterior previous
cómodo comfortable
completo full
final final
ideal ideal
igual same
importante important
incómodo uncomfortable
interior interior
lujoso luxurious
magnífico magnificent
mismo same
moderno modern
otro another

preciso necessary
privado private
viejo old

Verbs

afeitarse to shave
apagar to switch off (e.g. light)
aparcar to park
arrancar to start
barrer to sweep
calentar to heat
casarse to get married
cepillarse to brush (i.e. teeth)
cerrar to close
cerrar con llave to lock
cocinar to cook
coger to get
colgar to hang
colocar to place
compartir to share
congelar to freeze
dejar to let, to leave
descansar to rest
desnudarse to get undressed
despertarse to wake up (oneself)
dormir to sleep
dormirse to fall asleep
ducharse to have a shower
encender la luz to switch on the light
encontrar to meet, to find
encontrarse to be found
estar to be
fregar to scrub
freír to fry
funcionar to work (of machinery)
lavar to wash
lavar los platos to wash the dishes
lavarse to get washed
lavarse la cabeza to wash one's hair
lavarse los dientes to clean one's teeth
levantarse to get up
limpiar to clean
madrugar to get up early
manchar to stain
morder to bite
pasar la aspiradora to do the vacuuming
peinarse to comb one's hair
planchar to iron
poder to be able
poner la mesa to lay the table
quitar la mesa to clear the table
quitarse la ropa to take off clothes
rasgar to tear
renovar to renew
reparar to repair
sacar to take out, to buy (a ticket)
secar to dry
soñar to dream
utilizar to use
vaciar to empty
vestirse to get dressed

The living room

la alfombra carpet
la butaca armchair
el canapé settee
la cómoda chest of drawers
la estantería shelves
la moqueta carpet (fitted)
el sillón armchair
el sofá settee

The bedroom

la agenda diary
la almohada pillow
el cajón drawer
la cama bed
la cama de matrimonio double bed
el colchón mattress
el despertador alarm clock
el estante shelf
el guardarropa wardrobe
la manta blanket
el póster poster
la sábana sheet
el secador hairdryer
el tocador dressing table

The bathroom

el baño bath
el cepillo de dientes toothbrush
el champú shampoo
la ducha shower
el espejo mirror
el jabón soap
el lavabo washbasin
el maquillaje make-up
la máquina de afeitar electric shaver
el papel higiénico toilet paper
la pasta de dientes toothpaste
el peine comb
el perfume perfume
el taburete stool
las tijeras scissors
la toalla towel

The kitchen

el abrelatas tin-opener
el aparador sideboard
el armario cupboard
la bandeja tray
la cacerola saucepan
la cocina kitchen
la cocina cooker
la cocina de gas gas cooker
la cocina eléctrica electric cooker
el congelador freezer
el fregadero sink

el frigorífico fridge
el grifo tap
el horno oven
la jarra jug
la lata tin
la lavadora washing machine
el lavaplatos dishwasher
la mesa table
la nevera fridge
el olor smell
el sacacorchos corkscrew
la sartén frying pan
la silla chair
la taza cup
el tisú tissue
la vajilla crockery

The garden

el árbol tree
el arbusto shrub
el césped lawn
la flor flower
la hierba grass
el jardín garden
el manzano apple tree
el muro wall
la planta plant
la rama branch
la rosa rose
el sendero path
la violeta violet

Pets

la cobaya hamster
el conejo rabbit
el gato cat
el hámster hamster
el insecto palo stick insect
la jaula cage
los peces tropicales tropical fish
el periquito parakeet
el perro dog
el pez fish
el ratón mouse
la tortuga tortoise

The housework

la aguja needle
el agujero hole
el alfiler pin
la aspiradora vacuum cleaner
la basura rubbish
el cepillo brush
la faena de casa chore
el hilo thread
la mancha stain
el orden order (i.e. tidiness)
la plancha iron
el polvo dust
los quehaceres chores

Houses

la casa adosada semi-detached house
la casa de campo country house
la casa de un piso bungalow
la casa independiente detached house

School

In class

el acento accent
los apuntes notes
la asignatura subject
la atención attention
el aula (f) classroom
el bachillerato A-level
la cartelera notice board
la casilla box (on exam paper)
el castigo punishment
la clase class
el colegio school
el conocimiento knowledge
la contestación answer
los correcciones corrections
el COU pre-university year
el curso course
los deberes homework
el detalle detail
el dibujo drawing
el diccionario dictionary
la disciplina discipline
la educación education
el ejemplo example
el ejercicio exercise
el error mistake
el esfuerzo effort
los estudios studies
el examen exam
la excepción exception
la figura shape
la frase sentence
el gimnasio gymnasium
la gramática grammar
hacer preguntas to ask questions
el informe piece of information
el intercambio school exchange
el/la interno/a boarder
la lección lesson
la letra letter (e.g. of alphabet)
el método method
el modo way, manner
la nota mark
el número number
la orden command
la página page
la palabra word
el papel paper
el pasado past
el permiso permission
la pizarra blackboard

la pregunta question
el progreso progress
la prueba test
el pupitre desk
el recreo break
la respuesta answer
la sección section
la tarea homework
el timbre bell
la tiza chalk
el trimestre term
el uniforme uniform
el vocabulario vocabulary
la vuelta al colegio return to school

Subjects

el arte art
la biología biology
el castellano Spanish language
las ciencias sciences
el drama drama
la economía economics
la educación física PE
la física physics
la geografía geography
la gimnasia gym
la historia history
los idiomas languages
la informática IT
la literatura literature
las matemáticas maths
la mecanografía typing
la música music
la química chemistry
la tecnología technology
los trabajos manuales CDT

Adjectives

aburrido bored
afortunado fortunate
antiguo old, former
ausente absent
autorizado permitted
calificado qualified
católico Catholic
correcto correct
cristiano Christian
estricto strict
exigente demanding
fácil easy
festivo (día festivo) holiday
incorrecto incorrect
injusto injust
lógico logic
mixto mixed
necesario necessary
obligatorio compulsory
parecido similar
particular private
pobre poor
posible possible
presente present
probable probable
propio own
público public
querido dear (in a letter)
retrasado delayed
severo severe
sorprendente surprising

The places

la cantina/el comedor dining area
el colegio mixto mixed school
el colegio técnico technical school
la escuela primary school
el instituto school
el laboratorio lab

The equipment

el aparato piece of equipment
el boli pen
el bolígrafo pen
la calculadora calculator
la cosa thing
el cuaderno exercise book
la fotocopiadora photocopier
la goma rubber
la hoja de papel sheet of paper
el lápiz pencil
el libro book
el libro de texto text book
el ordenador computer
la regla ruler
el rotulador felt-tip pen
el sacapuntas pencil sharpener

The people

el/la alumno/a pupil
el conserje caretaker
el/la director/a headteacher
el/la estudiante student
el/la idiota idiot
el/la imbécil imbecile
el profesor teacher
el tutor tutor

Verbs

aburrirse to be bored
acabar de to have just
aguantar to put up with
añadir to add
aprender to learn
aprobar to pass (an exam)
arreglar to sort out
calcular to calculate
castigar to punish
comenzar to begin

comparar to compare
comprender to understand
continuar to continue
copiar to copy
corregir to correct
deber to have to
dejar el colegio to leave school
deletrear to spell
devolver to give back
dibujar to draw
doblar to double
educar to educate, to bring up
empezar to begin
empujar to push
enseñar to teach
entender to understand
escoger to choose
escuchar to listen
estudiar to study
examinarse to take an exam
explicar to explain
fracasar to fail
inquietarse to worry
interesarse por to be interested in
levantar la mano to raise one's hand
lograr to succeed
necesitar to need
ofrecer to offer
olvidarse de to forget
organizar to organise
pasar lista to call the register
pelear to fight
permitir to allow
poner to put
ponerse a to begin to
preguntar to ask
preocuparse to worry
preparar to prepare
prohibir to forbid
querer decir to mean
repasar to revise
repetir to repeat
responder to answer
resultar to turn out
revisar to check
sacar buenas notas to get good marks
sacar malas notas to get bad marks
significar to mean
sonar to sound
subrayar to underline
suspender to fail (exam)
sustituir to substitute
terminar to finish
traducir to translate
valer to be worth

Food and drink

Meals

el almuerzo lunch
la cena evening meal
el desayuno breakfast
la merienda snack/picnic

Vegetables

el ajo garlic
la cebolla onion
el champiñon mushroom
la col cabbage
las coles de Bruselas sprouts
la coliflor cauliflower
el espárrago asparagus
las espinacas spinach
el guisante pea
el haba (f) bean
las judías verdes green beans
la lechuga lettuce
las legumbres vegetables
la patata potato
el pepino cucumber
el pimiento pepper
las verduras vegetables
la zanahoria carrot

Fruit

el albaricoque apricot
la almendra almond
la cereza cherry
la ciruela plum
la frambuesa raspberry
la fresa strawberry
la fruta fruit
el higo fig
el limón lemon
la manzana apple
el melocotón peach
el melón melon
la naranja orange
la pera pear
la piña pineapple
el plátano banana
la sandía water melon
el tomate tomato
la uva grape

Meat

el biftec steak
el bistec steak
la carne meat
la carne de cerdo pork
la carne de cordero lamb
la carne de ternera veal
la carne de vaca beef
el chorizo garlic sausage
la chuleta chop
el cordero lamb
el filete fillet
el jamón ham
el jamón de York York ham

el jamón serrano cured ham
el pollo chicken
el salchichón garlic sausage
el solomillo sirloin
la ternera veal
el tocino bacon

On the table

el aceite oil
el azúcar sugar
los cubiertos cutlery
la cuchara spoon
el cuchillo knife
el mantel tablecloth
la pimienta pepper
el platillo saucer
el plato dish
el porrón wine jar
la sal salt
la salsa sauce
la servilleta serviette
el tenedor fork
el vinagre vinegar

Other food

el aceite de oliva olive oil
la aceituna olive
el arroz rice
la barra loaf
el bizcocho sponge cake
el bocadillo sandwich (French bread)
los bombones chocolates
el caramelo sweet
el chocolate chocolate
el churro fritter
el cocido stew
la ensalada salad
la ensaladilla Russian salad
la galleta biscuit
la hamburguesa hamburger
la harina flour
el helado ice-cream
el huevo egg
la mayonesa mayonnaise
el panecillo roll
las patatas fritas chips
el perrito caliente hot dog
la salchicha sausage
el sandwich sandwich
el termo thermos flask
la tortilla omelette
la tortilla española Spanish omelette
el yogur yogurt

Starters

el aperitivo appetiser
los entremeses starters
el gazpacho cold soup
la sopa soup

From the sea/river

el atún tunny fish
el bacalao cod
los calamares squid
el cangrejo crab
las gambas prawns
la langosta crab
el lenguado sole
los mariscos seafood
los mejillones mussels
la merluza hake
el pescado fish
la sardina sardine
la trucha trout

Desserts

el flan caramel custard
la nata cream
el pastel cake
el postre dessert
el pudín (bread) pudding
el queso cheese
la tarta cake, tart, pie
la torta cake
el turrón nougat

Breakfast

los cereales cereals
la mantequilla butter
la mermelada jam
el pan bread
el pan tostado toasted bread
la tostada toast

Drinks

el agua (m) water
el agua mineral con gas mineral water (fizzy)
el agua mineral sin gas mineral water (still)
la bebida drink
la cerveza beer
el champán champagne
la coca-cola coca-cola
el coñac coñac
la gaseosa lemonade
la ginebra gin
el gin tonic gin and tonic
la horchata almond drink
el jerez sherry
el jugo de fruta fruit juice
la leche milk
la limonada lemonade
la manzanilla manzanilla sherry
la naranjada orange squash
el refresco soft drink
la sangría sangria
la sidra cider
el té tea

el tinto red wine
el vino wine
el zumo de fruta fruit juice
el zumo de naranja orange juice

The restaurant

los aseos toilets
la bandeja tray
la botella bottle
el/la camarero/a waiter/waitress
la comida food
los cubiertos cutlery
la especialidad speciality
el menú del día set menu of the day
el plato combinado set meal
por aquí this way
el precio fijo fixed price
la receta recipe
el restaurante restaurant
el sabor flavour
el servicio service
los servicios toilets
el/la vegetariano/a vegetarian

The café

la bandeja tray
el café coffee
el café con leche white coffee
el café solo black coffee
la cafetería café
el cenicero ashtray
cobrar to charge
la copa glass
la cuenta bill
el hielo ice
el mostrador counter
nada más that's all
la propina tip
la ración portion
la ronda round (of drinks)
la sombra shade
las tapas bar snacks
la tarifa price list
la terraza terrace
el trapo rag, cloth
el vaso glass
el vino blanco white wine
el vino tinto red wine

Adjectives

asado roast
barato cheap
caro expensive
congelado frozen
costoso dear
delicioso delicious
dulce sweet
frito fried
gratis free
gratuito free
incluido included
inevitable inevitable
libre free
picante hot (to the taste)
potable drinkable
próximo next
variado varied

Restaurant verbs

almorzar to have lunch
aprovecharse to take advantage of
bastar to be enough
beber to drink
cenar to have dinner
comer to eat
desayunar to have breakfast
helar to freeze
hervir to boil
merendar to have a snack/picnic
oler a to smell of
pagar to pay
pedir to ask for, to order
probar to try out
quejarse to complain
quitar to remove
saber a to taste of
servir to serve
traer to bring
tragar to swallow

Health and fitness

Sports

el alpinismo climbing, mountaineering
el atletismo athletics
el baloncesto basketball
el balonvolea volleyball
el billar billiards
el ciclismo cycling
la corrida de toros bullfight
la equitación horse-riding
el esquí acuático water ski-ing
el fútbol football
el futbolín table football
la natación swimming
el patinaje skating
la pesca fishing
el ping-pong table tennis
el tenis tennis
el windsurf windsurfing

Sport words

la actividad activity
el balón ball
la bicicleta bicycle
el campeonato championship
la caña de pescar fishing rod
la carrera race
el centro polideportivo sports centre

la competición competition
el concurso competition
la copa mundial World Cup
la decisión decision
el deporte sport
el esquí ski
el estadio stadium
la etapa stage
el fracaso failure
el gol goal
las instrucciones instructions
el juego game
la liga league
el partido match
el paso step
la pelota ball
el peso weight
el premio prize
el punto point
la red net
el resultado result
el salto jump
la selección team
la temporada season
el terreno pitch
el torneo tournament
la vela sail
el vestuario dressing room

The people

el/la aficionado/a fan
el árbitro referee
el/la atleta athlete
el/la campeón/campeona champion
el/la ciclista cyclist
el equipo team
el/la espectador/a spectator
el/la futbolista footballer
el gamberro hooligan
el hincha fan
el/la jugador/a player
el matador bullfighter
el miembro member
el socio member
el/la tenista tennis player
el torero bullfighter

Verbs

agotar to exhaust
arrojar to throw
asistir a to be present at
asomarse to lean out of (e.g. a window)
buscar to look for, to fetch
caerse to fall
cansarse to get tired
celebrarse to take place
correr to run
dar to give
echar to throw
empatar to draw (a game)
entrenarse to go training
esconder to hide
estrenar to have its première
ganar to win
intentar to try
jugar to play
lanzar to throw
marcar un gol to score a goal
meter to put
montar a caballo to ride
nadar to swim
participar to take part
perder to lose
pisar to tread
practicar to practise
respirar to breathe
saltar to jump
silbar to whistle
sudar to sweat
tirar to pull
torear to bullfight
vencer to beat
zambullirse to dive

The body

la barba beard
el bigote moustache
la boca mouth
el brazo arm
el cabello hair
la cabeza head
la cara face
la cintura waist
el codo elbow
el corazón heart
el cuello neck
el cuerpo body
el dedo finger
el diente tooth
la espalda back
el estómago stomach
la frente forehead
la garganta throat
el hombro shoulder
el hueso bone
el labio lip
la lágrima tear
la lengua tongue
la mano hand
la mejilla cheek
la muñeca wrist
el muslo thigh
la nariz nose
el ojo eye
la oreja ear
el pecho chest/breast
el pelo hair
el pie foot
la piel skin

la pierna leg
la rodilla knee
el rostro face
el tobillo ankle
el vientre stomach
la voz voice

Illnesses

la aspirina aspirin
el catarro cold
la cita appointment (e.g. with doctor)
la clínica clinic
el comprimido tablet
la consulta doctor's surgery, examination
el consultorio doctor's surgery
la crema cream
la cura cure
el diente tooth
el dolor pain
la droga drug
el empaste filling
la enfermedad illness
la enteritis enteritis
el esparadrapo sticking plaster
la farmacia chemist's
la fiebre temperature
la gastritis gastritis
la gripe flu
la herida wound
la insolación sunstroke
la inyección injection
el jarabe syrup
el medicamento medicine
la medicina medicine
la muela tooth (molar)
la operación operation
la pastilla tablet
la picadura bite (insect)
la pomada cream
la quemadura burn
el remedio remedy
el resfriado cold
la salud health
el sarampión measles
el SIDA AIDS
el síntoma symptom
el supositorio suppository
la tirita sticking plaster
la tos cough
el tratamiento treatment
la venda bandage

The people

el dentista dentist
el doctor doctor
el/la enfermero/a nurse
el/la farmacéutico/a chemist
el/la médico/a doctor

Verbs

cortar to cut
descubrir to discover
desmayarse to faint
doler to hurt
empastar to put in a filling
estar bien to feel OK
estar constipado to have a cold
estar mal to feel ill
guardar cama to stay in bed
mantener to maintain
marearse to get dizzy
matar to kill
medir to measure
picar to bite
quemar to burn
quemarse to burn oneself
remediar to put right
resbalar to slip
sentirse to feel
temblar to shiver
torcer to turn, to twist
toser to cough
vendar to bandage
vivir to live
vomitar to vomit

4.5 Area of Experience B – Personal and social life

Self, family and personal relationships

Family

el apellido surname
el bebé baby
el beso kiss
la dirección address
el divorcio divorce
el domicilio address
la edad age
el estado civil status
la fecha de nacimiento date of birth
el lugar de nacimiento place of birth
el nacimiento birth
el noviazgo engagement

The people (in the family)

el/la abuelo/a grandfather/mother
el/la cuñado/a brother/sister-in-law
el/la esposo/a husband/wife

la familia family
los familiares relations
el gemelo twin
el/la hermano/a brother/sister
el/la hijo/a son/daughter
la madre mother
la mamá mum
el marido husband
la mujer wife
el/la nieto/a grandson/daughter
el/la niño/a child
el/la novio/a boy/girl friend
la nuera daughter-in-law
el padre father
los padres parents
el papá dad
el/la pariente relation
el/la primo/a cousin
el/la sobrino/a nephew/niece
el/la suegro/a father/mother-in-law
el/la tío/a uncle/aunt
el/la viudo/a widower/widow
el yerno son-in-law

Friends

el abrazo embrace
la amistad friendship
el amor love
el apodo nickname
la bienvenida welcome
la broma joke
el carácter character
el cariño affection
la carta letter
el chiste joke
la cita date (i.e. to meet friend)
la conversación conversation
la correspondencia correspondence
la culpa blame
los demás the rest
el deseo desire
el diálogo conversation
el favor favour
el gusto pleasure
el humor humour
la identidad identity
la invitación invitation
el matrimonio marriage
la pelea fight
la postal postcard
la promesa promise
la señal sign, signal
la sonrisa smile
la tarjeta card
la visita visit

People

el/la adolescente adolescent
el/la adulto/a adult
el/la amigo/a friend
el/la amigo/a por correspondencia penfriend
el caballero gentleman
el/la chico/a boy/girl
el/la compañero/a friend
el/la corresponsal correspondent
el desconocido stranger
el/la enemigo/a enemy
la gente people
el hombre man
el huésped guest
el/la invitado/a guest
el/la muchacho/a boy/girl
la pareja couple
la persona person
todo el mundo everybody
el/la vecino/a neighbour

Verbs

acompañar to accompany
acordarse to remember
ayudar to help
besar to kiss
cartearse to exchange letters
celebrar to celebrate
charlar to chat
citarse to arrange to meet
conocer to know
contar to tell, to count
contar con to rely on
crecer to grow
cumplir to reach (a birthday)
dar de beber to give a drink
dar de comer to feed
dar la mano to shake hands
dar las gracias to thank
darse cuenta de to realise
despedirse de to say goodbye to
detestar to hate
divorciarse to get divorced
echar de menos to miss (i.e. a person)
echar una carta to post
elegir to choose
emparejar to pair up
enamorarse to fall in love
encantar to delight
enfadarse to get angry
evitar to avoid
importar to be important
indicar to indicate
invitar to invite
llamarse to be called
llevarse bien con to get on well with
llevarse mal con to get on badly with
llorar to cry
morir to die
nacer to be born
odiar to hate
parecer to seem

parecerse a to be like
pedir un favor to ask a favour
ponerse to become
preferir to prefer
presentar to introduce
prometer to promise
proponer to propose
querer to love, to want
recoger to pick up
reconocer to recognise
recordar to remember
regalar to give a present
reírse to laugh
rogar to ask
salir to go out
saludar to greet
sonreírse to smile
tutear to use "tú"
ver to see
visitar to visit

Clothes

el abrigo overcoat
la americana jacket
el bañador swimsuit
la bata dressing gown
la blusa blouse
el bolsillo pocket
la bota boot
el botón button
los calcetines socks
el calzado footwear
la camisa shirt
la camiseta t-shirt
el chaleco waistcoat
el chándal tracksuit
la chaqueta jacket
la cinta ribbon
el cinturón belt
la corbata tie
la falda skirt
la gorra cap
el guante glove
el impermeable raincoat
el jersey jersey
los leotardos tights
la mantilla mantilla
las medias stockings/tights
el pantalón corto shorts
el pantalón vaquero jeans
los pantalones/el pantalón trousers
el panty/panti tights
el pañuelo handkerchief
el pijama pyjamas
la rebeca cardigan
la ropa clothes
la ropa interior underclothes
la sandalia sandal
el sombrero hat
los tejanos jeans
la tela cloth
el traje suit
el traje de baño swimsuit
los vaqueros jeans
el vestido dress
la zapatilla slipper
el zapato shoe
los zapatos de deporte trainers

Extras

el abanico fan
el anillo ring
el billetero wallet
el bolso de mano handbag
el broche brooch
la cartera briefcase/wallet
el collar necklace
el diamante diamond
las gafas glasses
las gafas de sol sun glasses
la joya jewel
las lentillas lenses
el monedero purse
el paraguas umbrella
el pendiente earring
la pulsera bracelet
el reloj de pulsera wristwatch
la sortija ring

Free time and social activities

Free time

el bañador swimsuit
la cámara camera
la caña de pescar fishing rod
la canción song
las cartas playing cards
el cigarillo cigarette
el cigarro cigar
la colección collection
el/la deportista sportsperson
la diapositiva slide (photo)
el disco record
la discoteca disco
la diversión entertainment
el encendedor cigarette lighter
el espectáculo show
el fin end
la foto(grafía) photo(graph)
la función function
la gana desire
el interés interest
el juego game
el juguete toy
la lotería lottery
la moda fashion
el ocio leisure
el pasatiempo hobby
el payaso clown
el premio gordo first prize

el puro cigar
los ratos libres free time
la risa laughter
el sorteo draw (i.e. lottery)
la sugerencia suggestion
el tabaco tobacco
el tiempo libre free time
el tocadiscos record player

Places

la bolera bowling alley
el circo circus
el club club
el club para jóvenes youth club
el concierto concert
la exposición exhibition
el parque de atracciones theme park
la piscina swimming pool
la pista de hielo ice rink
la sala room
la sala de fiestas dance hall
la taberna pub
el zoo zoo

Activities

el ajedrez chess
el baile dance
los bolos bowling
la caza hunting
la cerámica pottery
la cocina cooking
el corte y confección dressmaking
el crucigrama crossword
el deporte sport
el flamenco flamenco
el footing jogging
el monopatín skateboard
el paseo walk
el videojuego video game

Verbs (movement)

acercarse a to approach
acostarse to go to bed
adelantar to overtake
alejarse to go away
andar to walk
atravesar to cross
bajar to go down
darse prisa to hurry
dirigirse hacia to head for
ir to go
ir a buscar to fetch
ir a ver to go and see
irse to go away
marcharse to go away
moverse to move
mudarse to move house
regresar to return
subir to go up
venir to come
volver to return
volverse to turn round

Reading

la ciencia-ficción science fiction
el diario newspaper
el fascículo instalment
la lectura reading
el libro book
la novela novel
el periódico newspaper
la prensa press
la revista magazine
el tebeo comic

Cinema

el cine cinema
la comedia comedy
los dibujos animados cartoon
la estrella del cine cinema star
el éxito success
la fila row
la localidad seat, ticket
la obra de teatro play
la película film
la película de amor romantic film
la película de aventuras adventure film
la película de ciencia-ficción science-fiction film
la película de miedo horror film
la película del oeste western
la película policíaca detective film
la sesión performance

Music

la banda band
la canción song
el cassette cassette
clásico classical
el compact disc compact disc
el conjunto group
el coro choir
el disco compacto CD
el estéreo stereo
el grupo group
el instrumento instrument
la música music
la música clásica classical music
la música fuerte loud music
la música pop pop music
el/la músico/a musician
la orquesta orchestra
el teclado keyboard

Musical instruments

las castañuelas castanets
la flauta flute

la guitarra guitar
el piano piano
el violín violin

TV

la actriz actress
la charla chat
el documental documentary
el episodio episode
las noticias news
la pantalla screen
el programa programme
la publicidad advertising
la radio radio
la tele TV
el telediario TV news
la telenovela soap
la televisión TV
el televisor TV set
la TVE Spanish TV
el vídeo video

Verbs

abrazar to embrace
acudir to come
bailar to dance
cantar to sing
cazar to hunt
cesar de to stop (doing something)
coleccionar to collect
conseguir to manage
coser to sew
dar un paseo to go for a walk
dar una vuelta to go for a walk
divertirse to enjoy oneself
fabricar to make
fumar to smoke
gustar to please
huir to flee
ir de paseo to go for a walk
leer to read
pasarlo bien to have a good time
pasearse to go for a walk
patinar to skate
pescar to fish
pintar to paint
registrar to record
seguir to follow, to continue
señalar to point out
sentarse to sit down
separarse to separate
tocar to touch, to play
tumbarse to lie down
usar to use

Holidays

On holiday

el alojamiento lodgings
el alquiler rent
la cámara camera
la crema bronceadora sun cream
el descanso rest
la dificultad difficulty
el disgusto annoyance, bother
la distracción entertainment
el documento document
la estancia stay
la excursión trip
los gastos expenses
la información information
el mapa map
la máquina de fotos camera
la mochila rucksack
el regalo present
el regreso return
la tarjeta postal postcard
el trayecto journey
el/la turista tourist
el/la veraneante holiday maker

Camping

los aseos toilets
el camping campsite
el/la campista camper
la caravana caravan
la cerilla match
el espacio space
la facilidad facility
el gas gas
la pila battery
el saco de dormir sleeping bag
la sala de juegos games room
el sitio place, spot
la tienda de campaña tent

Hotel

el ascensor lift
los aseos toilets
la cadena (de hoteles) chain (of hotels)
con vista a with a view of
el/la dueño/a owner
la ficha form
la firma signature
fuera de servicio out of order
la habitación room
la habitación doble double room
la habitación individual single room
la habitación sencilla single room
la hoja form
el hotel hotel
el hotelero hotel-owner
el libro de reclamaciones complaints book
la llave key
el lujo luxury
la media pensión half board
la nacionalidad nationality
el nombre (de pila) (first) name
el país de origen country of origin

el parador government-run hotel
el pasaporte passport
la pensión boarding house
la pensión completa full board
el portero hotel porter
prohibida la entrada no entry
el/la propietario/a owner
la queja complaint
la recepción reception
el/la recepcionista receptionist
el retrete toilet
la salida exit
las señas address
la vista view
el wáter toilet

Verbs

abrir to open
abrir el grifo to turn on the tap
acampar to camp
aguardar to wait for
ahorrar to save
alegrarse to be happy
alojarse to stay (e.g. in a hotel)
alquilar to hire
asegurar to insure
aterrizar to land
atrasar to delay
averiarse to break down
bañarse to bathe
broncearse to get tanned
campar to camp
cerrar el grifo to turn off the tap
coger una insolación to get sunstroke
completar to complete
comprobar to check
comunicar to communicate
conducir to drive
desembarcar to disembark
despegar to take off (plane)
desviar to make a detour
detenerse to stop
durar to last
embarcarse to embark
entrar to enter
escaparse to escape
esperar to wait, to hope,to expect
esquiar to ski
estacionar to park
estropear to spoil
firmar to sign
flotar to float
frecuentar to frequent
frenar to brake
hacer camping to go camping
hacer las maletas to pack
hallar to find
hospedarse to stay
informarse to find out
ir de camping to go camping
ir de vacaciones to go on holiday
llegar to arrive
llegar tarde to be late
llenar to fill
llevar to take (a person),to wear
llevar retraso to be late
mojarse to get soaked
molestar to bother
pasar to spend (time),to happen
quedar(se) to stay
rellenar un formulario to fill in a form
reservar to book
rodear to surround
sacar fotos to take photos
soler to usually do something
tardar to take (time)
tenderse al sol to lie in the sun
tomar to take
tomar el sol to sunbathe
tostarse to sunbathe
transportar to transport
veranear to spend the summer
viajar to travel
volar to fly

Abstractions

la afición enthusiasm
la alegría happiness
la ambición ambition
el cariño affection
el consejo advice
el cuidado care
el destino destiny
la duda doubt
la escasez scarcity
la esperanza hope
el estado state
la fama fame
la forma shape
la hospitalidad hospitality
la importancia importance
la infancia childhood
la justicia justice
la juventud youth
la libertad freedom
la manera way
la memoria memory
la meta objective
el miedo fear
la muerte death
el orgullo pride
la paciencia patience
la pena pity
la seguridad security
el sentido feeling
la siesta nap
la suerte luck
el tamaño size
la verdad truth

Expressions

¡adelante! come in!
¡bienvenido! welcome!
¡Dios mío! gosh!
¡eso es! that's it!
¡igualmente! same to you!
¡Jesús! bless you!
¡lástima! what a shame!
¡madre mía! gosh!
¡ni hablar! out of the question!
¡oiga! excuse me!
¡ojalá! if only!
¡ojo! careful!
¡por Dios! please do!
¡que aproveche! enjoy your meal!
¡qué asco! how disgusting!
¡qué bien! how good!
¡qué horror! how terrible!
¡qué lástima! what a pity!
¡qué pena! what a pity!
¡qué va! no chance!
¡salud! cheers!
¡socorro! help!
¡suerte! good luck!
¡tráigame! bring me!
¡vale! OK!

¿cómo es? what is it like?
¿cómo estás? how are you?
¿cómo se dice ...? how do you say ...?
¿cómo se escribe ...? how do you spell ...?
¿de veras? really?
¿qué hay? what's new?
¿qué tal? how are you?
¿se puede? may I?

en absoluto absolutely not!
adiós goodbye
atentamente Yours faithfully
buenas noches good night
buenas tardes good evening, good afternoon
buenos días good day
claro of course
conforme agreed
de acuerdo agreed
de nada don't mention it
desde luego of course
¡enhorabuena! congratulations!
gracias thank you
hasta la vista see you soon
hasta luego see you soon, later
hasta mañana till tomorrow
hola hello
lo siento I'm sorry
me da igual I don't mind
mucha suerte good luck
muchas gracias many thanks
mucho gusto pleased to meet you
muy señor mío Dear Sir (in a letter)
perdón excuse me, sorry
perdona excuse me
por ejemplo for example
por eso for that reason
por favor please
por supuesto of course
¡que aproveche! enjoy your meal!
recuerdos best wishes
saludos greetings
vale la pena it's worthwhile

Verbs

aconsejar to advise
adivinar to guess
admitir to admit
advertir to warn
agradecer to thank
amenazar to threaten
avisar to warn
callarse to be silent
convencer to convince
decir to say, to tell
declarar to declare
disculparse to say sorry
discutir to discuss, to argue
felicitar to congratulate
mencionar to mention
mentir to lie
sugerir to suggest

Adjectives

agradecido grateful
alegre happy
animado excited
atónito astonished
cansado tired
cariñoso affectionate
constipado having a cold
contento happy
deprimido depressed
encantado delighted
enfadado angry
enfermo ill
favorito favourite
feliz happy
furioso furious
harto fed up
impaciente impatient
inquieto worried
ocupado busy
orgulloso proud
preocupado worried
satisfecho satisfied
triste sad

Special occasions

Occasions

¡feliz santo! Happy Saint's Day!
el Año Nuevo New Year
la bandera flag

la boda wedding
el Corpus Corpus Christi
la costumbre custom
la cruz cross
el cumpleaños birthday
el día de fiesta holiday
el día de mi santo Saint's Day
el día de Navidad Christmas Day
el día de Reyes 6th of January
el día festivo non-working day
el día laboral working day
Dios God
el domingo de Resurrección Easter Sunday
felices pascuas Happy Easter/Christmas
felicidades congratulations
feliz año nuevo Happy New Year
feliz cumpleaños Happy Birthday
feliz Navidad Happy Christmas
la feria fair
la fiesta holiday
los Juegos Olímpicos Olympic Games
la luna de miel honeymoon
la misa mass
la mudanza house move
la Navidad Christmas
la Nochebuena Christmas Eve
la Nochevieja New Year's Eve
las Pascuas Easter/Christmas
la procesión procession
el sacerdote priest
la Semana Santa Holy Week
la verbena fair
el Viernes Santo Good Friday

Incidents

el accidente accident
la acción action
la ambulancia ambulance
el asesinato murder
el atraco hold-up, mugging
la aventura adventure
el aviso warning
la ayuda help
la bomba bomb
la cárcel gaol
el caso case
el choque collision
las circunstancias circumstances
la contrabanda smuggled goods
el crimen crime
la Cruz Roja Red Cross
el cuento story
el daño damage
el delito offence
el desastre disaster
la descripción description
la desgracia misfortune
el engaño deceipt
la escena scene
el fuego fire
el fusil rifle
el golpe blow
el grito shout
el humo smoke
el incendio fire
la inundación flood
la mentira lie
el motivo motive
la multa fine
el peligro danger
la pérdida loss
la recompensa reward
el rescate rescue
el riesgo risk
el robo robbery
el salvavidas life belt/jacket
la sangre blood
el secuestro kidnapping
la sorpresa surprise
el suceso event
el susto fright
el testigo witness
la tragedia tragedy
la vida life

The people

el asesino murderer
el bombero fireman
el/la cobarde coward
el contrabandista smuggler
el/la delincuente delinquent
el drogadicto drug addict
el/la guardia policeman/woman
la Guardia Civil police
el ladrón thief
el/la policía police officer
la policía police
el ratero pickpocket
la víctima victim

Verbs

ahogarse to drown
apagar to put out (e.g. a fire)
aparecer to appear
apresurarse to hurry
asesinar to murder
asustarse to be frightened
atacar to attack
atar to tie
atracar to rob, to mug
atreverse (a) to dare (to)
atropellar to run over
batir to beat
batirse to fight
ceda el paso give way (when driving)
chocar (con) to collide (with)
cometer to commit
cruzar to cross
denunciar to report to the police

desaparecer to disappear
describir to describe
doblar la esquina to turn the corner
engañar to deceive
exigir to demand
girar to turn round
golpear to hit
gritar to shout
herirse to get injured
identificarse to identify oneself
imaginar to imagine
obligar to force
ocurrir to happen
parar to stop
pegar to hit
proteger to protect
quebrar to break
realizar to carry out
registrar to search
rescatar to rescue
robar to steal
romper to break
romperse to break
salvar to save
secuestrar to kidnap
suceder to happen

4.6 Area of Experience C – The world around us

Home town and local area

In the street

la acera pavement
el banco bench
el buzón post box
la cabina telefónica phone box
la calle street
el carnet de identidad ID card
el cartel poster
la circulación traffic
el embotellamiento traffic jam
la esquina corner
el estanco kiosk
la fuente fountain
el letrero sign
la ley law
el monumento monument
la parada de autobuses bus stop
el paso de peatones pedestrian crossing
el peatón pedestrian
la persona mayor adult
la persona menor young person
prohibido el paso no entry
el ruido noise
el semáforo traffic light
el silencio silence
el surtidor petrol pump
el tráfico traffic
el transeúnte passer-by

The town

las afueras outskirts
el alcalde mayor
los alrededores outskirts, surroundings
el aparcamiento car park
el apartamento flat
la arquitectura architecture
la avenida avenue
el ayuntamiento building
el banco bank
el bar bar
el barrio district
la bocacalle side street
la calle street
la capital capital
el castillo castle
el centro centre
el centro comercial shopping centre
la circulación traffic
la ciudad city
el ciudadano citizen
el cruce road junction
el edificio building
la estatua statue
la Guardia Civil police
el parking car park
el parque park
el parque infantil play ground
la parte part
el piso flat
el plano town map
la plaza square
la plaza mayor main square
la población population
el pueblo small town, village
el puente bridge
la situación situation
la torre tower
la urbanización housing estate
la vecindad vicinity
la vivienda dwelling
la zona area
la zona industrial industrial area

The buildings

el albergue de juventud youth hostel
el albergue juvenil youth hostel
la biblioteca library
la caja de ahorros savings bank
la catedral cathedral
el centro de deportes sports centre
la comisaría police station

correos post office
la estación de autobuses bus station
el hospital hospital
la iglesia church
el museo museum
el museo de arte art gallery
la oficina de correos post office
la oficina de objetos perdidos lost property office
la oficina de turismo tourist office
el palacio palace
la plaza de toros bullring
el polideportivo sports centre
el teatro theatre

The shops

la agencia de viajes travel agent's
la bodega wine cellar
la carnicería butcher's
la charcutería delicatessen
la churrería fritter stall
la confitería sweet shop
la droguería drug store
el estanco tabacconist's
la farmacia chemist's
la frutería fruit shop
la hamburguesería hamburger outlet
la joyería jeweller's
la lavandería laundry
la librería book shop
el mercado market
el/la modista dressmaker's
la panadería baker's
la papelería stationer's
la pastelería cake shop
la peluquería hairdresser's
la perfumería perfume shop
la pescadería fish shop
la relojería watch maker's
el tabacalero tobacconist's
la tienda de comestibles grocer's
la tienda de discos record shop
la tienda de recuerdos souvenir shop
la tienda de ultramarinos grocer's
la verdulería greengrocer's
la zapatería shoe shop

Shopping

a mitad de precio half price
la alimentación food
los almacenes stores
el artículo article
el autoservicio self-service
la bolsa bag
el bolso bag
el bote tin
la caja box
la caja cash desk
la calidad quality
el carro supermarket trolley
la cesta basket
el cesto basket
el/la cliente customer
la cola queue
los comestibles food
las compras shopping
el coste cost
el/la dependiente/a shop assistant
el descuento discount
el dinero money
el escaparate shop window
la falta lack
el frasco bottle
la ganga bargain
los grandes almacenes stores
el IVA VAT
el kiosco kiosk
la liquidación sale
la lista list
la muñeca doll
el precio price
el probador fitting room
el producto product
el puesto stall
el quiosco kiosk
la ranura slot
las rebajas reductions
el recibo receipt
el recuerdo souvenir
la sección de discos record section
el segundo piso second floor
el supermercado supermarket
la talla size
el tercer piso third floor
la tienda shop
el tipo type
los ultramarinos groceries
el valor value
el/la vendedor/a salesperson
la venta sale

Shopping verbs

anunciar to advertise
comprar to buy
costar to cost
desear to wish
entregar to deliver
enviar to send
envolver to wrap up
faltar to lack
gastar to spend (money)
introducir to insert
ir de compras to go shopping
mirar to look at
mostrar to show
pagar to pay
pertenecer to belong
pesar to weigh
probarse to try on
satisfacer to satisfy
vender to sell

The post office

el buzón post box
la cabina telefónica phone box
el código postal post code
Correos post office
la entrega delivery
el paquete parcel
el sello stamp

The bank

el billete de banco banknote
el cajero automático cashpoint
el cambio change
el céntimo hundredth of a peseta
el cheque cheque
el cheque de viajero traveller's cheque
la comisión commission
la cuenta de banco bank account
el duro five-peseta piece
la libra esterlina pound sterling
la moneda coin, currency
el penique penny
la peseta (pta) peseta
la sucursal branch
el suelto change
el talonario de cheques cheque book
la tarjeta de crédito credit card

Bank verbs

aceptar to accept
aumentar to increase
cambiar to change
mandar to send
obtener to obtain
pedir prestado to borrow
prestar to lend
recibir receive

The natural and made environment

Environment

el aire air
la aldea village
el aldeano villager
el ambiente atmosphere
el árbol tree
el arroyo stream
la bahía bay
el bosque wood
el camino path
el/la campesino/a peasant
el campo countryside
la carretera road
el cielo sky
la colina hill
el color colour
la cosecha harvest
el embalse dam
la especie type
la estrella star
la flor silvestre wild flower
la granja farm
la isla island
el lago lake
la luna moon
la marea tide
la montaña mountain
el mundo world
la oscuridad darkness
el país country
el paisaje countryside
la península peninsula
la piedra stone
la pista track
el prado meadow
la provincia province
la región region
el río river
la sierra mountain range
el sonido sound
la subida climb
la tierra earth, land
la valle valley
la vertiente slope

Animals

la abeja bee
el animal animal
la avispa wasp
el burro donkey
el caballito pony
el caballo horse
la cabra goat
el cerdo pig
el elefante elephant
la gallina hen
el insecto insect
la mosca fly
la oveja sheep
el pájaro bird
la paloma dove
el pato duck
el pavo turkey
la rata rat
la serpiente snake
el tigre tiger
el toro bull
la vaca cow

At the seaside

la arena sand
la barca de pesca fishing boat
el barco boat
el chalet villa
el colchón de aire inflatable mattress
la costa coast

el cubo bucket
el mar sea
la ola wave
el parasol parasol
la playa beach
el puerto port

The colours

amarillo yellow
azul blue
blanco white
castaño brown
el color naranja orange
gris grey
marrón brown
moreno dark
negro black
rojo red
rosa pink
rubio blond
verde green

Adjectives

actual present-day
apropiado suitable
árido arid
ecológico ecological
eficaz effective
físico physical
internacional international
militar military
montañoso mountainous
en paro unemployed
plástico plastic
tranquilo quiet

Situations

¿por dónde se va a …? how do I get to …?
al aire libre in the open air
allá/allí there
arriba above, upstairs
la distancia distance
en el suelo on the floor
el fondo bottom, far end
a la izquierda on the left
el lado side
el lugar place
a orillas del mar at the seaside
al revés back to front
situado situated
todo derecho straight on
todo recto straight on

Compass locations

el este east
el noreste northeast
el noroeste northwest
el norte north
el oeste west
el sudeste southeast
el sur south
el suroeste southwest

Places

la Costa Brava Costa Brava
la Costa Cantábrica Cantabrian Coast
la Costa del Sol Costa del Sol
la Costa Verde Green Coast
Londres London

How much?

apenas scarcely
aproximadamente approximately
bastante enough
completamente completely
demasiado too much
más more
menos less
mucho a lot
poco little
solamente only
solo alone
sólo only
suficiente sufficient
también also

Where?

abajo below, downstairs
adentro inside
afuera outside
ahí there
allí there
aquí here
atrás behind
dentro inside
a la derecha to the right
en alguna parte somewhere
en casa at home
en/por todas partes everywhere
a la izquierda to the left

How?

a pie on foot
abierto open
absolutamente absolutely
afortunadamente fortunately
andando on foot
bien well
casi almost
de golpe suddenly
de prisa quickly
de veras truly
desafortunadamente unfortunately
desgraciadamente unfortunately
despacio slowly
exactamente exactly
francamente frankly
igualmente equally

juntos together
lentamente slowly
mal badly
muy bien very well
naturalmente of course
normalmente normally
perfectamente perfectly
por completo completely
rápidamente quickly
en realidad really
sin duda doubtless

When?

¿qué hora es? what's the time?
a eso de about
a menudo often
a partir de from
antes de before
aún still
al cabo de at the end of
el comienzo beginning
de costumbre usually
de nuevo again
de repente suddenly
de vez en cuando from time to time
dentro de poco soon
después after
el día day
en punto on the dot
entonces then
la época time
esta noche tonight
la fecha date
a fines de at the end of
generalmente usually
la hora hour
la hora de comer lunch time
el instante instant
mientras tanto meanwhile
muchas veces often
otra vez again
a partir de from
pocas veces rarely
por fin finally
por lo general in general
el principio beginning
pronto soon
de pronto suddenly
raramente rarely
un rato a short while
en seguida straight away
siempre always
todavía still
unas veces sometimes
a veces at times
la vez occasion
ya already

How long?

el año year
el cuarto de hora quarter of an hour
el fin de semana weekend
la mañana morning
media hora half an hour
el mes month
el minuto minute
el momento moment
la noche night
ocho días week
quince días a fortnight
la semana week
el siglo century
la tarde evening

Time expressions

actualmente at present
ahora now
ahora mismo right now
algunas veces sometimes
el año pasado last year
anoche last night
anteayer the day before yesterday
ayer yesterday
al día siguiente on the following day
esta mañana this morning
hace una hora an hour ago
hoy today
inmediatamente straight away
las seis y pico just after six o'clock
luego then
la madrugada very early in the morning
la medianoche midnight
el mediodía midday
pasado mañana the day after tomorrow
por la mañana in the morning
por la noche at night
al principio at the beginning
a principios at the beginning of
recientemente recently
las seis en punto six o'clock exactly
temprano early
todos los días every day
últimamente recently
la víspera eve

The weather

bajo cero below zero
la borrasca storm
la brisa breeze
la bruma mist
el buen tiempo good weather
el calor heat
el chubasco shower
el cielo sky
el clima climate
la escarcha frost
la estación del año season
la gota drop
el grado degree
hace buen tiempo the weather is nice

hace fresco the weather is cool
hace mal tiempo the weather is bad
hace sol the weather is sunny
hace viento the weather is windy
hacer calor to be hot
hacer frío to be cold
el hielo ice
la humedad humidity
la lluvia rain
el mal tiempo bad weather
la neblina mist
la niebla fog
la nieve snow
la nube cloud
la nubosidad cloudiness
el pronóstico del tiempo weather forecast
el relámpago lightning
el sol sun
la temperatura temperature
la tempestad storm
el tiempo weather
la tormenta storm
el trueno thunder
el viento wind

Weather adjectives

caluroso hot
cubierto cloudy
despejado clear
fresco cool, fresh
frío cold
húmedo humid
nublado cloudy
oscuro dark
soleado sunny
templado mild

Weather verbs

brillar to shine
cosechar to harvest
guardar to keep
llover to rain
nevar to snow
soplar to blow
tronar to thunder

Shapes and sizes

alto tall
ambos both
amplio wide
ancho wide
bastante enough
cada each
corto short
cuadrado square
delgado thin
doble double
enorme enormous
estrecho narrow
flaco thin
gordo fat
grande big
grueso fat
inmenso immense
insuficiente insufficient
largo long
máximo maximum
mayor bigger
mediano middling
medio average, half
menor smaller
mínimo minimum
normal normal
pequeño small
profundo deep
tanto so much, so many
todo all
varios several

People and things

Positive adjectives

activo active
agradable pleasant
amable pleasant
ambicioso ambitious
aplicado hard-working
atrevido daring
capaz capable
célebre famous
chulo amusing, attractive
cortés polite
curioso curious
de buen humor good-humoured
de buena salud healthy
deportivo sporting (i.e. likes sport)
directo direct
dispuesto ready
divertido amusing
elegante elegant
emocionante exciting
encantador delightful
enérgico energetic
espléndido splendid
Estimado Dear (in letters)
estupendo marvellous
excelente excellent
famoso famous
fantástico fantastic
fenomenal marvellous
formal well-behaved
fuerte strong
generoso generous
gracioso funny
guapo handsome, pretty
histórico historic
honesto honest
honrado honorable
inocente innocent

inteligente intelligent
interesante interesting
justo just, fair, right
limpio clean
lindo pretty
listo ready, clever
maravilloso marvellous
mejor better
nuevo new
paciente patient
perfecto perfect
positivo positive
práctico practical
precioso lovely
sano healthy
santo holy
seguro safe
sensible sensitive
serio serious, reliable
simpático nice
sobresaliente outstanding
trabajador hardworking
útil useful
valiente brave
verdadero true
vivo alive

Negative adjectives

agresivo aggressive
antipático unpleasant
borracho drunk
callado quiet
celoso suspicious, jealous
cruel cruel
culpable guilty
de mal humor bad-humoured
débil weak
desafortunado unfortunate
desagradable unpleasant
descortés rude
difícil difficult
egoísta selfish
equivocado mistaken
estúpido stupid
falso false
fatal very bad
feo ugly
goloso greedy
grave serious
hablador talkative
horrible horrible
imposible impossible
insoportable unbearable
inútil useless
loco mad
mal educado rude
malo bad
mareado sea-sick, dizzy
mentiroso lying
nervioso nervous
peor worse
perezoso lazy
regular so so
roto broken
ruidoso noisy
salvaje wild
sospechoso suspicious
sucio dirty
terrible terrible
tonto silly
torpe clumsy
travieso naughty
vacío empty

Physical adjectives

agudo sharp
anticuado old
automático automatic
bello beautiful
breve brief
bueno good
caliente warm, hot
céntrico central
cercano nearby
cerrado closed
cierto certain, true
comercial commercial
con retraso late
concurrido crowded
dañino harmful
de moda in fashion
delantero front
diferente different
distinto different
duro hard
eléctrico electric
electrónico electronic
especial special
espeso thick
exterior exterior
extraño strange
extraordinario extraordinary
ferroviario rail
flojo weak
futuro future
hermoso beautiful
industrial industrial
intacto intact
lejano distant
lento slow
ligero light
liso smooth
lleno full
mojado soaked, wet
nacido born
natural natural
peligroso dangerous
pesado heavy
quieto still
rápido fast

raro strange
real royal
reciente recent
redondo round
seco dry
sencillo single (ticket)
sentado sitting
siguiente following
suave soft
tibio lukewarm
tímido shy
típico typical
trasero rear
último last
único only
urgente urgent

4.7 Area of Experience D – The world of work

Job applications

Work

el acuerdo agreement
la ambición ambition
el anuncio advertisement
la carrera race
el comercio trade
la compañía company
el contrato contract
el despacho office
el ejército army
el empleo job
la empresa firm
la entrevista interview
el escritorio desk, office
la fábrica factory
la finca farm
la formación training
el formulario form
la fotocopia photocopy
la ganancia profit
la hoja de solicitud job application form
el impuesto tax
la industria industry
la máquina machine
la máquina de escribir typewriter
los negocios business
la oferta offer
la oficina office
el ordenador computer
la profesión profession
el proyecto plan
la reunión meeting
el salario salary
el sindicato trades union
el sueldo pay
el taller workshop
la taquigrafía shorthand
el trabajo work
el turismo tourism
la universidad university

The people

el amo owner
el/la aprendiz/a apprentice
el/la colega colleague
el/la empleado/a employee
el empresario businessman
el/la encargado/a employee in charge
el/la gerente manager
el/la jefe/a boss
el patrón boss
el/la responsable person in charge
el sindicalista trades union member

Verbs

acostumbrarse to get used to
cubrir to cover
cuidar to take care of
cultivar to grow
diseñar to design
disfrutar to enjoy
distinguir to distinguish
emplear to employ
escribir to write
escribir a máquina to type
estar de pie to be standing
estar en paro to be unemployed
estar sentado to be sitting
ganarse la vida to earn your living
haber to have
hablar to speak, to talk
hacer to do, to make
hacer falta to need
hacer una encuesta to conduct a survey
hacerse to become
interpretar to play the part
jubilarse to retire
pagar to pay
recomendar to recommend
recompensar to reward
remitir adjunto to enclose
reunirse to meet together
ser to be
tener to have
trabajar to work
trabajar de canguro to babysit

Jobs

el abogado lawyer
el actor actor
la actriz actress
el aduanero customs officer
el/la agente agent
el ama de casa (f) housewife
el arquitecto architect
el/la artista artist
el/la autor/a author
la azafata air hostess
el basurero rubbish collector
el bombero fireman
el/la camarero/a waiter/waitress
el camionero lorry driver
el/la cantante singer
el carnicero butcher
el carpintero carpenter
el cartero postman
el chófer driver
el científico scientist
el/la cocinero/a cook
el/la comerciante shopkeeper
el cómico comedian
el/la conductor/a driver
la criada maid
el cura priest
el dentista dentist
el/la dependiente/a shop assistant
el doctor doctor
el/la electricista electrician
el/la enfermero/a nurse
el/la escritor/a writer
el/la espía spy
el/la farmacéutico/a chemist
el/la florista florist
el fontanero plumber
el fotógrafo photographer
el frutero fruitseller
el funcionario civil servant
el/la garajista garage attendant
el granjero farmer
el/la guardia policeman/woman
el guardián warden
el/la guía guide
el hombre de negocios businessman
el ingeniero engineer
el inspector inspector
el jardinero gardener
el juez judge
el lechero milkman
el/la maestro/a teacher (primary school)
el marinero sailor
el mecánico mechanic
la mecanógrafa typist
el minero miner
la mujer de negocios businesswoman
el negociante trader
el obrero worker
el panadero baker
el/la peluquero/a hairdresser
el/la periodista journalist
el pescador fisherman
el piloto pilot
el pintor painter
el profesor teacher (secondary)
el químico chemist
el/la recepcionista receptionist
el/la representante representative
el sastre tailor
el/la secretario/a secretary
el soldado soldier
el técnico technician
el tendero shopkeeper

Communication

The telephone

la central telefónica telephone exchange
el cobro revertido reverse-charge
la conferencia long-distance call
el contestador automático answering machine
la guía telefónica telephone book
la llamada call
el número de teléfono phone number
el prefijo code
el recado message
el teléfono telephone

Telephone verbs

contestar to answer
descolgar to pick up the phone
equivocarse to make a mistake
estar equivocado to be mistaken
llamar to call
llamar por teléfono to phone
marcar to dial
oír to hear
telefonear to phone

Telephone expressions

¡al aparato! speaking!
¡diga! hello!
¡dígame! hello!
está comunicando engaged
no cuelgue Vd. hold the line

Useful IT vocabulary

reserva; de seguridad; salvaguardar back-up
lenguaje BASIC BASIC
negrita bold
inicialización; inicializar; cebar boot
exploración; examen (de la información) browsing
error; gazapo; basura bug
Enseñanza Asistida por Ordenador (EAO) Computer-Assisted Learning

técnico informático computer professional
cursor cursor
desplazar; trasladar (la información en la pantalla) cut and paste
dato; referencia datum
base de datos database
sistema de gestión de base de datos database management system
borrar; suprimir delete
autoedición (producción autónoma de publicaciones de calidad) desktop publishing
directorio; repertorio directory
sistema operativo en disco (DOS) disc operating system (DOS)
unidad de disco disc-drive
visualizar; presentar display
telecarga de programas downloading of programs
transcribir (imprimir una presentación de pantalla) dump (print out a screen)
revisar; corregir; modificar; preparar (el texto) edit
revisión; corrección; edición editing
programas de aplicación didácticos (equipo lógico) educational software
correo electrónico electronic mail
facsímil (fax) facsimile (fax)
campo; sección (en una base de datos) field (on database)
ficha; fichero; archivo file
disquete; disco flexible floppy disc
formatear (un disquete virgen o una visualización) format (a blank disc or display)
tecla de función function key
copia integral (presentación impresa); copia impresora hard copy (a print-out)
disco duro; disco rígido hard disc
hardware; aparatos integrantes hardware
realce; realzar highlighting
informática; tecnología de la información information technology
input; entrada input
interactivo interactive
tecla key
teclado keyboard
palabra clave; palabra reservada keyword
cargar un programa load a program
carga loading
menú menu
unir; fusionar merge
microprocesador; microplaqueta microchip
microordenador; microcomputadora microcomputer
módem modem
monitor; pantalla monitor
ratón mouse
calidad correspondencia; impresión de alta calidad Near Letter Quality (NLQ)
red informática network
desconectado; fuera de línea; autónomo off-line
ofimática office technology
conectado; en línea on-line
salida output
paquete; juego de programas package
contraseña password
periférico peripheral
gráfico de sectores pie chart
impresora printer
programa program
señal; indicación visible (demanda de respuesta) prompt (input request)
memoria de acceso aleatorio (RAM); memoria de lectura- escritura Random Access Memory (RAM)
memoria de lectura solamente (ROM); memoria permanente Read Only Memory (ROM)
registro (en una base de datos) record (in a database)
archivar; almacenar save
pantalla screen
visualización en pantalla screen display
corrimiento; movimento de avance/ retroceso de imagen en la pantalla scrolling
programa; software software
hoja electrónica spreadsheet
pila stack (Apple Hypercard)
cadena de caracteres string (unit of characters/numbers)
telecomunicaciones telecommunications
videotexto teletext
terminal terminal
programa de servicio; utilidad utility (program to support software)
información visualizada videotex/teletex viewdata
sintetizador de voz voice synthesiser
tratamiento de textos word-processing
procesador de textos word-processor
(lo que usted ve es lo que se imprimirá) = salida visualizada definitiva (SVD) WYSIWYG (what you see is what you get)

4.8 Area of Experience E – The international world

Tourism at home and abroad

Transport

la aduana customs
el aeropuerto airport
la agencia de viajes travel agent's
el asiento seat
el aterrizaje landing
la autopista motorway
el autostop hitchhiking
la autovía main road
el billete ticket
el billete de ida single ticket
el billete de ida y vuelta return ticket
la bolsa bag
el bonobús bus pass
el canal canal
la carretera road
el control de pasaportes passport check
el cruce road junction
la curva peligrosa dangerous bend
la demora delay
con destino a heading for
el equipaje luggage
la estación de autobuses bus station
la estación de servicio service station
el extranjero abroad
el folleto brochure
la frontera border
el gasoil diesel oil
el/la guía guide
la guía guide-book
el horario timetable
la huelga strike
la línea aérea airline
la llegada arrival
la maleta suitcase
el metro underground train
las obras roadworks
el peaje motorway toll
la prisa speed
la reserva reservation
el retraso delay
el terminal terminal
el transporte transport
las vacaciones holidays
el viaje journey
el/la viajero/a traveller
el vuelo flight
la vuelta return

The people

el aduanero customs officer
el/la autostopista hitchhiker
la azafata air hostess
el cobrador ticket-collector
el/la fumador/a smoker
el/la garajista garage attendant
el/la habitante inhabitant
la motocicleta motorcyclist
el/la pasajero/a passenger
el revisor ticket inspector

Vehicles

el autobús bus
el autocar coach
el avión plane
el camión lorry
el ferry ferry
el helicóptero helicopter
la moto motorcycle
el taxi taxi
el tranvía tram

By car

el aceite oil
el asiento seat
el auto car
el/la automovilista driver
la avería breakdown
la batería battery
el carnet de conducir driving licence
el cinturón de seguridad safety belt
el coche car
el depósito fuel tank
el desvío detour
el embotellamiento traffic jam
el faro headlight
los frenos brakes
la gasolina petrol
la gasolinera filling station
la marca make
el mecánico mechanic
el modelo model
el motor engine
el neumático tyre
el parabrisas windscreen
el permiso de conducir driving licence
el pinchazo puncture
la portezuela door (of vehicle)
la reparación repair
la rueda wheel
sin plomo lead-free
el súper high-grade petrol
el tornillo screw
el vehículo vehicle

la velocidad speed
la ventanilla window (of vehicle)
el volante steering wheel
la zona azul blue zone (parking)

By train

el andén platform
el asiento seat
el billete sencillo single ticket
el coche cama sleeping car
el coche restaurante dining car
la consigna left-luggage
la correspondencia rail connection
el departamento compartment
el despacho de billetes ticket office
la estación station
la estación del ferrocarril railway station
el ferrocarril railway
de largo recorrido long distance
el mozo porter
la primera clase first class
procedente de coming from
la red network
RENFE Spanish Railways
la sala de espera waiting room
la segunda clase second class
el suplemento supplement
Talgo luxury train
la taquilla ticket office
transbordar to change trains
el transbordo connection
el tren train
el tren expreso express train
la vía track

Countries

Alemania Germany
América del Sur South America
Argentina Argentina
Australia Australia
Austria Austria
Bélgica Belgium
Chile Chile
EE.UU USA
Escocia Scotland
España Spain
Estados Unidos U.S.A.
Europa Europe
Francia France
Gales Wales
Gran Bretaña Great Britain
Grecia Greece
Holanda Holland
Inglaterra England
Irlanda Ireland
Irlanda del Norte Northern Ireland
Italia Italy
Méjico/México Mexico
el País de Gales Wales
Perú Peru
Portugal Portugal
el Reino Unido United Kingdom
Rusia Russia
Suecia Sweden
Suiza Switzerland
Venezuela Venezuela

Nationalities

alemán (alemana f) German
americano American
argentino Argentinian
austríaco Austrian
belga Belgium
británico British
chileno Chilean
escocés (escocesa f) Scottish
español Spanish
europeo European
extranjero foreigner
francés (francesa f) French
galés (galesa f) Welsh
griego Greek
holandés Dutch
inglés (inglesa f) English
irlandés (irlandesa f) Irish
italiano Italian
mejicano/mexicano Mexican
norteamericano American
peruano Peruvian
portugués (portuguesa f) Portuguese
ruso Russian
sudamericano South American
sueco Swedish
suizo Swiss
venezolano Venezuelan

Life in other countries and communities

Rivers

el Duero Duero River
el Ebro Ebro River
el Guadalquivir Guadalquivir River
el Manzanares Manzanares River
el Tajo Tagus River

Regions

Andalucía Andalusia
Asturias Asturias
Castilla Castille
Cataluña Catalonia
Euskadi Basque Country
Extremadura Extremadura
Galicia Galicia
Mancha Mancha Region
el País Vasco Basque Country
Vizcaya Biscay province

People

andaluz Andalusian
asturiano from Asturias
cantábrico Cantabrian
castellano native of Castille
catalán (catalana f) Catalan
el forastero stranger
el gallego native of Galicia
el judío Jew
vasco Basque

Mountains

los Alpes the Alp
la Sierra de Guadarrama Guadarrama mountains
los Pirineos the Pyrenees
la Sierra Nevada Sierra Nevada mountains

Seas

el Atlántico Atlantic
el Mediterráneo Mediterranean Sea

World events and issues

Problems

la actitud attitude
la agricultura agriculture
la basura rubbish
la causa cause
la comparación comparison
la conclusión conclusion
la contaminación pollution
el desempleo unemployment
la diferencia difference
la discusión argument
en mi opinión in my opinion
la encuesta survey
la ética ethics
la explicación explanation
la guerra (mundial) (world) war
el hambre (f) hunger, famine
el hecho fact
la idea idea
el inconveniente disadvantage
la inmigración immigration
la lucha struggle
la manifestación demonstration
la mayoría majority
la medida measure
el medio ambiente environment
el Mercado Común Common Market
el nivel level
la ocasión opportunity
la opinión opinion
el partido party (political)
la paz peace
la política politics
el problema problem
la razón reason
la reacción reaction
la religión religion
la seguridad social social security
el servicio militar military service
el sueño dream
la tendencia tendency
la tradición tradition
UE (Unión Europea) European Community
la ventaja advantage

People

el gobierno government
la marina navy
la muchedumbre crowd
la ONU UNO
el/la optimista optimist
el/la pesimista pessimist
el político politician
la princesa princess
el príncipe prince
el/la protestante Protestant
la reina queen
el rey king
la sociedad society
el/la terrorista terrorist

Verbs

conservar to conserve
construir to build
contaminar to pollute
contener to contain
creer to believe
decidir to decide
depender de to depend on
destruir to destroy
dudar to hesitate
eliminar to eliminate
estar a favor de to be in favour of
estar al día to be up to date
estar de acuerdo to agree
estar en contra de to be against
existir to exist
hacer la mili to do military service
hay there is, there are
hay que it is necessary
justificar tu opinión to justify your opinion
juzgar to judge
manifestar to demonstrate
mejorarse to improve
opinar to think that
pensar to think
preguntarse to wonder
saber to know
suponer to suppose
tender to tend
tratar de to try to

Chapter 5
Listening

5.1 Introduction to Foundation Tier

This is what you need to know about the listening test for the Foundation Tier:

- You must be entered for either the Foundation Tier or the Higher Tier of the listening test. You cannot opt out.
- You cannot be entered for both tiers: you must choose one or the other.
- Your teacher will ask you in about January which tier you wish to take.
- You will have to listen to a cassette recorded by native Spanish speakers.
- The scenarios for the recordings will be taken from the five Areas of Experience listed in the introduction to this book.
- Most of the questions will be in Spanish. You must answer in Spanish or tick a box or give a visual answer (e.g. draw a symbol in a box). You must not answer in English. *However* a small percentage of the questions will be in English and when you see that the rubric is in English then you should answer in English.
- Each recording will be heard twice and the recordings will be relatively short.
- For the Foundation Tier you will be asked to understand specific detail (for the Higher Tier you will have to draw conclusions).
- You are not expected to understand every single word.

5.2 How to prepare for the Foundation Listening Test

- You must get a cassette or CD with Spanish GCSE practice material.
- You must have the transcript of what is on the cassette or CD so that you can look up words when you get stuck.
- This book is accompanied by a CD of GCSE-type questions and the transcripts.
- After you have equipped yourself with a suitable cassette or CD you must spend time listening to it. Listen to each item many times over. Then check the transcript, make a list of the words you do not know and learn them.
- If travelling by car listen to a Spanish cassette on the way. If on a coach take a Walkman and listen to a Spanish cassette.
- Get a friend to read out the transcript and then do the same for him/her.
- There is certain vocabulary which is always going to be needed because this test is looking for specific items:

  jobs and professions

  relatives

physical descriptions
items of clothing
numbers
days of the week, months of the year, seasons
weather
places in a town
shops
landmarks in the country
directions (e.g. left, right)
time expressions (e.g. last week, yesterday)
school subjects

5.3 During the exam

- Fill in the front of your booklet quickly (have your candidate and centre number ready) so that you can spend as much time as possible reading through the questions.
- The rubrics to the questions will nearly always be in Spanish. You must be able to understand the rubrics.
- There is often a clue to the answer in the rubric so read the rubric carefully.
- You may find that it helps to write things down in Spanish as you hear them to give you time to work them out in English. For example if you know the answer is a number, then when you hear, say, **mil cuatrocientos** write it down in Spanish and then take your time working out that it is 1,400.
- Remember that you do not have to answer in full sentences. Many of the questions will be box-ticking types but if you do have to write in Spanish then a short or one-word answer scores full marks.
- If you are really stuck, guess! Do not leave the question space blank.

5.4 Foundation Tier examination questions

TRACK 1

- The following questions are on the CD available with the book (track references are in the margin). They are the type of question you can expect at GCSE.
- All the text of what is said is written out for you in the transcripts (see 5.5).
- In the GCSE you will hear each recording twice. However on the CD you will hear it only once. Stop the CD and replay it.
- Answers are provided at the end of the section (see 5.6), but do not look at the answers until you have attempted the questions.

TRACK 2

Recording 1

En el restaurante

(a)

(b)

(c)

(d)

(e)

(f)

¿Qué van a tomar? Pon la letra adecuada en cada casilla.

1 ☐
2 ☐
3 ☐
4 ☐

Examiner's tip

If you think that these questions are far too hard for you then your lack of vocabulary is at fault. Spend time learning the vocabulary in the vocabulary section in this book.

(4)

Recording 2

Luis

Enrique

Jaime

Carlos

Rafael

José

Escribe el nombre del chico que habla en el espacio adecuado.

1 ....
2 ....
3 ....
4 ....
5 ....
6 ....

Examiner's tip

Read the questions thoroughly. Make sure you have learnt the Spanish rubrics in the introduction to this book. *Before* the recording begins you should have a clear idea of what the question expects you to do.

(6)

Recording 3

Para cada pregunta pon una x en la casilla correcta.

1 ¿Qué busca?

(a) ☐

(b) ☐

(c) ☐

(d)

2 ¿Qué regalo compra?

(a) ☐
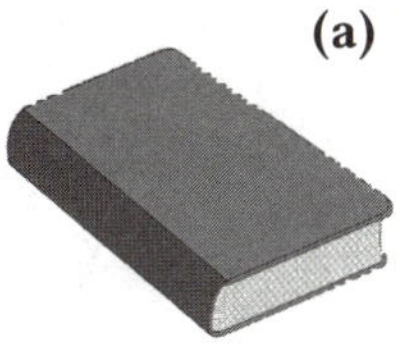

(b) ☐

(c) ☐

(d) ☐

3 ¿Qué deporte prefiere?

(a) ☐ **(b)** ☐ **(c)** ☐ **(d)** ☐

4 ¿Dónde está el dinero?

(a) ☐ **(b)** ☐ **(c)** ☐ **(d)** ☐

5 ¿Qué visitarán?

(a) ☐ **(b)** ☐ **(c)** ☐ **(d)** ☐

6 ¿Dónde está la librería?

(a) ☐ **(b)** ☐ **(c)** ☐ **(d)** ☐

7 ¿Cuándo sale el autobús?

(a) ☐ **(b)** ☐ **(c)** ☐ **(d)** ☐

8 ¿Cómo viaja Isabel?

(a) ☐ **(b)** ☐ **(c)** ☐ **(d)** ☐

9 ¿Dónde quiere ir Isabel?

(a) ☐ **(b)** ☐ **(c)** ☐ **(d)** ☐

10 ¿Cuándo vuelve Isabel?

(a) ☐ 04:08

(b) ☐ 05:09

(c) ☐ 06:03

(d) ☐ 07:10

(10)

Examiner's tip

Don't think that once you have heard a recording and attempted the question, that recording is no further use to you. Listen again and again to each recording: come back to it a few days later.

TRACK 5

Recording 4

Cuatro españoles se describen. Escucha el CD y rellena las casillas.

nombre	asignatura preferida	deporte favorito	transporte al colegio
Juan			
Elena			
Sofía			
Enrique			

(12)

Examiner's tip

Make sure you look at the mark allocation in brackets at the end of each question. It will help you to understand the question.

TRACK 6

Recording 5

En el hotel. Escucha lo que dice el recepcionista y pon una x en la casilla adecuada.

		verdadero	falso
1	La familia no ha reservado.	☐	☐
2	La familia quiere quedarse una semana.	☐	☐
3	Desde las habitaciones se ve el mar.	☐	☐
4	Las dos habitaciones tienen una cama de matrimonio.	☐	☐
5	Se paga un suplemento para el desayuno.	☐	☐
6	El desayuno se sirve a las ocho.	☐	☐

(6)

Examiner's tip

Never leave an answer blank. If you have to guess, then guess. If your Exam Board allows you to use a dictionary at the end, then write 'G' in the margin to remind yourself which questions you have guessed at. If you can, make a note of any key Spanish words so that you can look them up in the dictionary.

Recording 6

Información personal

Rellena los espacios en esta ficha.

Apellidos	Alvarez Díaz
Nombre	Jorge
Edad	....
Fecha de nacimiento	el trece de ....
Año	....
Profesión del padre	....
Profesión de la madre	....

(5)

Examiner's tip

Very often the words for people's jobs are tested. Make sure you know the vocabulary.

Recording 7

Estás en un restaurante y oyes esta conversación. Contesta en español.

1 ¿Qué quiere saber el camarero? ....
2 ¿Dónde está la mesa? ....
3 ¿Qué va a traer el camarero? ....
4 ¿Qué recomienda el camarero? ....
5 ¿Qué hay en la tortilla? ....
6 ¿Qué quiere el cliente para empezar? ....
7 ¿Qué quiere el cliente de postre? ....
8 ¿Qué bebe el cliente? ....

(8)

Examiner's tip

Nothing annoys an examiner more than illegible handwriting. If you have a handwriting problem, PRINT the answers. One letter at a time. The written answers in the exam are usually very short so you will have time to do this.

Recording 8

Rellena los espacios en el horario.

HORA	MIERCOLES	JUEVES	VIERNES
08.30	Geografía	Historia	4..............
09.30	Historia	Geografía	Arte
10.30	1..............	2..............	Matemáticas
11.30	Recreo	3..............	Recreo
12.00	Música	Inglés	Español
13.30	Comida	Comida	5..............
15.30	Arte	Música	Inglés

(5)

Examiner's tip

This last question is the hardest so far. Why not spend time going through the transcript and learning all the vocabulary?

5.5 Transcripts for examination questions

Recording 1

1 Una botella de vino tinto, por favor.
2 Un café con leche, por favor.
3 Para mí, pescado.
4 Quiero una cerveza.

Recording 2

1 ¿Mi familia? Pues soy hijo único pero tenemos dos gatos.
2 No vivo con mis padres. Vivo con mi hermano mayor y mis hermanitas.
3 Mis padres han muerto. Vivo con mi abuela.
4 ¿Detalles de mi familia? Pues vivo con mis padres y mis dos hermanas.
5 Yo vivo con mi hermano y tenemos dos perros.
6 Me gustaría tener un hermano pero tengo solamente una hermana.

Recording 3

1 Quiero escribir a mi amiga Isabel pero no encuentro un sello. ¿Dónde están los sellos?
2 Voy a comprar un regalo para Isabel. Voy a comprarle un libro.
3 Esta tarde voy a salir a hacer deporte. Mi deporte favorito es la natación.
4 No sé dónde está mi dinero. ¡Ay sí! Lo he dejado en mi dormitorio.
5 Cuando salga con Isabel vamos a visitar el puente romano.
6 Compraré el regalo en el Corte Inglés. La librería está en la segunda planta.
7 Voy a ir al centro en autobús. El autobús sale a las diez y media.
8 Isabel me dice que se va de vacaciones a Turquía en avión.
9 Isabel me dice que va a pasar todo el día en la playa.
10 Isabel me dice que va a volver el cuatro de agosto.

Recording 4

Hola. Me llamo Juan. Odio todas mis asignaturas menos el arte. Me encanta el fútbol pero no me gusta el tenis. Normalmente voy al instituto en bicicleta. No me gusta ir andando.

Buenos días. Me llamo Elena. Me gustan casi todas mis asignaturas pero no me gusta la historia. Mi favorita es el inglés. También me encantan todos los deportes menos el tenis. Me gusta especialmente el baloncesto. Por la mañana mi padre me lleva al instituto en coche porque el autobus es caro.

Hola. Me llamo Sofía. Nací en Francia así que me gusta mucho el francés pero mi asignatura predilecta es el alemán. Mi hermano me da clases de natación porque él es profesional pero yo prefiero el ciclismo. Es peligroso ir al instituto en bicicleta así que tomo el autobús.

Buenas tardes. Me llamo Enrique. Quiero ser químico así que paso mucho tiempo haciendo química. Las otras asignaturas – el inglés, etcétera – me aburren. Me encanta el hockey. No me gusta el fútbol. No hay autobuses así que voy al instituto andando.

Recording 5

Buenos días. La familia Smith ¿no? Han hecho la reserva por teléfono. Sí, la reserva es para siete noches y han pedido dos habitaciones con vistas al mar. Una habitación tiene cama de matrimonio y la otra tiene dos camas individuales. El desayuno está incluído en el precio y se sirve a las siete y media.

Recording 6

Me llamo Jorge Alvarez Díaz y tengo 18 años. Nací el trece de junio de mil novecientos setenta y ocho en Madrid. Tengo cuatro hermanos y mi padre es médico y mi madre da clases de inglés en un instituto.

Recording 7

Camarero ¿Una mesa para dos personas?
Hay una mesa aquí en el rincón. Lejos de la ventana abierta.
Les voy a traer el menú del día. Primero deme el paraguas.
Tenemos tortilla muy buena pero mariscos no tenemos.
Sólo tenemos tortilla de jamón.

Cliente Voy a pedir una tortilla pero primero quiero una ensalada.
Y de postre no quiero nada.
Y de beber quiero vino tinto.

Recording 8

Lo que no me gusta es que tenemos una clase de inglés todos los días ¡qué aburrido! El jueves no está mal pero antes del recreo tenemos química y no me gusta mucho. Tenemos recreo a las once y media todos los días y la comida es a la una y media todos los días. Tenemos cinco clases al día y el viernes empieza muy mal porque tenemos biología y no me entiendo bien con el profesor. El viernes después del español tengo mi clase favorita: deporte.

5.6 Suggested answers to examination questions

Recording 1

1 (b)
2 (f)
3 (d)
4 (a)

Recording 2

1 Carlos
2 Rafael
3 Luis
4 Jaime
5 Enrique
6 José

Recording 3

1 (b)
2 (a)
3 (c)
4 (a)
5 (b)
6 (c)
7 (d)
8 (b)
9 (a)
10 (a)

Recording 4

nombre	asignatura preferida	deporte favorito	transporte al colegio
Juan	arte	fútbol	bicicleta
Elena	inglés	baloncesto	coche
Sofía	alemán	ciclismo	autobús
Enrique	química	hockey	andando

Recording 5

1 falso
2 verdadero
3 verdadero
4 falso
5 falso
6 falso

Recording 6

18
junio
1978
médico
profesora

Recording 7

1 Si necesitan una mesa para dos.
2 En el rincón.
3 El menú del día.
4 La tortilla.
5 Jamón.
6 Ensalada.
7 No quiere postre.
8 Tinto.

Recording 8

1 Inglés.
2 Química.
3 Recreo.
4 Biología.
5 Deporte.

5.7 Introduction to Higher Tier

This is what you need to know about the exam:

- If you are entered for the Higher Tier you cannot do the Foundation Tier.
- The recordings will be faster than for the Foundation Tier and the vocabulary will be beyond the Minimum Core Vocabulary List issued by your Board.
- The recordings will be of native speakers and there may be background noises.
- The recordings are longer and harder. They may be split into sections. Then you will hear either the whole recording through and then hear it repeated in sections, or you will hear one section and that section repeated, then the second section and that section repeated, and so on. Listen out for the instructions.
- There are likely to be more:
  - long conversations and discussions
  - arguments
  - requests and instructions
- One major difference between Foundation Tier and Higher Tier is that for the Higher Tier you will be asked to draw conclusions and detect emotions. You will meet examples of this in the examination questions in this book.

5.8 During the exam

These are the points to remember on the exam day:

- Listen carefully to the instructions and make sure you have learnt all the possible rubrics in Spanish, so that you will understand the instructions written on the paper.
- Remember that the mark allocation for each question will give you a clue as to what information and how much information is required.
- Always attempt every question even if you have to guess.
- Remember that questions asking for specific detail follow the order of the information in the recording. However a question which asks you to detect emotions or draw conclusions may require you to draw upon information given throughout the recording.

5.9 Higher Tier examination questions

The following questions are on the CD which accompanies this book. They are written by a GCSE Chief Examiner. There is an overlap in questions for Foundation and Higher Tier, so do the Foundation Tier Listening tests first. Also remember that in your exam each extract will be repeated after a pause. On the accompanying CD the recordings are not repeated, so when you have listened to a recording reset and listen again.

TRACK 10

Recording 9

Un intercambio

Llegas a casa de tu amigo español. ¿Qué te dice? Pon una x en la casilla correcta.

1 La comida se sirve
   (a) antes de ver el dormitorio ☐
   (b) después de ver el dormitorio ☐
   (c) ahora mismo ☐

2 La habitación
- (a) está lejos de allí ☐
- (b) tranquila ☐
- (c) ruidosa ☐

3 Puedes poner tus cosas
- (a) en el armario ☐
- (b) sobre la cama ☐
- (c) debajo de la cama ☐

4 Para la comida hay
- (a) carne ☐
- (b) ensalada ☐
- (c) pescado ☐

5 Más tarde vas a
- (a) bailar ☐
- (b) dormir ☐
- (c) ver la tele ☐

6 ¿Quién vuelve más tarde?
- (a) su hermana ☐
- (b) su hermano ☐
- (c) su amigo inglés ☐

(6)

Examiner's tip

If you have to correct one of your ticks make sure your alterations are absolutely clear. If the examiner is in doubt, he/she will not give a mark.

TRACK 11

Recording 10

Someone is telling you about sport in Lima. The conversation is being translated.

1 The most popular sport is ....

2 Why is the level of golf so high? ....

3 Why is the city-centre pool famous? ....

4 New York hosted a competition for which sport? ....

5 What did the Peruvian team win? ....

(5)

Examiner's tip

20% of the questions will be asked in English and you answer in English.

TRACK 12

Recording 11

Isabel y Antonio hablan sobre el tabaco. Pon una x en la casilla correcta.

		verdadero	falso
1	Antonio no fuma por el olor.	☐	☐
2	La novia de Antonio fuma tabaco.	☐	☐
3	Isabel empezó a fumar cuando tenía quince años.	☐	☐
4	Isabel empezó a fumar porque sus amigos eran fumadores.	☐	☐
5	Isabel fuma muy poco.	☐	☐
6	Isabel ya no quiere fumar más.	☐	☐
7	Los padres de Isabel son fumadores.	☐	☐
8	Los padres de Isabel no quieren que ella fume.	☐	☐
9	Isabel fuma en casa.	☐	☐
10	Isabel gana dinero trabajando.	☐	☐
11	Isabel bebe vino de vez en cuando.	☐	☐

(11)

Examiner's tip

Some of these questions expect you to be able to draw a conclusion. Expect this kind of question in the Higher Tier.

Recording 12

Pon una x en las casillas correctas.

1 Pablo y Conchita
(a) se conocieron en la universidad ☐
(b) eran colegas ☐
(c) eran camaradas de clase ☐

2 La madre de Pablo
(a) es cocinera ☐
(b) es profesora ☐
(c) es camarera ☐

3 Escoge *tres* de estas actividades que Conchita y Pablo van a hacer juntos. Pon una x en tres de las casillas.

(a) ☐

(b) ☐

(c) ☐

(d) ☐

(e) ☐

(f) ☐

(5)

Examiner's tip

Again more questions requiring you to draw a conclusion. Do not expect the exact words in the questions to be said on the CD. For instance none of the three jobs in question 2 is actually stated.

Recording 13

Escucha a estas personas vendiendo cosas en el mercado. Rellena el espacio con una palabra de la lista.
El primer puesto vende **1**........................ y el vendedor dice que sus productos son los más **2**........................ del mercado.

El segundo puesto vende cosas para **3**........................y el vendedor menciona la calidad **4**........................ de sus productos.

El tercer puesto vende **5**........................y el vendedor dice que ofrece un servicio **6**........................ de transporte.

gratuito	superior	coches
niños	baratos	buena
relojes	baratas	muebles
paredes	legumbres	
bueno	armas	

(6)

Examiner's tip

'Los' for question 2 tells you that you are looking for a masculine plural noun. 'La' for question 4 tells you that you are looking for a feminine singular adjective. 'Un' in question 6 tells you that you are looking for a masculine singular noun.

Recording 14

Películas

Carla y Fernando discuten los tipos de película. Escribe en la columna correcta el nombre de la persona correcta.

Película	Le gustan mucho	Le gustan un poco	No le gustan nada
películas de miedo			
películas del oeste			
películas de amor			
películas de aventura			

(8)

Examiner's tip

Make sure you look at the mark allocation in brackets at the end of each question. It will help you to understand the question. Here it tells you that you have to put two names beside each type of film.

Recording 15

Escucha lo que dice la radio sobre una tenista famosa. Luego completa los detalles.

Laura Gabarda ha vuelto de los Estados **1** .... y va a hacer una gira en España en el mes de **2** .... Laura va a jugar **3** .... veces y las entradas cuestan **4** .... Para comprarlas hay que tener una **5** .... de crédito.

(5)

Examiner's tip

Sometimes you have a list of possible words to put into the blanks and sometimes you don't. Be ready for both types of question.

Recording 16

Tres alumnos

Tres alumnos hablan de su instituto. ¿Quién dice qué? Pon una x en las casillas correctas.

		Pedro	Pilar	Enrique
1	¿A quién le gusta ir al instituto?	☐	☐	☐
2	¿Quién no va a sus clases?	☐	☐	☐
3	¿Quién espera el fin del trimestre con impaciencia?	☐	☐	☐
4	¿Quién quiere ser profesor?	☐	☐	☐
5	¿Quién menciona un profesor que le gusta?	☐	☐	☐
6	¿Quién menciona un profesor que no le gusta?	☐	☐	☐

(6)

Examiner's tip

This type of question requires a good memory. It is essential that you read and memorise the whole question before the recording starts.

Recording 17

Tomar una decisión

¿Verdadero o falso? Pon una x en las casillas adecuadas.

		verdadero	falso
1	José tiene planes para ir a Inglaterra en otoño.	☐	☐
2	José quiere aprender inglés.	☐	☐
3	Los padres de José no van a Inglaterra.	☐	☐
4	Los padres de José quieren veranear en la costa.	☐	☐
5	José nunca va de vacaciones con sus padres.	☐	☐
6	La novia de José se llama Angela.	☐	☐
7	Angela quiere que José la acompañe a la Costa del Sol.	☐	☐
8	Angela se puso muy enfadada.	☐	☐
9	Jaime dice que José no debe ir a Inglaterra.	☐	☐
10	José va a seguir saliendo con Angela.	☐	☐

(10)

Examiner's tip

In this type of question you have to sort out which voice is José and which voice is Jaime. You will be given clues in the recordings. Listen out for them.

Recording 18

Estás en España viajando en autocar con un grupo organizado. El guía habla por el altavoz. Pon una x en la casilla correcta.

1 Vas a llegar al hotel
- **(a)** en veinte minutos ☐
- **(b)** en treinta minutos ☐
- **(c)** en cincuenta minutos ☐
- **(d)** en sesenta minutos ☐

2 Antes de llegar al hotel
- **(a)** vamos a parar para ver la catedral ☐
- **(b)** vamos a ver los sitios de interés ☐
- **(c)** vamos a ver la catedral ☐
- **(d)** vamos a ver un vídeo ☐

3 Esta tarde
- **(a)** vamos a cenar, luego ver un vídeo ☐
- **(b)** vamos a ver un vídeo y luego cenar ☐
- **(c)** vamos a visitar los sitios de interés ☐
- **(d)** vamos a hacer un vídeo ☐

4 Mañana
- **(a)** la mañana es libre y por la tarde veremos la catedral ☐
- **(b)** todo el día está libre ☐
- **(c)** visita organizada por la mañana y nada organizado por la tarde ☐
- **(d)** hay dos visitas organizadas ☐

5 Nos quedaremos en Zaragoza
- **(a)** un día ☐
- **(b)** dos días ☐
- **(c)** tres días ☐
- **(d)** cuatro días ☐

6 Si tenemos un problema en el hotel
- **(a)** hay que telefonear al guía ☐
- **(b)** hay que ir a la recepción ☐
- **(c)** hay que ir a la habitación tres ☐
- **(d)** hay que llamar al hotel ☐

(6)

TRACK 20

Recording 19

Tres españoles explican que no tienen tiempo libre. Pon una x en la casilla correcta.

1 Alfonso es una persona
- **(a)** que quiere divertirse mucho ☐
- **(b)** que se dedica a sus estudios ☐
- **(c)** caritativa ☐
- **(d)** vaga ☐

2 Jaime es una persona
- **(a)** que quiere divertirse mucho ☐
- **(b)** que se dedica a sus estudios ☐
- **(c)** caritativa ☐
- **(d)** vaga ☐

3 Ana es una persona
- **(a)** que quiere divertirse mucho ☐
- **(b)** que se dedica a sus estudios ☐
- **(c)** caritativa ☐
- **(d)** vaga ☐

(3)

TRACK 21

Recording 20

Un turista llama a un hotel. Escucha la conversación y rellena los huecos con las palabras correctas.

El turista telefonea de **1** .... El recepcionista le dice que una habitación **2** .... cuesta 3.000 pesetas y una habitación doble cuesta **3** .... pesetas. Por desgracia, no hay **4** .... en las habitaciones. El turista se va del hotel el **5**...................... de setiembre y si toma el desayuno en su habitación tendrá que pagar **6** .... pesetas.

(6)

Examiner's tip

Nothing annoys an examiner more than illegible handwriting. If you have a handwriting problem, PRINT the answers, one letter at a time. The written answers in the exam are usually very short so you will have time to do this.

5.10 Transcripts for examination questions

Recording 9

Un intercambio

No tenemos tiempo para poner tus cosas en tu dormitorio. Vamos a comer en seguida.

Después vamos a ver tu dormitorio. No te preocupes. Está muy lejos de los ruidos de la calle.

No hay mucho espacio en tu dormitorio porque la cama es grande pero puedes poner tus cosas en el armario.

Si quieres comer aún tenemos un poco de bacalao.

Y después vamos a salir a una discoteca con otro amigo inglés.

Y al volver estará mi hermano y puedo presentaros.

Recording 10

El deporte en el Perú

En Lima hay mucho interés por todo tipo de deporte pero sin duda el más popular es el patinaje sobre hielo. Es un deporte nuevo pero entre los jóvenes es más popular que el fútbol. En algunas zonas se puede jugar al golf: todos los clubs aquí están dirigidos por profesionales. En el centro de la ciudad se encuentra la Piscina Nacional y es famosa porque el equipo olímpico del Perú se entrenó allí. El equipo de baloncesto del Perú también es muy famoso porque hace dos semanas ganó una medalla de oro en un concurso en Nueva York.

Recording 11

Isabel Oye Antonio ¿quieres un cigarillo?
Antonio No gracias – no fumo.
Isabel ¿Por qué no?
Antonio La ropa de la gente que fuma huele mal y además a mi novia no le gusta. Dice que es una cosa sucia.
Isabel Pues yo empecé a fumar a la edad de quince años.
Antonio ¿Por qué empezaste?
Isabel Pues salía entonces con un grupo de jóvenes que fumaban. Yo hacía como ellos. Ahora fumo más de veinte cigarillos al día. Para mí es un placer y no quiero parar.
Antonio ¿Qué dicen tus padres?
Isabel Como los dos fuman también no dicen nada. Me dejan fumar pero no en casa. Si quiero fumar tengo que salir.
Antonio Pero cuesta mucho dinero ¿no?
Isabel Sí pero como trabajo en casa de una señora limpiando la casa tengo bastante dinero.
Antonio Y ¿bebes alcohol?
Isabel Nunca en mi vida.

Recording 12

Pablo habla de su día

Voy a pasar el día con una amiga muy especial. Se llama Conchita y nos conocemos desde hace mucho tiempo: íbamos a la escuela juntos. Como mi madre tiene que dar clase sería mejor no almorzar en casa y conozco un sitio que ofrece los platos que a Conchita le gustan. Luego como ponen una película de miedo en el centro de la ciudad iremos a verla. Y más tarde como a Conchita le gusta bailar iremos a 'La Mariposa' hasta las diez de la noche.

Recording 13

En el mercado

Habas, zanahorias, cebollas, patatas ... y ¡qué precios! Nosotros tenemos los precios más bajos de este mercado.

Muñecas, coches eléctricos, juegos, trenes, juguetes ... ofrecemos productos de la mejor calidad.

Mesas, sillas, sillones, armarios, camas ... y el transporte a tu casa es gratis.

Recording 14

Carla Oye Fernando vamos a ver una película. Yo quiero ver una película de miedo. Son mis favoritas.
Fernando Las películas de miedo me dan asco. No quiero ver esa película.
Carla Entonces ¿qué quieres ver?
Fernando Yo prefiero una película del oeste. Son mis favoritas.

Carla Una película del oeste ... me da igual pero ¿no sería mejor ver una película de amor? Me gustan bastante.

Fernando Si vas a una película de amor vas sola. Ni hablar. Pero si quieres me gustaría mucho ver una película de aventura.

Carla Bueno. Una película de aventura ... si quieres ... supongo que sí.

Recording 15

La tenista española Laura Gabarda volvió hoy de su gira en los Estados Unidos para empezar otra gira aquí en España a principios de junio. La gira durará dos semanas y Laura jugará un total de seis partidos en seis regiones distintas de España. Las entradas costarán 10.000 pesetas y sólo se pueden comprar por teléfono usando una tarjeta de crédito.

Recording 16

Tres alumnos

Me llamo Pedro. Estoy harto de mi instituto. Muchas veces digo a mi madre que estoy enfermo para poder quedarme en casa. Y a veces con ciertos profesores no voy a las clases: me quedo en el café. La única cosa que me gusta es ... pues ... las vacaciones.

Me llamo Pilar. Me aburro en el instituto aunque voy todos los días. Me fastidia lo que tenemos que hacer. No me gustan mis asignaturas menos una: la clase de geografía. Es que el profesor es tan guapo.

Me llamo Enrique. Me encanta ir al instituto. Aprendo muchísimo y me gustan todas mis asignaturas menos una: geografía. No me entiendo bien con el profesor. Lo curioso es que un día quiero ser profesor de geografía.

Recording 17

Jaime ¿Qué te pasa, José?

José Pues no sé lo que voy a hacer este verano.

Jaime Pero te vas a Inglaterra a hacer un curso de inglés ¿no?

José Ya ... ya ... pero las cosas han cambiado.

Jaime ¿Qué ha pasado?

José Pues ya sabes que tengo que aprender inglés para mi próximo trabajo y por eso iba a pasar el verano en Inglaterra aprendiendo inglés. Mis padres han alquilado un apartamento en la Costa del Sol y por primera vez no voy a ir de vacaciones con ellos.

Jaime Ya lo sé ... ya lo sé.

José Ahora mi novia Angela dice que va a la Costa del Sol también y quiere verme allí. Dice que no debo ir a Inglaterra. Dice que tengo que ir a la Costa del Sol con ella. Cuando le dije que prefiero ir a Inglaterra se puso furiosa. Dijo que si quiero seguir siendo su novio tengo que abandonar la idea de ir a Inglaterra.

Jaime Me parece que debes dedicarte a tus estudios y si Angela no está de acuerdo entonces no salgas más con ella.

José Tienes razón. No salgo más con ella.

Recording 18

Señoras, señores, estamos llegando a Barcelona y estaremos delante del hotel en media hora. En unos momentos pasaremos cerca de la catedral – podrán verla a la izquierda – pero no tenemos tiempo para visitarla ahora. Esta tarde la cena en el hotel será a las nueve, y a las diez y media voy a poner un vídeo mostrando los sitios de interés en Barcelona. Mañana por la mañana volveremos allí a verla con más tranquilidad. Y mañana por la tarde tienen tiempo libre para conocer la ciudad e ir de compras. Pasado mañana nos marchamos a Zaragoza y pasaremos tres días allí. Bueno señoras y señores, espero que el hotel les guste y si tienen algún problema hay que marcar el número tres para poder hablar conmigo.

Recording 19

Oye Alfonso ¿quieres salir esta tarde?

Lo siento pero no puedo ... es decir que ya he quedado con mi novia: vamos ahora a patinar. Luego vamos a comer en un restaurante. Después vamos al cine y por último vamos a una discoteca. Lo siento pero no tengo tiempo.

Hola Jaime ¿quieres salir esta tarde?

Lo siento, no puedo. Tengo exámenes dentro de dos meses y tengo que estudiar. Si no apruebo no puedo ir a la universidad. Voy a estudiar todo el día todos los días. Lo siento pero no puedo salir.

¿Qué tal, Ana? ¿quieres salir esta tarde?

Lo siento pero no tengo tiempo. Esta mañana voy a misa. Luego voy a ayudar al sacerdote a limpiar la iglesia. Después tengo que visitar a los enfermos en el hospital y más tarde tengo que escribir a los periódicos quejándome de la pobreza que existe en algunos barrios de esta ciudad. No, no puedo salir.

Recording 20

Turista	Buenos días. Llamo desde Inglaterra. Quiero reservar dos habitaciones, por favor.
Recepcionista	Muy bien. ¿Qué tipo de habitaciones quiere?
Turista	Pues una habitación para una persona y una habitación para dos personas.
Recepcionista	No hay problema. La habitación doble costará 5.000 por noche y la habitación individual costará 3.000 por noche.
Turista	Y ¿hay ducha en las habitaciones?
Recepcionista	Ambas tienen baño: lo siento pero no hay ducha en ninguna.
Turista	Vale.
Recepcionista	¿Cuál es la fecha de su llegada?
Turista	Estaremos allí del 7 al 14 de setiembre. ¿El desayuno está incluído en el precio?
Recepcionista	Lo siento, no. El desayuno en el comedor cuesta 550 pesetas. Si toman el desayuno en su habitación costará cien pesetas más.

5.11 Suggested answers to examination questions

Recording 9

1 (c) **2** (b) **3** (a) **4** (c) **5** (a) **6** (b)

Recording 10

1 Ice-skating **2** Clubs are run by professionals **3** Olympic team trained there
4 Basketball **5** A gold medal

Recording 11

1 verdadero **2** falso **3** verdadero **4** verdadero **5** falso **6** falso **7** verdadero **8** falso
9 falso **10** verdadero **11** falso

Recording 12

1 (c) **2** (b) **3** (b)(c)(f)

Recording 13

1 legumbres **2** baratos **3** niños **4** superior **5** muebles **6** gratuito

Recording 14

Película	Le gustan mucho	Le gustan un poco	No le gustan nada
películas de miedo	Carla		Fernando
películas del oeste	Fernando	Carla	
películas de amor		Carla	Fernando
películas de aventura	Fernando	Carla	

Recording 15

1 Unidos **2** junio **3** seis **4** 10.000 **5** tarjeta

Recording 16

		Pedro	Pilar	Enrique
1	¿A quién le gusta ir al instituto?			x
2	¿Quién no va a sus clases?	x		
3	¿Quién espera el fin del trimestre con impaciencia?	x		
4	¿Quién quiere ser profesor?			x
5	¿Quién menciona a un profesor que le gusta?		x	
6	¿Quién menciona a un profesor que no le gusta?			x

Recording 17

1 falso **2** verdadero **3** verdadero **4** verdadero **5** falso **6** verdadero **7** verdadero **8** verdadero **9** falso **10** falso

Recording 18

1 (b) **2** (c) **3** (a) **4** (c) **5** (c) **6** (a)

Recording 19

1 (a) **2** (b) **3** (c)

Recording 20

1 Inglaterra **2** individual **3** 5000 **4** duchas **5** 14 **6** 650

Chapter 6
Speaking

6.1 Introduction

This is what you need to know about the Speaking exam:
- It is compulsory; you cannot opt out of it.
- The speaking test in Spanish is the equivalent of the course-work that you do in other subjects.

The Edexcel (London) Board offers coursework as an alternative to an oral test: check with your teacher.

The SEG Board requires staged assessment of oral work: check with your teacher and with the analysis of Boards at the beginning of this book.

- It is made up of either two or three parts: role-play tests, a conversation and if you are doing MEG or NEAB you will have to do a presentation as part of your conversation.
- The exam will take place between March and May.
- It will be conducted by your teacher, who will usually be the one who decides when and where the exam takes place.
- It will be recorded on cassette and either marked by your teacher or marked by an external examiner.
- It will last between eight and twelve minutes.
- You will have time before the exam to prepare the role-play situations. You can use a dictionary during the preparation time but not during the actual exam.
- You can keep the role-play cards in front of you during the exam.
- Your teacher will play the role of a native speaker who speaks no English. This means you cannot ask him/her what words mean.

6.2 Role-play situations

The role-play situations will be based on the Areas of Experience used by every Board. However there are certain situations which lend themselves to role-play and you should be aware of this. These situations are:

at cafés and restaurants

asking the way

public transport

at the campsite, youth hostel, hotel

at the doctor's/scene of an accident

shopping for food/drink/clothes

at the post office

on the telephone

at the bank/exchange office

lost property

tourist information office

at the cinema

visiting and receiving an exchange partner

When you are revising for or attempting role-plays you should be aware of the following points:

- The instructions at the top of your card will be in English. These English instructions will set the scene. After that the cues to guide you towards what you have to say are either in Spanish or are pictorial.
- The drawings used by the Boards can be very confusing. You must try to get used to the kind of pictures you will have to interpret before the exam.
- You must try and listen to and understand what your teacher is saying to you. He/she will guide you in Spanish into completing the task even if you do not understand what the picture is telling you to do.
- Most Exam Boards issue a booklet with a list of pictures and drawings. They are sometimes called visuals or icons. Ask your teacher if you can look at the booklet.

In the Foundation Tier the skill lies in identifying what are the key words needed. If you can communicate the key words then you will almost certainly gain full marks even if you make grammar mistakes. So for instance if the visual shows a return ticket to Málaga you need to know **ida y vuelta a Málaga** The **quiero** normally placed before it is not required to gain the mark.

There are three types of role-play situation. You will take two of them. The two you take depends on whether you are entered for Foundation Tier or for Higher Tier. If you are entered for Foundation Tier you take types one and two. If you are entered for Higher Tier you take types two and three.

In this book there are 20 role-play situations. The teacher's script and suggested student's answers are on the accompanying CD. There is a tone which tells you to stop your machine and give the appropriate response. You can then play on and hear the suggested answer. The teacher's role and suggested answers are also written out at the end of each section (see 6.4 and 6.6).

6.3 Role-play type 1

This is a series of about five tasks based on pictures, words in Spanish or a mixture of both. You will be assessed on to what extent you fulfil the task. Minor errors will not count against you.

Each task will be one item. (In Role-play type 2 you may have two or more items to deal with.) Here is an example of a Role-play type 1.

Look at the task first, prepare your answers using a dictionary if you need one, then listen to your CD.

Role-play 1

You are in a café in Spain. Your teacher will play the part of the waiter/waitress.

1

2

3

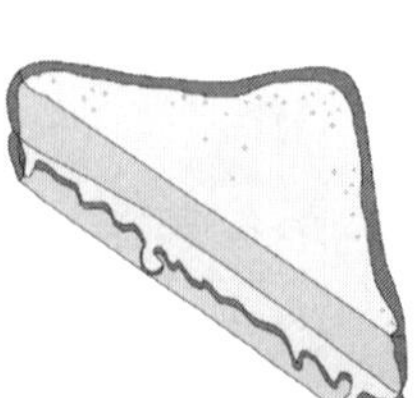

4

5

Teacher's role and suggested answers

Teacher	Estás en un café y yo soy el camarero/la camarera. Buenos días, señor(ita).
You	Buenos días. Una mesa para una persona, por favor.
Teacher	Muy bien. ¿Qué quieres tomar?
You	Una limonada, por favor.
Teacher	¿ Algo más?
You	Un bocadillo de queso, por favor.
Teacher	Muy bien.
You	¿Hay un teléfono?
Teacher	En el rincón.
You	Gracias. ¿Cuánto cuesta, por favor?
Teacher	Son cuatrocientas pesetas.

E xaminer's tip

You need to know the question words **¿quién?** = who? **¿dónde?**= where? **¿qué?** = what? **¿cuándo?**=when? **¿por qué?** = why? **¿cómo?** = how? **¿cuánto?** = how much? **¿cuántos/as?** = how many?

Now here are some more to practise on. Remember to prepare first, then listen to the CD and only later should you use the text and answers at the end of this section.

Role-play 2

You are in a Spanish station and you want a first-class return to Madrid. You must find out the platform the train leaves from, how much the ticket costs and what time it departs.

1

2

3

4

5

E xaminer's tip

Be sure you know your railway vocabulary: first-class **(de primera clase)** second-class **(de segunda clase)** single **(de ida)** return **(de ida y vuelta)**

Role-play 3

You are in a service-station in Spain. Your teacher will play the part of the attendant and will start the conversation.

1

2

3

4

5

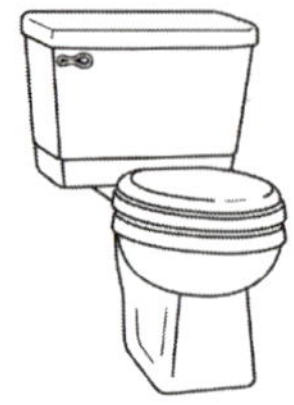

E xaminer's tip

Make sure you know the two types of petrol: **súper** = 4-star and **sin plomo** is lead-free.

TRACK 37

Role-play 4

You go into a hotel in Spain. Your teacher will play the part of the receptionist and will start the conversation.

1 Saluda al/a la recepcionista.

2 Pide esta habitación.

3 Para estas fechas.

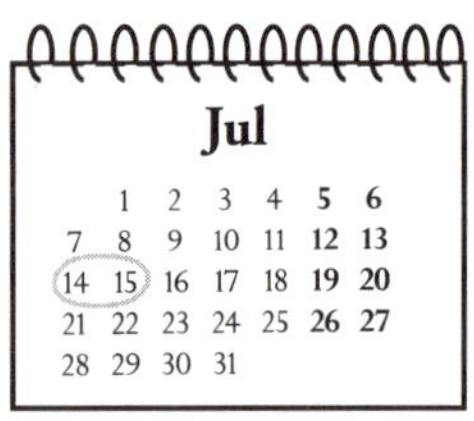

4

5

TRACK 38

Role-play 5

You see this advertisement for work in Spain and you decide to apply for the job. You have an interview. Your teacher will be your interviewer and will start the conversation.

Se necesita urgentemente
Camarero/a – 16- 25 años
Debe hablar español e inglés

Tel: Madrid 4164338

Examiner's tip

Remember that **nombre** means first-name and **apellido** means second-name.

Role-play 6

You enter a tourist information office in order to enquire about changing English money into pesetas. You want to know how many pesetas to the pound. Your teacher will play the part of the assistant and will start the conversation.

1

2

£1 = ?

3

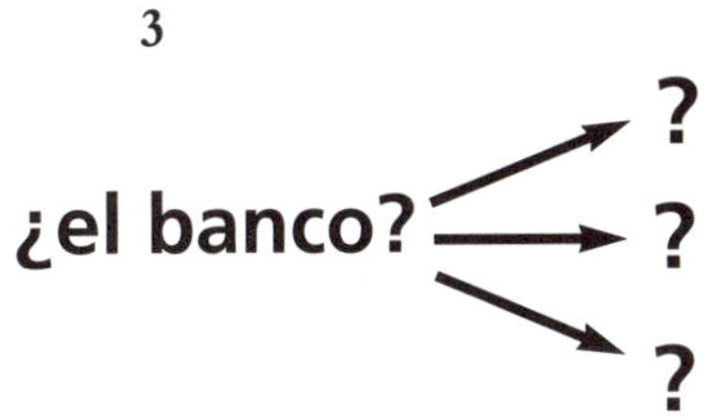

4

5

6.4 Teacher's role and suggested answers

Role-play 2

Teacher	Estás en una estación y yo soy el empleado/la empleada. ¿Qué quieres, joven?
You	Quiero un billete de ida y vuelta a Madrid.
Teacher	Muy bien.
You	Primera clase, por favor.
Teacher	Aquí tienes.
You	¿Qué andén, por favor?
Teacher	Andén número ocho.
You	¿Cuánto cuesta?
Teacher	Tres mil.
You	¿A qué hora sale el tren?
Teacher	A las diez y media.

Role-play 3

Teacher Entras en una gasolinera. Yo soy el empleado/la empleada. ¿En qué puedo servirle?
You Veinticinco litros, por favor.
Teacher ¿Algo más?
You ¿Puede Vd. comprobar los neumáticos?
Teacher Sí. No hay problema.
You ¿Para ir a Madrid, por favor?
Teacher Todo seguido. ¿Algo más?
You ¿Hay helados?
Teacher Lo siento, no.
You ¿Dónde están los servicios?
Teacher Aquí, a la derecha.

Role-play 4

Teacher Entras en un hotel. Yo soy el/la recepcionista. Buenos días.
You Quiero una habitación individual con ducha.
Teacher Muy bien. ¿Para cuándo?
You El catorce y quince de julio.
Teacher Muy bien.
You ¿Cuánto cuesta la habitación?
Teacher Cuatro mil pesetas por noche.
You Bueno. ¿Hay ascensor?
Teacher Aquí a la izquierda.

Role-play 5

Teacher Buscas trabajo en España y estoy entrevistándote. Buenos días. Su nombre, por favor.
You Me llamo John.
Teacher ¿Su apellido?
You Es Brown.
Teacher ¿De dónde es Vd.?
You Soy inglés/inglesa.
Teacher ¿Cuántos años tiene?
You Tengo dieciséis años.
Teacher ¿Qué idiomas habla?
You Hablo inglés y español.
Teacher ¿Tiene Vd. experiencia?
You Trabajé en un bar el año pasado. ¿Cuánto dinero ganaré?
Teacher Quinientas pesetas a la hora. ¿Puede empezar mañana?
You Sí, no hay problema.

Role-play 6

Teacher Estás en una oficina de turismo y yo soy el empleado/la empleada. Buenos días.
You Buenos días. ¿Puedo cambiar dinero inglés aquí?
Teacher Lo siento, no. Tiene que ir al banco.
You ¿Una libra vale cuántas pesetas?
Teacher No sé. Hay que preguntar en el banco.
You ¿Dónde está el banco?
Teacher Está enfrente, joven.
You ¿Está abierto?
Teacher No. Lo siento. Está cerrado.
You ¿A qué hora se abre?
Teacher A las cuatro, señor(ita).

6.5 Role-play type 2

This is what you need to know about this type of role-play.

- Whether you do Foundation Tier or Higher Tier you have to do this type of role-play. It overlaps between Foundation and Higher Tier.
- The tasks may be more open-ended. That means that instead of just one item you have to communicate, you may have to communicate a more complex idea, a number of items or make a choice.
- The examiner is looking for a higher level of Spanish from you but minor errors will still be tolerated.
- There will be one task where you must respond to an unprepared question from the examiner. Read this section in order to be ready for this.

The 'unprepared' questions

You will have to face a role-play question which you do not know beforehand. On your card it will say something like: **'Contesta a la pregunta'** or for Edexcel (London) there will be an exclamation mark on your card. Your teacher will have a script which tells him/her what to ask you. You have to understand what your teacher says so be ready for it! There are several ways you can prepare for these questions:

- Read the setting carefully. For instance if the setting says: 'You get oil on your jeans while cleaning your bicycle so you take them to the cleaner's', there is a good chance that the 'unprepared' question will ask you how you got your jeans dirty.
- The majority of 'unprepared' questions are linked to the previous role-play command. Think carefully. Can you predict what it will be? For instance if the prompt is: **'Di lo que has perdido'**, you can be fairly sure that the examiner will ask you to give more details of the loss, when? where? what was in it? what colour was it? Remember that you will have a dictionary for you to use in the preparation period.
- Remember that a short answer scores full marks and you have no need to use a full sentence. So have a short answer ready for 'what time?', 'when?', 'how much ?' 'where?' 'what did you buy?' 'what did you do?' 'what did you eat? drink?'.

For example:

¿A qué hora te levantarás?	A las ocho.
¿Cuándo llegas? ¿cuándo llegaste?	Mañana/ayer.
¿Cuánto dinero quieres cambiar?	Veinte libras.
¿Dónde lo perdiste?	En la playa.
¿Qué compraste?	Un libro.
¿Qué comiste/bebiste?	Pescado/leche.

Here is an example of a Role-play type 2.

Role-play 7

TRACK 40

You go into a Spanish bank to change some traveller's cheques. Your teacher will play the part of the bank employee and will start the conversation.

1. Tienes cheques de viaje. ¿Qué dices?
2. Di cuántos cheques tienes y cuánto vale cada cheque.
3. No tienes tu pasaporte. Explica por qué no lo tienes.
4. No sabes si el banco estará cerrado cuando vuelvas con tu pasaporte. Pregunta.
5. Contesta a la pregunta.

Examiner's tip

When you are asked the 'unprepared' question candidates very often ask for a repetition out of nervousness and to give themselves time to think. You may well lose a mark if you ask for a repetition. When asked this question THINK! Do not ask for a repeat unless you are really at a loss for an answer.

Teacher's role and suggested answers

Teacher Entras en un banco y yo soy el empleado/la empleada. ¿Qué quiere Vd.?
You Quiero cambiar mis cheques de viaje en dinero español.
Teacher ¿Qué cheques tiene Vd.?
You Tengo dos cheques de cincuenta libras.
Teacher Déme su pasaporte, por favor.
You Lo siento. Lo he dejado en mi hotel.
Teacher ¿Puede Vd. volver más tarde con el pasaporte?
You ¿El banco estará abierto a las cinco?
Teacher Sí. ¿A qué distancia está su hotel?
You A un kilómetro.

Here are some more examples of Role-play type 2. Remember to prepare them with a dictionary before switching on your CD player. The teacher's role and the suggested answers are given at the end of the examples.

TRACK 41

Role-play 8

You are staying with your friend in Spain during an exchange. He/she wants to go out with you one evening so you show him/her your diary. Negotiate with your friend the best time to go out and also decide where you are going. He/she will start the conversation.

Lunes	al colegio por la mañana	a la playa por la tarde con Elena
Martes	nada	nada
Miércoles	al colegio por la mañana	baloncesto con Pablo
Jueves	al colegio por la mañana	un paseo en las montañas con Pablo y Elena
Viernes	nada	nada
Sábado	vuelvo a Inglaterra	

1 ¿Adónde?
2 ¿Qué día?
3 ¿A qué hora?
4 ¿Con quién?

TRACK 42

Role-play 9

You are in Spain on a touring holiday with your family and your car breaks down ten kilometres from Valencia on the way to Alicante. You telephone a garage. Your teacher will play the part of the garage owner and will start the conversation.

1 Da tus datos personales y di lo que ha pasado.
2 Di dónde estás.
3 Di la marca, nacionalidad y color del coche.
4 Di dónde esperaréis.
5 Contesta a la pregunta.

Role-play 10

You arrive at a hotel but it is very late. They have no record of your booking, the hotel is full and the hotel restaurant is closed. You are tired and hungry. Your teacher will play the part of the receptionist and will start the conversation.

1 Da la fecha en que reservaste la habitación.
2 Pregunta si pueden encontrar una habitación en otro sitio.
3 Tienes hambre. Pide ayuda.
4 Contesta a la pregunta.
5 Dile cuándo llegarás al restaurante.

Role-play 11

You are buying food at a market for a picnic. Your teacher will play the part of the stall-holder.

1 Dile lo que haces y pregúntale si puede sugerir cosas de comer.
2 Quieres fruta. Dile qué fruta quieres.
3 Contesta a la pregunta.
4 Escoge dos cosas de comer.
5 Escoge dos bebidas.

Role-play 12

You are discussing with your Spanish friend what you are going to do today. Say what you want to do and say what you do not want to do. The exclamation mark means that you will be asked a question.

1

2

3

4

Examiner's tip

If you take the Edexcel (London) exam you need to know that an exclamation mark means that you will be asked an unprepared question.

6.6 Teacher's role and suggested answers

Role-play 8

Teacher	Bueno, a mí me gusta ir al cine o ir a la discoteca. ¿Qúe prefieres?
You	Prefiero ir al cine.
Teacher	¿Qué días tienes libre?
You	Tengo el martes libre y el viernes libre.
Teacher	Esos dos días tengo demasiados deberes. ¿Qué haces el miércoles por la tarde?
You	Juego al baloncesto con Pablo.
Teacher	¿A qué hora termina el partido?
You	A las ocho.
Teacher	Bueno vamos después de las ocho. ¿Con quién vamos?
You	Vamos con Pablo y Elena.

Role-play 9

Teacher	Estás en España y tienes un problema con el coche. Yo soy el mecánico. Dígame.
You	Me llamo John Smith. Soy turista inglés y hemos tenido una avería.
Teacher	¿Dónde está?
You	Estamos a diez kilómetros de Valencia en la carretera de Alicante.
Teacher	¿Cómo es el coche?
You	Es un Ford, es inglés y es verde.
Teacher	¿Vds. van a esperar en el coche?
You	No, estaremos en un café muy cerca del coche.
Teacher	¿Qué tipo de problema tiene Vd. con el coche?
You	Tenemos un problema con la batería/los neumáticos/los frenos/el motor.

Role-play 10

Teacher	Llegas a un hotel. Yo soy el/la recepcionista. Lo siento, no encuentro su reserva y el hotel está completo.
You	Pero hice la reserva el dos de mayo.
Teacher	Lo siento.
You	¿Quiere llamar a otro hotel?
Teacher	No hace falta. El Hotel Sol siempre tiene habitaciones.
You	Tengo hambre. ¿Dónde puedo comer?
Teacher	Yo llamaré al restaurante en el Hotel Sol para reservarle algo de comer.¿Qué quiere Vd. comer?
You	Un bocadillo de jamón.
Teacher	¿Cuándo va al Hotel Sol?
You	Estaré allí en diez minutos.

Role-play 11

Teacher	Estás en un mercado y yo soy el vendedor/la vendedora. Buenos días, señor(ita).
You	Buenos días. Estoy comprando cosas para una merienda. ¿Puede sugerir cosas?
Teacher	Pues fruta claro.
You	Déme unas manzanas y unos plátanos.
Teacher	¿Cuántos quiere?
You	Cuatro manzanas y tres plátanos.
Teacher	Aquí tiene.
You	También pan y sardinas.
Teacher	Y ¿de beber?
You	Vino y limonada.
Teacher	Que aproveche.

Role-play 12

Teacher	Yo soy tu amigo/a español/a. ¿Qué quieres hacer hoy?
You	Me gustaría o ir al cine o ir al teatro.
Teacher	¿No quieres nadar?
You	No quiero ir ni a la piscina ni a la playa.
Teacher	Vale. Vamos al cine. ¿Qué tipo de película te gusta?
You	Me gustan las películas de miedo.
Teacher	Vamos a la sesión de noche. ¿A qué hora quieres acostarte esta noche?
You	A la una.

6.7 Role-play type 3

This is what you need to know about this type of role-play.

- This type of role-play will contain a greater degree of unpredictability.
- The kind of role-play you will get varies depending on your Exam Board.
- For instance you may have a series of pictures and you have to tell the story of the pictures in the past tenses (MEG). You may have to come to an agreement with someone about where to go and what to do and what time to go (NEAB). You may have a role-play just like role-play type 2 but with two unpredictable elements instead of one (WJEC/London).

Role-play Type 3 – MEG

Role-plays 13 and 14 are MEG-type role-plays. These role-plays take the form of a series of pictures telling a story, telling how someone spent a day or a series of days. You can usually decide if the subject of the story is you or someone else. It is important to realise that the past tenses (preterite, pluperfect and imperfect) are going to be extremely important, so revise them from the grammar section in this book.

How to approach the MEG role-play 3. Most of these tasks require you to talk about things that 'I' did or that 'we' did. So you should concentrate on those parts of the verb. If you want to make things simpler, then instead of saying 'we went' just say 'I went with my friend/family' so then you only have to concentrate on the 'I' part of the verb.

Examiner's tip

Learn this list of preterites and see how often they occur in the suggested answers that follow:

bebí	I drank	**fui**	I went
comí	I ate	**llegué**	I arrived
compré	I bought	**perdí**	I lost
conocí a	I met	**tomé**	I took
decidí (+ inf.)	I decided	**vi**	I saw
di un paseo	I went for a walk	**viajé**	I travelled
empecé a (+ inf.)	I started to	**visité**	I visited
encontré	I found	**volví**	I returned
entré en	I went in		

- Try and introduce an imperfect tense into the account. Mention the weather or what you were wearing:

  Hacía buen tiempo. It was nice weather.
  Hacía sol. It was sunny.
  Llovía a cántaros y estábamos mojados hasta los huesos. It was pouring and we were soaked to the skin.
  Llevaba mi jersey nuevo. I was wearing my new jersey.

- Try to build up a collection of mark-winning phrases. For example:

al (+ inf.)	
al llegar	on arriving
para (+ inf.)	
para reservar un billete	in order to book a ticket
sin perder un momento	without wasting a moment
antes de (+ inf.)	
antes de comer	before eating
después de (+ inf.)	
después de comer	after eating
¡Qué día!	What a day!
¡Qué barbaridad!	How awful!

See how these expressions are used in the suggested answers that follow.

Role-play 13

The notes and pictures below give an outline of a cycle ride in Spain. Say what happened. You do not need to mention every detail but you must cover the whole day's events.

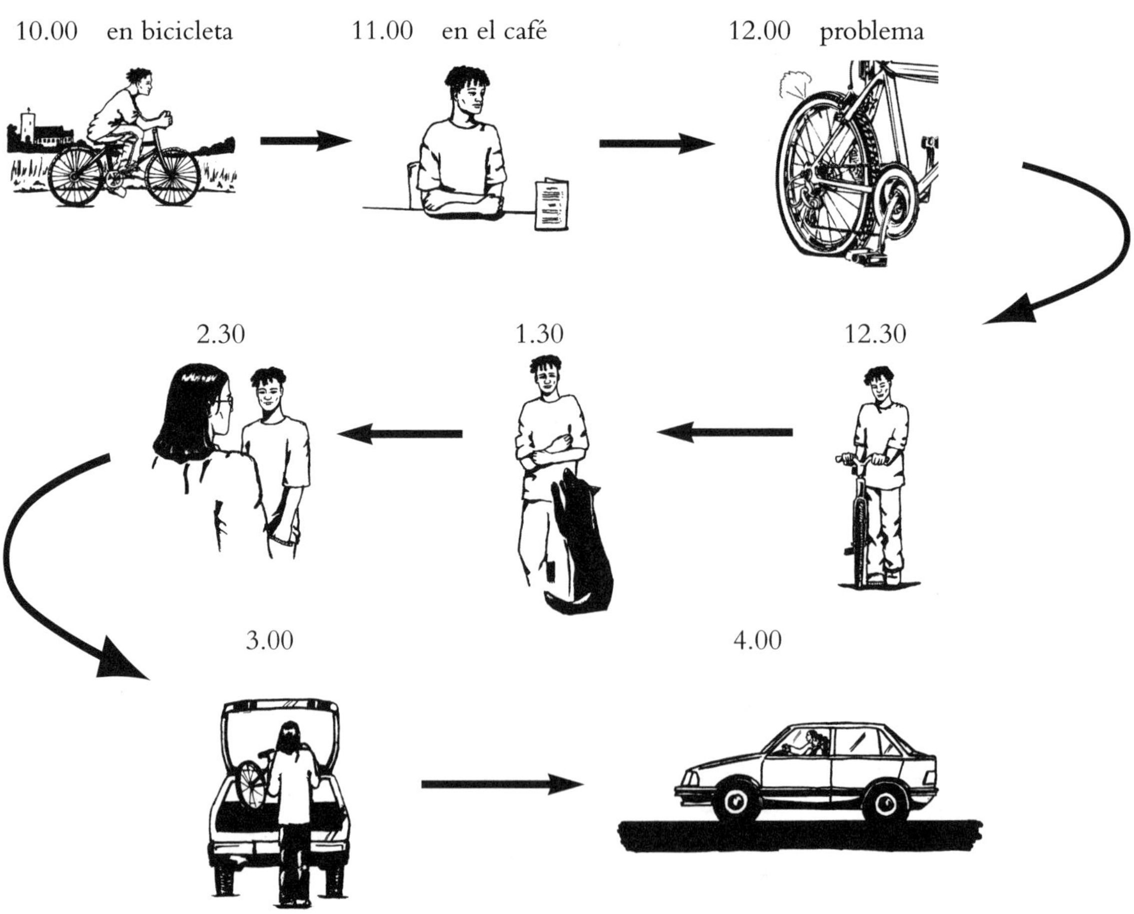

Teacher's role and suggested answers

Teacher ¿Qué pasó?

You Esta mañana, fui de paseo en bicicleta. Lo pasé bomba. Hacía sol y hacía calor. Llevaba mi jersey amarillo. Vi muchos edificios interesantes y visité una iglesia antigua. Bebí una limonada y comí un bocadillo en un café.

Teacher ¿Qué pasó después?

You Después de salir del café, decidí volver a casa. Desgraciadamente cinco minutos más tarde tuve un pinchazo. Estaba en el campo y no había nadie para ayudarme.

Teacher ¡Qué barbaridad!

You Empecé a andar con la bicicleta. Dos horas más tarde, estaba triste, tenía hambre y sed. Luego hubo un incidente. Un perro me atacó y tuve que huir. Más tarde conocí a un hombre muy simpático. El hombre me ayudó. Puso mi bicicleta en su coche y me llevó a casa.

Teacher ¡Qué bien! ¿Cómo era el hombre?

You Era bastante viejo, tenía los ojos azules y el pelo largo y negro. Llevaba gafas. Era muy simpático. ¡Qué día!

Role-play 14

The notes and pictures below give an outline of a few days that you spent touring in Spain with your family. You tell a Spanish friend about the tour. Your teacher will play the part of the Spanish friend. You need not mention every detail and you may add extra information.

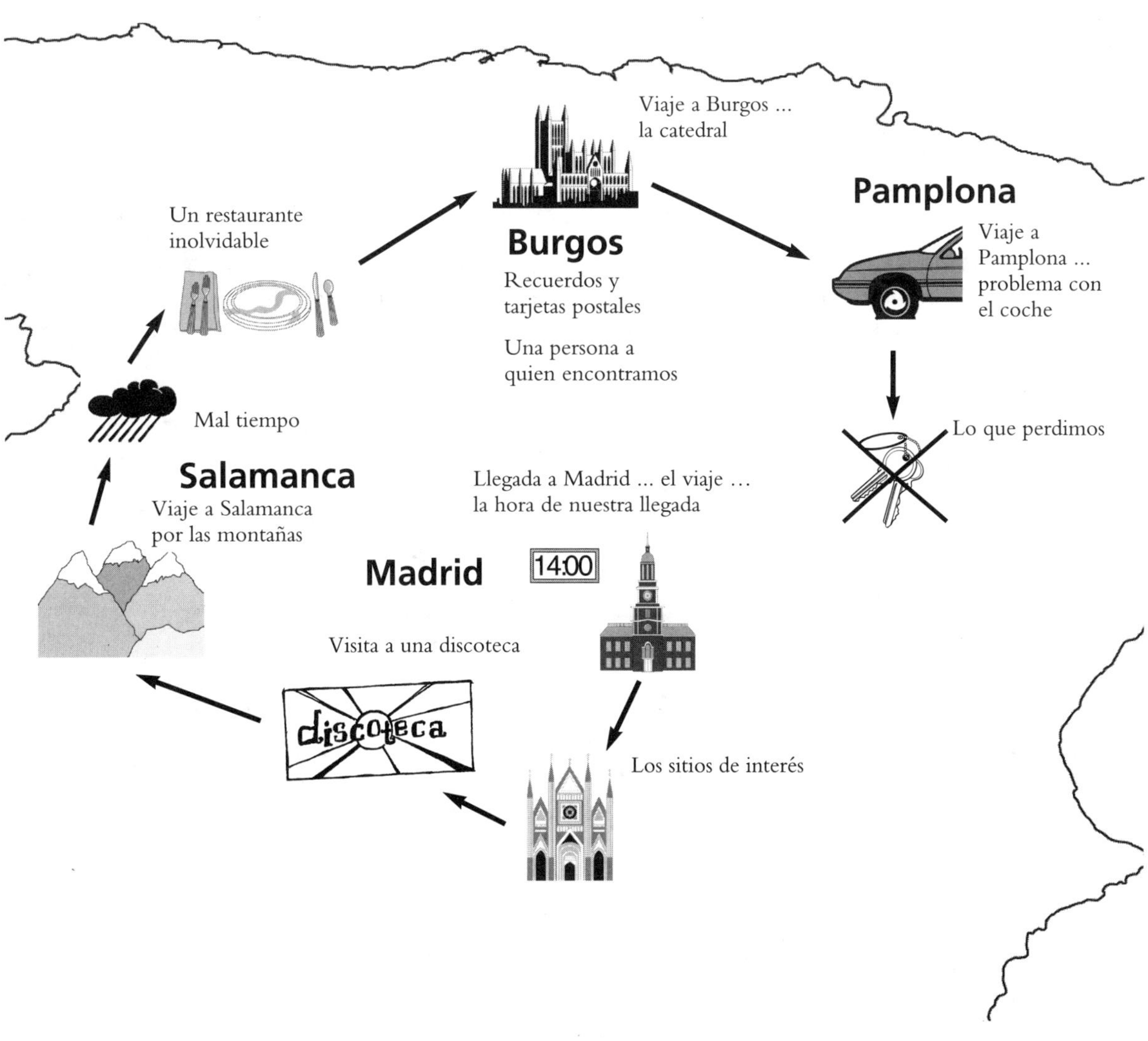

Teacher's role and suggested answers

Teacher ¿Qué pasó?

You Después de viajar dos horas, llegué a Madrid en coche con mi familia a las dos de la tarde. Sin perder un momento, encontré un hotel y fui a visitar los sitios de interés. Visité la catedral y vi el Palacio Real. Más tarde fui a una discoteca y bailé y charlé con la gente.
Al día siguiente, viajé con mi familia en coche a Salamanca. Fuimos por las montañas y llovía a cántaros. ¡Estábamos mojados hasta los huesos! Fuimos a un restaurante inolvidable. Comí mariscos, una chuleta de cerdo con patatas, queso y fruta. Bebí agua mineral.

Teacher ¿Qué pasó después?

You Al día siguiente, viajamos a Burgos. Visité la catedral y compré recuerdos y tarjetas postales. También compré regalos para mis amigos de Inglaterra. Conocí a mi amigo por correspondencia en Burgos. Vive allí y fuimos al cine juntos.

Teacher Fuisteis a Pamplona, ¿no?

You Sí pero cerca de Pamplona tuvimos un problema con el coche. Tuvimos un pinchazo pero mi padre lo reparó. Pero más tarde perdió las llaves del coche. ¡Mi madre las encontró en su bolsillo! ¡Qué día!

Role-play type 3 – NEAB

You may well have to come to an agreement about something, persuade someone about something or sort out a problem. You may well have to start off by saying that you want to do something or that you like something. The examiner/your teacher will then disagree with you.

Look at this example:

Role-play 15

TRACK 48

Your Spanish friend is in England and is amazed that you have to wear school uniform. You hate having to wear school uniform. He/she likes the idea.

1 Describe tu uniforme.
2 Da tu opinión sobre la ausencia de uniforme en España.
3 Cuando tu amigo dice que el uniforme es una buena idea, di que no estás de acuerdo y da razones.

Examiner's tip

Your teacher will be under instructions to argue with you. You must convince him/her that uniform is a bad idea.

Teacher's role and suggested answers

Teacher Me gusta la idea de llevar uniforme. ¿Cómo es el tuyo?

You Tengo que llevar un pantalón gris/una falda gris, calcetines grises, zapatos negros, una camisa/camiseta blanca y una corbata azul y gris.

Teacher ¡Qué raro!

You ¿Llevas uniforme en España?

Teacher Nunca. Pero me parece una buena idea.

You No estoy de acuerdo.

Teacher ¿Por qué?

You Es muy caro.

Teacher Pero no es más caro que otra ropa.

You Sí pero mis padres no me compran otra ropa. Tienen que comprar uniforme y me quedo sin buena ropa.

Teacher Entiendo.
You Además es muy feo.
Teacher No estoy de acuerdo.
You Tú ves el uniforme un día o dos. Yo veo el uniforme todos los días. Es espantoso, sobre todo el color.

Here are two more examples of NEAB-style role-plays.

Role-play 16

You are on a driving holiday in Spain and you are almost out of petrol. You arrive at a filling station. The filling station is about to close and they do not want to serve you. Find out if there are other filling stations and persuade the attendant that it is an emergency. Your teacher will play the role of the attendant and will start the conversation.

Teacher's role and suggested answers

Teacher Lo siento. Está cerrado.
You Lleno, por favor.
Teacher Está cerrado.
You ¿Hay otra gasolinera por aquí?
Teacher Sí, a cincuenta kilómetros. Todo seguido.
You No tenemos bastante gasolina para cincuenta kilómetros.
Teacher Pues lo siento pero está cerrado.
You Pero ¿puede Vd. abrir unos segundos para darnos gasolina?
Teacher No tengo tiempo.
You Le daré una propina.
Teacher ¿Una propina? ¿Lleno ha dicho?

Role-play 17

You see this poster advertising three films. You and your Spanish friend discuss which one to see. Say which type of film you like and give a reason. Say that you do not want to see the films that your friend wants to see and give reasons. Finally suggest another activity and again give a reason. Your teacher will play the part of the friend and will start the conversation.

Examiner's tip

In this type of role-play very often the examiner is going to disagree with whatever you decide so be sure to have an alternative suggestion worked out.

Teacher's role and suggested answers

Teacher Hay tres películas, una película de amor, una película de horror y una película del oeste ¿Qué tipo de película te gusta?
You Me gustan las películas del oeste.
Teacher ¿Por qué?
You Me gusta la animación.
Teacher Pues a mí no me gustan. Vamos a ver *El amor es para siempre*. ¿Quieres?
You No me gusta.

Teacher ¿Por qué?
You Esas películas son muy lentas.
Teacher Entonces vamos a *El monstruo y el vampiro.*
You No me gustan. Me dan miedo.
Teacher Pues vamos a hacer otra cosa.
You ¿Por qué no vamos a la discoteca? Tengo ganas de bailar.
Teacher Muy bien.

Role-play type 3 – WJEC

You may well be asked to answer an unpredictable question more than once, to ask questions to your teacher/examiner and to give your opinions on matters. For example:

Role-play 18

TRACK 51

Your Spanish friend has arrived in Britain and is not happy with the British weather. Your teacher will play the part of your Spanish friend and will begin the conversation.

1 Contesta a la pregunta de tu amigo/a.
2 Dile por qué te gusta o no te gusta el campo cerca de tu casa.
3 Contesta a la pregunta de tu amigo/a.
4 Pregunta a tu amigo/a qué le gusta de Gran Bretaña.
5 Da tu opinión de España.

Teacher's role and suggested answers

Teacher ¿Te gusta el clima de tu país? ¿Por qué (no)?
You Sí, me gusta. No me gusta el calor intenso de España.
Teacher Y ¿el campo por aquí te gusta?
You Me gusta muchísimo. Me gustan los ríos y las montañas.
Teacher ¿Conoces España?
You He visitado España una vez. Pero ¿cuál es tu opinión de Gran Bretaña?
Teacher Me gusta todo ... salvo el clima.
You A mí me encanta España ... por la gente y la cocina.

Role-play type 3 – Edexcel (London examinations)

London says that there will be two unpredictable questions in their role-plays and also a visual stimulus e.g. a menu or an advertisement. Below the visual stimulus there will be prompts in Spanish. Here are two examples.

Role-play 19

TRACK 52

You are in Spain and a few hours before you fly back to England you lose something. You go to the lost property office. Your teacher will play the part of the employee and will start the conversation.

> OFICINA DE OBJETOS PERDIDOS
>
> abierto de 8.00–20.00
> abierto todo el año

Examiner's tip

Be sure that you can always describe the *contents* of something. The word **contenía** (it contained) is invaluable.

- lo que has perdido
- dónde y cuándo
- el contenido

Teacher's role and suggested answers

Teacher	Buenos días. ¿En qué puedo servirle?
You	Buenos días. He perdido una maleta negra.
Teacher	¿Dónde y cuándo?
You	La he perdido en la estación a las diez y media.
Teacher	¿Qué había en la maleta?
You	Ropa, nada más.
Teacher	Lo siento, no tenemos una maleta. ¿Puede Vd. volver mañana?
You	Imposible. Vuelvo a Inglaterra a las cinco de la tarde.
Teacher	Entonces ¿qué hacemos si encontramos la maleta?
You	¿Puede Vd. mandarla a Inglaterra?
Teacher	Sí, déme su dirección.

Examiner's tip

Note how the two unpredictable questions were strongly hinted at in the English introduction. It is important to scan this for clues.

Here is another example:

TRACK 53

Role-play 20

You and a friend are on holiday in Spain. Your friend becomes so ill that you have to curtail your holiday and fly home earlier than you planned. You go to a travel agent. Your teacher will play the part of the travel agent and will start the conversation.

AGENCIA DE VIAJES SEU
vuelos-seguros –
viajes a todo el mundo
Abierto: 10 a 13, 17 a 20

- el cambio ¿por qué?
- cuándo queréis volver
- transporte al aeropuerto

Teacher's role and suggested answers

Teacher	¿Sí, señor(ita)?
You	Mi amigo está muy enfermo. Nuestro vuelo de regreso es para el día doce. Queremos volver antes, por favor.
Teacher	¿Cuándo quieren volver?
You	Lo antes posible.
Teacher	¿A qué aeropuerto quieren volver?
You	A Heathrow.
Teacher	¿Cómo se escriben su nombre y apellido, por favor?
You	John Brown. J-o-h-n B-r-o-w-n.
Teacher	Hay un vuelo a las dos. ¿Cómo van Vds. al aeropuerto?
You	Vamos a tomar un taxi.

6.8 Conversation – presentation

This is what you need to know about the conversation part of your exam.

First read through the Analysis of Boards (and check with your teacher) to find out what to expect in the conversation part of your Speaking exam. If you are doing MEG or NEAB you will start off with a presentation. If you are doing other Boards you need not read this section.

MEG says you may use illustrative material, NEAB says you must use it. This means that if you want to talk say about your stamp collection or a book or an article you should bring those items into the exam. You can then point out things during your presentation and your teacher will ask you questions on them.

- MEG gives you a separate mark for your presentation. For NEAB you get one mark overall for your presentation and your conversation.
- MEG says that you can take some notes into the exam to remind you of what you are going to say. You can take in a piece of paper with *five short headings.* You will not be allowed just to read from written notes. NEAB do not allow you to take any notes in at all.

Your teacher will be looking out for the following things:

- Use of past, present and future tenses. The Boards do recognise that it may be difficult for you to use all three in the presentation but you should try. Bear this in mind when choosing the title of your presentation.
- Unusual vocabulary and structures.
- Your ability to give a good presentation but also your ability to be able to answer any unpredictable questions he/she asks.
- Choice of Topic. Do not choose 'Myself' because it is too broad and may overlap with other topics during the conversation section. Some suggestions might be:
  - mi revista favorita
  - mi profesor(a) favorito/a
  - mis vacaciones
  - mi familia
  - mi hermana
  - mi deporte favorito
  - mi música favorita
  - mi estrella favorita
  - mi pasatiempo favorito
  - el intercambio
  - mi visita a España
  - mi futuro

Here is an example of a presentation. You should not use it yourself because your presentation must be your own work. However this presentation may give you ideas.

Presentation

Illustrative material could be a photo of yourself playing tennis and also a photo of your favourite tennis star.

Voy a hablar de mi deporte favorito: el tenis. *Jugué* al tenis por primera vez cuando *tenía* ocho años y me encantó en seguida. *Pedí* una raqueta a mis padres y *me* regalaron una como regalo de cumpleaños. Tengo suerte porque cerca de mi casa hay unas canchas de tenis y *solía* ir con mi hermana a jugar todos los fines de semana. Ahora soy miembro de un club de tenis y *no sólo* me mantiene en buena condición fisica *sino también* me da la oportunidad de conocer a gente interesante de mi edad.

También me encanta el tenis profesional y veo los partidos en la televisión. En el verano paso muchas horas viendo el torneo de Wimbledon y los otros torneos por todo el mundo. Este año *iré* a Wimbledon si consigo entradas. Un día me *gustaría* ser tenista profesional. Mi estrella favorita es ....

Note that this would take about a minute to say.

Look at the points in italics in this presentation. There are examples of the preterite, the imperfect, the present, the conditional and the future tenses. There is a direct object pronoun **me**, and advanced structures like **no sólo sino también**, and **solía**.

The presentation would then be developed by your teacher. He/she would probably ask you:

¿Cuántas veces a la semana juegas al tenis?
¿Contra quién juegas?
Describe tu club de tenis.
¿Cuánto cuesta?
Háblame de tu estrella favorita.

6.9 Foundation Tier conversation

If you are being entered for Foundation Tier you should be able to answer these questions.

You and your family

¿Cómo te llamas?	Me llamo ...
¿Cuántos años tienes?	Tengo ... años.
¿Cuántos sois en tu familia?	Somos ...
¿Quiénes son?	Son mi padre, mi madre, mi hermano y yo.
¿Qué hace tu padre?	Es ...
¿Qué hace tu madre?	Es ...
¿En qué año naciste?	Nací en mil novecientos ochenta y siete.
¿Cuánto mides?	Mido un metro ochenta.
¿Tienes animales en casa?	Tengo un perro/un gato.
¿Cuándo es tu cumpleaños?	Es el veintisiete de setiembre.

House and home

¿Vives en una casa o un piso?	Vivo en una casa/un piso.
¿Cómo es tu casa?	Mi casa es pequeña y cómoda.
¿A qué distancia se encuentra tu casa del colegio?	Se encuentra a cinco kilómetros de mi colegio.
¿Cuántas habitaciones hay en tu casa?	Hay ... habitaciones.
¿Qué ves por la ventana de tu dormitorio?	Veo las casas de mis vecinos.
¿Qué hay en tu jardín?	Hay flores y árboles.
¿Qué hay en tu dormitorio?	Hay una cama, una mesa y una silla.

Your region

¿Qué sitios de interés hay cerca de tu casa?	Hay una iglesia interesante y un parque.
¿A qué distancia se encuentra tu casa de Londres/del mar?	Se encuentra a cien kilómetros de Londres/del mar.
Cuántos habitantes hay en tu pueblo/ciudad?	Hay ocho mil habitantes más o menos.
¿Qué hay en tu pueblo/ciudad?	Hay cines, discotecas y un club para jóvenes.

Your pastimes and interests

¿Cuál es tu pasatiempo favorito?	Me gusta jugar al tenis.
¿Dónde juegas al tenis?	Juego en el parque.
¿Con quién juegas?	Juego con mi amigo/a.
¿Sabes tocar algún instrumento musical?	Sé tocar el piano.
¿Qué programa prefieres en la televisión?	Prefiero *Vecinos*.
¿Vas al cine algunas veces?	Sí, voy cuando tengo dinero.
¿Te gusta la jardinería?	Odio la jardinería.
¿Qué deportes practicas?	Juego al hockey/al fútbol.
¿Qué tipo de música te gusta?	Me gusta la música pop.

School

¿Qué asignatura prefieres?	Prefiero el español.
¿Por qué?	Me gusta el/la profesor/a.
¿Qué asignatura te gusta menos?	Lo que menos me gusta es el francés.
¿Qué deportes practicas en el colegio?	Juego al fútbol/al tenis/al hockey.
¿Cómo vienes al colegio por la mañana?	Vengo a pie/en coche/en autocar.
¿Cómo viniste al colegio esta mañana?	Vine a pie/en coche/en autocar.
¿A qué hora llegas?	Llego a las nueve menos cuarto.
¿A qué hora empiezan las clases?	Empiezan a las nueve y veinte.
¿Cuántas clases tienes cada día?	Tengo cinco clases cada día.
¿Cuánto tiempo dura cada clase?	Cada clase dura una hora.

¿A qué hora es el recreo? — El recreo es a las once y veinte.
¿Cuánto tiempo dura el recreo? — El recreo dura veinte minutos.
¿Qué haces durante el recreo? — Hablo con mis amigos/as y como un bocadillo.
¿Cuántos alumnos hay en tu colegio? — Hay seiscientos alumnos en mi colegio.
¿En tu clase de español? — Hay veinte alumnos en mi clase de español.
¿Cuántos profesores hay en tu colegio? — Hay cuarenta profesores.
¿Qué haces durante la hora de comer? — Como mis bocadillos y juego al tenis.

Holidays

¿Adónde fuiste de vacaciones el año pasado? — Fui a España.
¿Has visitado otros países? — He visitado Francia, España y Alemania.
¿Con quién fuiste? — Fui con mi familia.
¿Cómo fuiste? — Fui en avión/en barco/en coche.
¿Has visitado España? — Sí, visité España el año pasado.
¿Dónde te alojaste? — Me alojé en un hotel.
¿Cuánto tiempo estuviste en España? — Estuve en España dos semanas.
¿Qué tiempo hizo? — Hizo sol todos los días.
¿Qué hiciste allí? — Tomé el sol y nadé en el mar.
¿Adónde irás este verano? — Iré a España otra vez.

Daily routine

¿A qué hora te despiertas? — Me despierto a las siete.
¿A qué hora te levantas? — Me levanto a las siete y cuarto.
¿Qué haces para prepararte? — Me lavo, me visto y tomo el desayuno.
¿A qué hora sales para el colegio? — Salgo a las ocho y media.
¿A qué hora vuelves del colegio? — Vuelvo a las cuatro.
¿Qué haces al volver a casa? — Hago mis deberes.
¿A qué hora cenas? — Ceno a las seis y media.
¿Qué haces después de cenar? — Veo la televisión.
¿A qué hora te acuestas? — Me acuesto a las diez.

6.10 Higher Tier conversation

This is what you need to know about the exam:

- You will be assessed on your communication skills and also on the quality of your language.
- You will be asked to show your knowledge of tenses by being asked questions about what you did in the past, what you do normally and what you will do in the future. Your future grade depends on how well you produce the different tenses.
- Your answers need to be longer than in the Foundation Tier. You will be asked open-ended questions (questions that allow you to answer at length, e.g. **describe tus vacaciones**) and you must show that you can talk at length using impressive vocabulary and structures.
- You will not be allowed to give a pre-learnt speech. Your teacher will interrupt when he/she realises this is what you are doing.
- Your teacher will have a list of topics on which the conversation will be based. He/she may give you a list of topics and questions and you should concentrate on these.
- The topics that you are most likely to encounter are:

  family
  house and home
  your village, town or region
  your school
  your friends
  shopping
  food and meals

daily routine
special occasions
the world of work
pocket money
your future plans
your hobbies and leisure
your holidays

In the exam

- Try to give long answers.
- Try to use any impressive vocabulary that you know.
- Try to put expression into what you say.
- Prepare a few phrases and words that your classmates do not know. Spring them on your teacher in the exam (make sure they are right first!). He/she may be impressed to the point of increasing your mark.

6.11 Example questions and answers

Although your answers must not be a pre-learnt speech, it is nevertheless important that you are able to speak for about a minute or so on these topics. Why not record these answers on a cassette and listen to them as often as you can? Get a friend or parent to ask you the questions and see if you can talk for a minute. Ask them to interrupt you and ask you an unexpected question.

Your family

Describe tu familia.

En mi familia somos cuatro, mi madre, mi padre, mi hermana y yo. Tenemos también un perro. Mi padre trabaja en una oficina. No sé exactamente lo que hace. Mi madre es dentista.

¿Cómo es tu padre?

Mi padre es grande y tiene los ojos negros. Tiene cuarenta y cinco años y le gusta leer periódicos y ver la televisión.

¿Cómo es tu madre?

Mi madre es pequeña y bonita. Tiene los ojos marrones y el pelo largo y negro. Tiene cuarenta y dos años y le gusta trabajar en el jardín y salir con mi padre.

¿Cómo es tu hermana?

Mi hermana tiene trece años y es muy simpática. Tiene los ojos azules, el pelo largo y rubio y lleva gafas. Le gusta la música pop y ver la televisión.

¿Tienes otros parientes?

Sí, tengo otros parientes, muchos sobrinos, muchos tíos, muchos primos. Mis abuleos nos visitan a menudo.

¿Qué animal te gusta más?

Me gustan los perros porque son muy cariñosos y limpios.

Your house and home

Describe tu casa.

Mi casa es muy bonita. Hay tres dormitorios, una cocina, un comedor, una sala de estar y un cuarto de baño.

Describe tu dormitorio.

Mi dormitorio es muy cómodo. Hay una cama, una silla, una mesa, un estéreo, un televisor y muchos libros. Es mi habitación favorita.

¿Qué haces en tu dormitorio?

Hago muchas cosas. Hago mis deberes, leo, escucho música, veo la televisión y duermo, por supuesto.

Describe tu cocina.

Mi cocina es muy moderna. Hay una nevera, un lavaplatos, una lavadora y una mesa con cuatro sillas. Desde la cocina se ve el jardín.

Describe tu sala de estar.

Mi sala de estar es muy cómoda. Hay un sofá, dos sillones, una alfombra roja, un televisor, un estéreo y cortinas muy bonitas.

¿Tienes un jardín?

Sí, tenemos un jardín detrás de la casa. Es muy bonito. Tiene césped, árboles, plantas y flores. También hemos plantado patatas, cebollas, guisantes y zanahorias. A mis padres les gusta trabajar en el jardín.

Your village/town/region

Describe tu pueblo/ciudad/región.

A mí me gusta esta región. Por aquí hay mucho de interés. Tiene canal, un río, un parque bonito y muchos campos de deporte y un cine. No lejos de aquí hay fábricas pero también hay campo bonito.

¿En qué parte de Gran Bretaña se encuentra tu región?

Se encuentra en el norte/sur/este/oeste/centro de Inglaterra/Gales/Escocia/Irlanda.

¿Cuántos años hace que vives aquí?

Vivo aquí desde hace quince años, es decir toda mi vida.

¿Cuáles son los edificios interesantes?

Hay la biblioteca, el cine, el ayuntamiento, la iglesia antigua, la piscina y el hospital. También hay muchos edificios muy antiguos.

Your hobbies

¿Quieres describir tus pasatiempos?

Tengo muchos pasatiempos. Me gusta jugar al fútbol/hockey/tenis/baloncesto. También me gusta leer, ver la televisión, ir al cine y salir con mis amigos.

¿Cuál es tu deporte favorito?

Mi deporte favorito es la natación. Normalmente voy a la piscina los sábados con mis amigos.

¿Qué tipo de película te gusta?

Me gustan las películas de aventura. No me gustan las películas románticas, las películas de horror ni las películas de guerra.

¿Qué cosas lees?

Me gusta leer novelas pero también leo revistas y periódicos.

¿Tocas algún instrumento musical?

Toco la guitarra/el piano/el clarinete/el violín.

¿Qué haces normalmente por las tarde después de tus deberes?

Leo, veo la televisión, escucho música, doy un paseo con el perro y visito a mi amigo.

¿Qué hiciste anoche después de tus deberes?

Leí, vi la televisión, escuché música, di un paseo con el perro y visité a mi amigo.

¿Qué harás esta tarde después de tus deberes?

Leeré, veré la televisión, escucharé música, daré un paseo con el perro y visitaré a mi amigo.

School

¿Cómo te preparas para el colegio por la mañana?

Me despierto a las siete, me levanto a las siete y cuarto, me lavo, me visto y tomo el desayuno. Luego preparo mis libros y salgo.

Describe un día en tu colegio.

Llego a las nueve menos cuarto. Voy a mi aula y el profesor pasa lista. Luego voy a la primera clase. Hay otra clase y luego es el recreo.

¿Qué haces durante el recreo?

Charlo con mis amigos, como patatas y bebo limonada.

Y ¿después?

Tenemos una clase más y luego es la hora de comer. A veces vuelvo a casa para comer, a veces como bocadillos y a veces como en el comedor del colegio. Luego hay dos clases más y vuelvo a casa y hago mis deberes.

Describe tu colegio.

Una parte del colegio es muy vieja y la otra parte es moderna. Hay campos de fútbol, pistas de tenis, laboratorios, un laboratorio de lenguas y una biblioteca. No tenemos piscina pero hay una muy cerca.

Háblame de tus asignaturas y tus clases.

Estudio ocho asignaturas – el inglés, las matemáticas, el español, la física, la química, la biología, la tecnología y el francés. Hay novecientos alumnos y sesenta profesores más o menos. Tenemos cinco clases diarias y cada clase dura una hora.

¿Cuánto tiempo hace que estudias español?

Estudio español desde hace tres años.

Future plans

¿Qué vas a hacer el año que viene?

Voy a seguir con mis estudios. Voy a estudiar inglés, francés, y por supuesto español.

Cuando termines el colegio, ¿qué quieres hacer?

Quiero ir a una universidad a estudiar idiomas.

Y ¿después de la universidad?

Quiero ser músico/a. Quiero hacer mucho dinero y ser muy famoso/a.

Holidays

¿Adónde fuiste de vacaciones el año pasado? ¿Qué hiciste allí?

El año pasado fui a España con mi familia. ¡Lo pasé bomba! Comí muchísimo, bebí muchísimo, salí con mis amigos, bailé mucho y tomé el sol.

¿Qué tiempo hizo?

Casi todos los días hizo buen tiempo. Hizo sol y calor. Sin embargo, un día llovió a cántaros y nos mojamos hasta los huesos.

¿Cómo viajaste a España?

Fuimos en coche al aeropuerto, tomamos el avión y al llegar tomamos un taxi al hotel.

¿Adónde irás de vacaciones este año?

Iré otra vez a España con mi familia.

¿Qué harás allí?

¡Lo pasaré bomba! Comeré muchísimo, beberé muchísimo, saldré con mis amigos, bailaré mucho y tomaré el sol.

¿Cómo viajarás a España?

Iré en coche al aeropuerto, tomaré el avión y al llegar tomaré un taxi al hotel.

Examiner's tip

Most of these questions are very predicable so be sure to have a little speech worked out to describe your family, your school, your holidays, your pastimes and your town or region.

Chapter 7
Reading

7.1 Introduction

This is what you need to know about the exam:

- You must opt for either the Foundation Tier or the Higher Tier. You cannot do both.
- Most people consider Reading as the easiest of the four skills.
- You will have to deal with authentic material: i.e. material that you might expect to encounter in Spain rather than material written by an English person. The Exam Boards are under instructions to set questions on:

  signs

  notices

  advertisements

  brochures

  letters

  tourist and leisure guides

  extended texts

- Most of the questions will be asked in Spanish. About 20% will be asked in English. The rule is: if the rubric (i.e. the instructions at the top of the question) and the questions are in English, answer in English. If the rubric and the questions are in Spanish then you answer in Spanish.
- Many of the questions will be of a box-ticking or form-filling nature.
- If you have to answer by writing Spanish words, then you are usually required to write a very short answer. You will only lose marks for your Spanish if it is so bad that the examiner does not understand it. The odd minor mistake does not matter.
- You may use a dictionary throughout. Make sure you know the dangers of over-use of the dictionary. Read the section on dictionary use at the beginning of this book.
- If you are doing the Short Course the questions will be restricted to two Areas of Experience, usually Areas B and D. If you are doing the Full Course expect questions from all the Areas of Experience. See the section on Areas of Experience at the beginning of this book.
- In the Foundation Tier, you will need to be able to identify specific points of detail. In the Higher Tier you will have to be able to:

  understand the gist of texts

  understand agreement and disagreement

  identify attitudes, emotions, ideas

  draw conclusions

  identify relationships between ideas

7.2 How to prepare for the Reading examination

You can often guess what kind of questions are going to appear. You must learn all the words from the vocabulary section in this book which could be used as signs. Here are some guidelines:

Learn all the names of the shops, e.g. **carnicería** – butcher's.
Learn all the places in a town, e.g. **ayuntamiento** – town hall.
Learn all the signs you might find in a bus or train station, e.g. **la salida** – exit.
Learn all the places and features of a hotel, e.g. **el ascensor** – lift.
Remember **abierto** (open) and **cerrado** (closed) are always cropping up.
The days of the week, the months and seasons of the year are always cropping up.
Learn all the words used in weather forecasts.
Learn all the foods and drinks that you are likely to find on a menu.

7.3 During the exam

- Remember to read the setting of each question. It can often give a clue to the answer. Often there is information in the setting of the question which is essential for the understanding of the question.
- Remember to look at the mark allocation for each question. If two marks are allocated you know that the examiner is looking for two elements.
- If writing in Spanish, keep your answers short. If, say, you are asked **'¿En qué dirección...?'** and the anwer is that you must turn left, do not write **'Para ir al ayuntamiento, hay que ir a la izquierda'** and do not write **'hay que ir a la izquierda'**. Just write **'izquierda'**. This is sufficient to get full marks.
- Always attempt each question even if you have to guess. But remember that if you have more than one guess the examiner will only look at the first answer you write.
- In a multiple-choice question you will get no marks if you tick more than one box when asked to tick one only.
- In a multiple-choice question if you have to correct your original choice make sure that the examiner knows which option you have finally chosen.

7.4 Foundation Tier examination questions

These questions are either from past papers or have been prepared by a Chief Examiner. The suggested answers are given after this Section. Note that some of the questions are set in Spanish and some in English.

Reading Test 1

1 On a visit to Spain you see the following signs.

(a) At a garage.

SERVICIOS

What does this sign tell you? (1)

(b) At a railway station.

(i) CONSIGNA

(ii) SALA DE ESPERA

What do these signs tell you? (2)

(c) In a street.
What does this sign tell you? (1)

PASO DE PEATONES

2 You are exploring Spain by car with your parents. Your father, who does not speak Spanish, asks you about some signs that you see.

(a) Why must you be careful on this road? (1)

(b) Could you park here? (1)

(c) You follow this sign, in what part of Villajoyosa would you find yourself? (1)

(d) What *two* things are you *not* allowed to do here? (2)

(e) Name *two* things advertised on this van. (2)

WJEC

Reading Test 2

1 Travelling to Spain by car with your family, you see this sign while looking for a place to park in a Spanish town.

Why should you not park here? (1)

2 Later, at a junction, you see this sign:

Which vehicles are allowed to turn left, apart from buses and taxis? (1)

3 You see this advertisment in the window of a small supermarket.

What would you expect to be given free with a packet of Ariel washing powder? (1)

4 You pick up an economy sized packet of RUFFLES crisps.

What gift will you find inside? (1)

5 On the way out you see these notices at the check-out.

What are you being asked to do? (1)

6 Returning to your car, you find a handbill under the windscreen-wiper. Your parents ask you what it is advertising.

(a) What sort of clothing does this shop sell? (1)

(b) What types of sports equipment can you buy here? Give *two* details. (2)

Edexecl (London)

Reading Test 3

1 En una estación quieres leer algo. ¿Qué letrero signes?

(a) ☐ **(b)** ☐ **(c)** ☐ **(d)** ☐

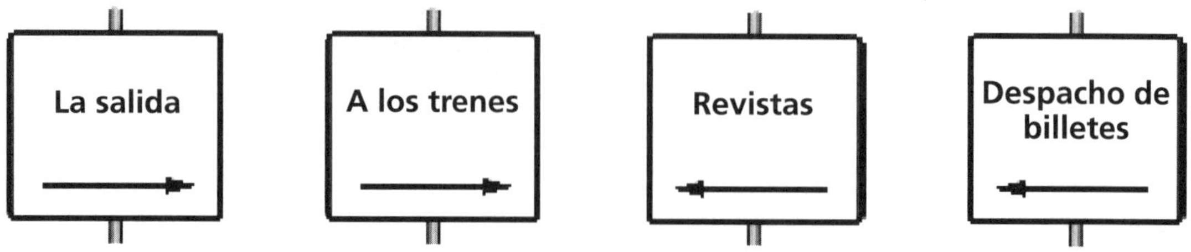

2 En el tren quieres comer algo ¿Qué letrero sigues?

(a) ☐ **(b)** ☐ **(c)** ☐ **(d)** ☐

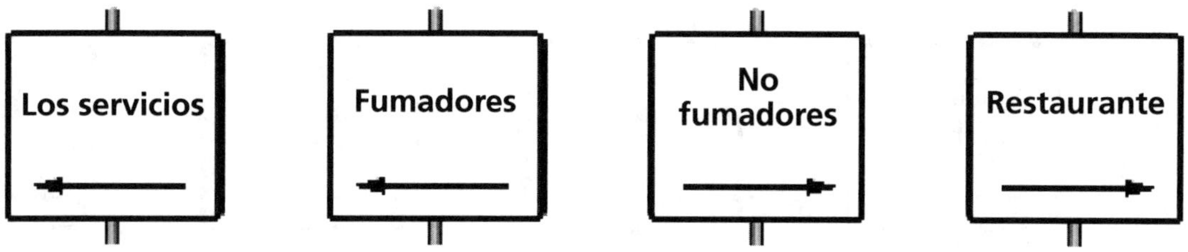

3 En tu hotel quieres subir a tu habitación ¿Qué letrero sigues?

(a) ☐ **(b)** ☐ **(c)** ☐ **(d)** ☐

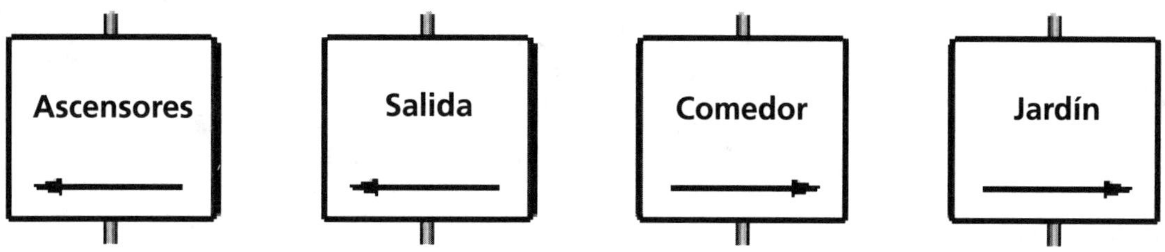

4 Quieres comprar un jersey. ¿Qué letrero sigues?

(a) ☐ **(b)** ☐ **(c)** ☐ **(d)** ☐

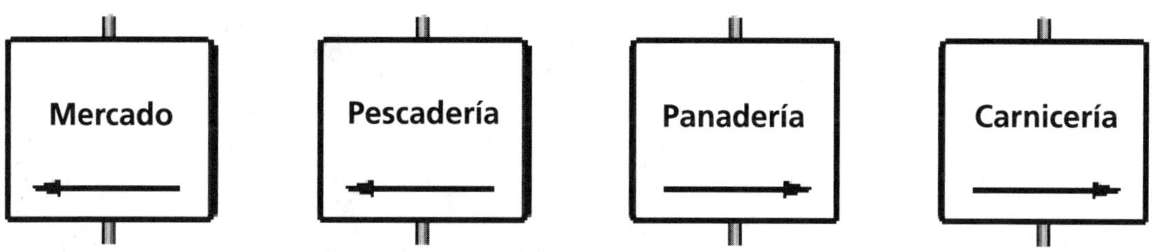

5 Estás en una tienda de comestibles. ¿Cuánto cuesta la fruta?

(a) 120 ☐
(b) 140 ☐
(c) 90 ☐
(d) 80 ☐

PRECIOS

Huevos	120
Sardinas	140
Leche	90
Naranjas	80

6 Quieres beber un refresco en un café. ¿Cuánto cuesta?

(a) 180 ☐
(b) 90 ☐
(c) 220 ☐
(d) 85 ☐

BEBIDAS

cerveza	180
café	90
coñac	220
Fanta de limón	85

7 Quieres mandar una carta a Inglaterra. ¿Qué letrero sigues?

(a) ☐ **(b)** ☐ **(c)** ☐ **(d)** ☐

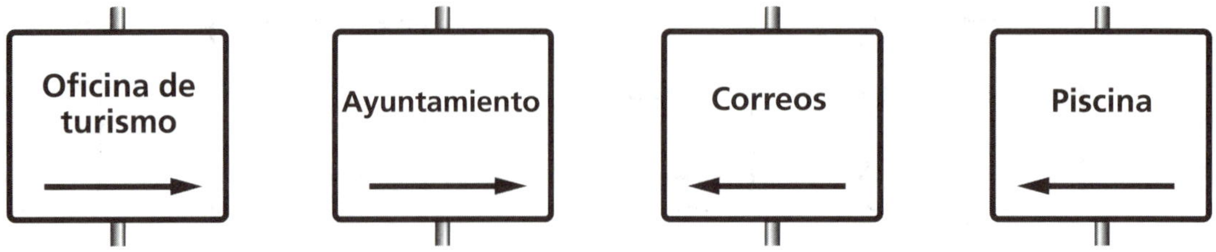

(7)

E xaminer's tip

You can see how important it is to learn the vocabulary that deals with places in a town and items of food and drink.

Reading Test 4

¿Qué se puede comprar aquí?

(a) salchichas ☐
(b) pescado ☐
(c) libros ☐
(d) relojes ☐

(1)

Reading Test 5

Recibes esta carta de tu amigo Pablo.

Hola Peter

¡Qué día! Esta mañana el despertador no sonó y me levanté tarde. Luego cogí un autobús al instituto pero hubo una avería. Más tarde jugué al fútbol y ¡ganamos! Luego mi profesor miró mi trabajo y dijo que mi trabajo era estupendo. Al volver a casa mi padre dijo que no puedo salir. Además dijo que no tiene bastante dinero para regalarme la bicicleta que me prometió. Hace cinco minutos llamó María diciendo que quiere salir conmigo. ¡Qué día!

Pablo

¿Qué aspectos han salido bien? ¿Qué aspectos han salido mal? Pon una señal en la casilla correcta.

		Ha salido bien	Ha salido mal
1		☐	☐
2		☐	☐
3		☐	☐
4		☐	☐
5		☐	☐
6		☐	☐
7		☐	☐

(7)

Examiner's tip

The pictures and symbols used by the Exam Boards can be confusing. Take some time to look at them to ensure you understand what you are being asked for.

Reading Test 6

Lees estos anuncios.

BUSCO TRABAJO
Soy especialista en plantas de invierno y árboles frutales.
Llámame.
Luis: 2347234

Soy estudiante y puedo trabajar de las 7 a las 11. Mis clases empiezan a mediodía. Llama
Teresa 9837264

Me encantaría trabajar con caballos. Por favor, llámame.
Raquel 8358346

Soy estudiante y puedo trabajar en junio, julio y agosto.
Cualquier cosa.
José 2349123

Hablo cuatro lenguas y doy clases. Servicio profesional.
Pablo 3203849

Necesito trabajo para los fines de semana. Soy mecánico.
Pedro 5467382

¿Estas declaraciones son verdaderas o falsas? Pon una señal en la casilla correcta.

		verdadero	falso
1	Luis es jardinero.	☐	☐
2	Teresa quiere trabajar por la tarde.	☐	☐
3	Raquel no quiere trabajar con animales.	☐	☐
4	José busca trabajo en invierno.	☐	☐
5	A Pedro no le molesta trabajar los sábados.	☐	☐
6	Pablo es profesor.	☐	☐

(6)

Examiner's tip

The word **lengua** can mean 'language' or 'tongue'. Incidentally the two words for language, **lengua** and **idioma**, are constantly coming up in exam questions.

Reading Test 7

Lees este folleto.

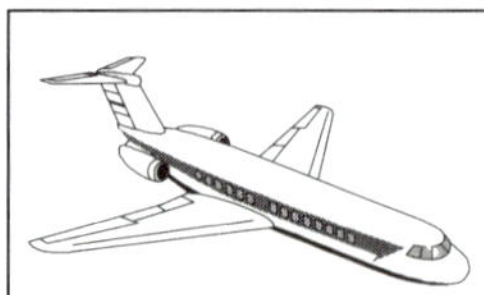

Londres: un fin de semana en la capital de Inglaterra

Vuelo directo de Madrid a Londres

Salida: viernes a las 1800
Vuelta: domingo a las 1800

Precio incluye hotel y media pensión
Niños pagan 50%
Entrada a la Torre de Londres gratis

Precio global: 40.000 pesetas.

Llama Viajes SEU 4163456

Indica si estas declaraciones son verdaderas o falsas. Pon una señal en la casilla correcta.

		verdadero	falso
1	El avión para en París.	☐	☐
2	El viaje de ida sale por la mañana.	☐	☐
3	El precio no incluye el almuerzo.	☐	☐
4	El precio incluye la cena.	☐	☐
5	Es gratuito para los niños.	☐	☐
6	Hay que pagar la entrada para la Torre de Londres.	☐	☐

(6)

Examiner's tip

You need to know the difference between full board and half board. The answer is lunch! For full board you get all your meals but for half board you get breakfast and an evening meal. So the difference is lunch!

Reading Test 8

Lees el pronóstico del tiempo en el periódico.

PRONOSTICO DEL TIEMPO

Hoy habrá un viento fuerte hasta mediodía. Luego el viento desaparecerá y habrá niebla en todas partes. Más tarde las temperaturas van a bajar.

Mañana se preve lluvia en todo el país por la mañana pero por la tarde el sol va a volver y tendremos cielos despejados con mucho calor. Pero cuidado. Mañana por la noche, va a nevar.

(a)

(b)

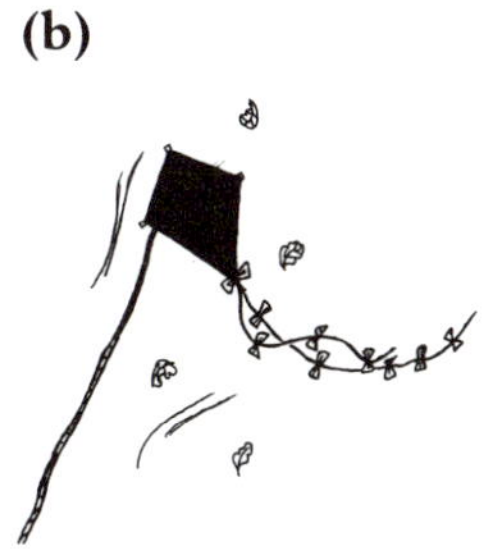

(c)

(d)

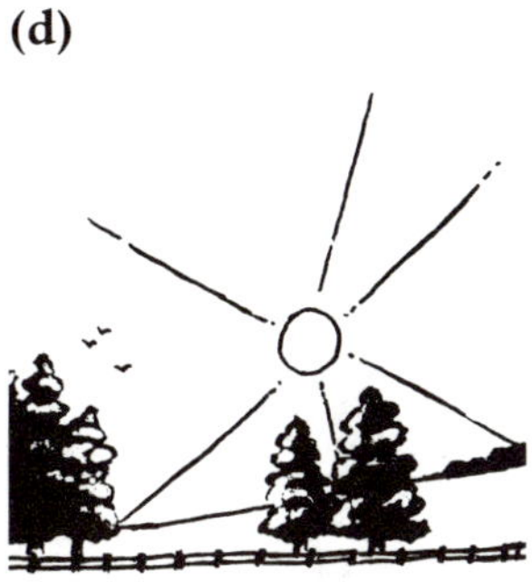

(e)

(f)

¿Qué tiempo hace a estas horas? Pon la letra correcta en la casilla.

HOY
1 09:00-1200 ☐
2 1200-1700 ☐
3 1700-2400 ☐

MAÑANA
4 0900-1200 ☐
5 1200-1700 ☐
6 1700-2400 ☐

Examiner's tip

The weather vocabulary is absolutely essential. See the vocabulary section in this book.

(6)

Reading Test 9

Acabas de llegar a una ciudad que no conoces. Pon una señal en la casilla correcta.

1 Quieres comer algo. ¿Adónde vas?
- **(a)** Comisaría ☐
- **(b)** Heladería ☐
- **(c)** Cine ☐
- **(d)** Corrida de toros ☐

2 Quieres beber algo. ¿Adónde vas?
- **(a)** lechería ☐
- **(b)** carnicería ☐
- **(c)** panadería ☐
- **(d)** paso subterráneo ☐

3 Pon la letra adecuada en la casilla correcta.

(a) el ayuntamiento **(b)** un estanco **(c)** una farmacia **(d)** la comisaría
(e) una carnicería **(f)** un banco **(g)** Correos

1 Quieres cambiar tu dinero ☐
2 Un ladrón se ha llevado tu maleta ☐
3 Te sientes enferma ☐
4 Quieres comprar una postal ☐
5 Buscas un buzón ☐
6 Quieres quejarte al alcalde ☐

4 ¿Qué se prohibe en el parque? Mira el letrero.

(a) ☐ **(b)** ☐ **(c)** ☐ **(d)** ☐

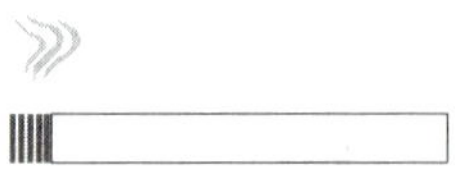

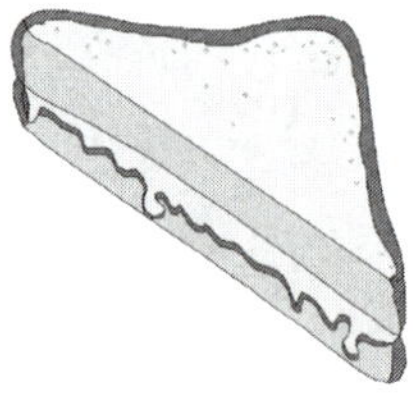

(9)

Reading Test 10

CAMPING MUNDO

- bar - supermercado - piscina - pesca
- cine - TV - baloncesto - periódicos

¿Qué puedes hacer en este camping? Pon una señal en la casilla correcta.

		verdadero	**falso**
1		☐	☐
2		☐	☐
3		☐	☐
4		☐	☐
5		☐	☐

(5)

Reading Test 11

MUEBLES
SERVICIO PROFESIONAL
MADRID 23435432

Mira la tarjeta de Alvaro Díaz. ¿Qué cosas vende? Pon una señal en la casilla correcta.

(a) Joyas etc ☐
(b) Sillones etc ☐
(c) Coches etc ☐
(d) Revistas etc ☐

(1)

Reading Test 12

ADELA

LUISA

MARTA

MARIA

¿Quién es? Escribe el nombre en la casilla correcta.

		Nombre
1	Tengo el pelo negro. Es rizado y corto.	☐
2	Tengo el pelo rubio. Es largo y liso.	☐
3	Tengo el pelo negro. Es liso y largo. No llevo gafas.	☐
4	Tengo el pelo negro. Es liso y largo. También llevo gafas.	☐

(4)

7.5 Suggested answers to examination questions

Reading Test 1

1 **(a)** Toilets.
(b) **(i)** Left luggage.
(ii) Waiting room.
(c) Pedestrian crossing.

2 **(a)** Because lorries come out onto it.
(b) No.
(c) The port.
(d) Bathe and go onto the boats.
(e) Toys and presents.

Reading Test 2

1 It is reserved for motorcycles.
2 Two-wheeled vehicles.
3 A digital watch.
4 Earrings.
5 Show the inside of your bag to the cashier.
6 **(a)** Sports clothes.
(b) Equipment for fishing and windsurfing.

Reading Test 3

1 (c)
2 (d)
3 (a)
4 (a)
5 (d)
6 (d)
7 (c)

Reading Test 4

(a)

Reading Test 5

1 mal
2 mal
3 bien
4 bien
5 mal
6 mal
7 bien

Reading Test 6

1 v
2 f
3 f
4 f
5 v
6 v

Reading Test 7

1 f
2 f
3 v
4 v
5 f
6 f

Reading Test 8

1 (b)
2 (c)
3 (e)
4 (a)
5 (d)
6 (f)

Reading Test 9

1 (b)
2 (a)
3 1 (f)
  2 (d)
  3 (c)
  4 (b)
  5 (g)
  6 (a)
4 (d)

Reading Test 10

1 v
2 v
3 f
4 f
5 v

Reading Test 11

(b)

Reading Test 12

1 Luisa
2 Adela
3 María
4 Marta

7.6 Higher Tier examination questions

- This is what you need to know about the Higher Tier.
- Most of the questions will be asked in Spanish. About 20% will be asked in English. The rule is: if the rubric (i.e. the instructions at the top of the question) and the questions are in English, answer in English. If the rubric and the questions are in Spanish then you answer in Spanish.
- Many of the questions will be of a box-ticking or form-filling nature.
- If you have to answer by writing Spanish words, then you are usually required to write a very

short answer. You will only lose marks for your Spanish if it is so bad that the examiner does not understand it. The odd minor mistake does not matter.

- You may use a dictionary throughout. Make sure you know the dangers of over-use of the dictionary. Read the section on dictionary use at the beginning of this book.
- If you are doing the Short Course the questions will be restricted to two Areas of Experience, usually Areas B and D. If you are doing the Full Course expect questions from all the Areas of Experience. See the section on Areas of Experience at the beginning of this book.
- At Higher Tier you will have to be able to:

  understand the gist of texts
  understand agreement and disagreement
  identify attitudes, emotions, ideas
  draw conclusions
  identify relationships between ideas

- If you are being entered for Higher Tier do not think that the questions in the Foundation Tier section of this chapter will be too easy for you. There is an overlap in the questions between Foundation Tier questions and Higher Tier questions for each Exam Board. Do the Foundation Tier Reading Tests first.

The following questions are either past papers or have been written by a Chief Examiner.

Reading Test 13

Lee este artículo sobre un hombre rico.

JUAN SECADA: MILLONARIO

La casa de Juan Secada es una casa de lujo. Pero Juan no nació en este lujo. Nació en Alicante en 1965, hijo de un pescador pobre. A la edad de dieciocho años fue a Valencia a vender pescado en el mercado. Ganó el suficiente dinero para poder llevar a Isabel al altar. Alquilaron un piso pequeño e Isabel tuvo dos hijos, Marta y Pepe. La vida era dura pero un día Juan decidió cambiar su estilo. En vez de vender pescado empezó a vender fruta. Fue un éxito total. A los pocos meses compró un coche, luego un camión para transportar la fruta. Hoy miles de personas trabajan en su empresa pero nunca olvida la pobreza de su juventud.

Mira la lista de las etapas de la vida de Juan Secada. Indica con los números 1-8 el órden correcto.

(a) Se casa.
(b) Empieza a vender fruta.
(c) Empieza a vender pescado.
(d) Se marcha de Alicante.
(e) Compra un camión.
(f) Nacen sus hijos.
(g) Deja de vender pescado.
(h) Juan nace en 1965. (ejemplo 1)
(i) Empieza a vivir en un piso.

1	2	3	4	5	6	7	8	9
(h)								

(8)

Examiner's tip

This kind of question, i.e. placing things in order, can be very confusing. It is a good idea to write out the phrases in rough in the right order. You are given the first phrase, so write out **Juan nace en 1965**; then write out the phrase that logically comes next. Notice that **dejar** means 'to leave' but **dejar de** means 'to stop doing something'.

Reading Test 14

Tu amiga Consuelo te ha mandado una carta pero no ha escrito las frases en el orden correcto.

(a) Escribo para decirte que no puedo visitarte en Inglaterra este año.
(b) Pues porque mi hermana se casa en agosto y tengo que comprar un regalo.
(c) Creo que voy a comprarle un microondas.
(d) Querida Ana: (ejemplo 1)
(e) En España las marcas japonesas son las mejores.
(f) La razón es que no tengo bastante dinero para el vuelo.
(g) Bueno nada más, amiga. Te escribiré después de la boda.
(h) Un abrazo, tu amiga Consuelo.
(i) El vuelo costaría 30.000 mil pesetas y las necesito - ¿sabes por qué?

El orden correcto es:

1	2	3	4	5	6	7	8	9
(d)								

(8)

Examiner's tip

Use a lot of scrap paper for this. Do not be afraid to ask the invigilator for scrap paper. You can make a right mess of your exam paper very easily with this type of question by putting numbers and drawing arrows.

Reading Test 15

Lee este anuncio de unos almacenes en España.

EL CORTE INGLES
REBAJA ESPECIAL

HOY OFRECEMOS UN DESCUENTO DEL 20% EN LOS ARTICULOS DE CUERO, GUANTES, BOLSAS, ZAPATOS, ABRIGOS, BUFANDAS, PANTALONES.

SEÑORAS, SEÑORES, CHICOS, CHICAS, PAREJAS, ANCIANOS, ANCIANAS VENGAN A NUESTROS ALMACENES PARA ESTA REBAJA EXCEPCIONAL.

TRAIGA ESTA HOJA PARA CONSEGUIR SU DESCUENTO.
ABIERTO HASTA LAS 22.00

Busca en el texto las palabras definidas.

1	Un precio reducido.	(1)
2	Piel de un animal.	(1)
3	Prenda que se lleva en la mano.	(1)
4	Un hombre y una mujer.	(1)
5	Un papel que anuncia cosas.	(1)
		(5)

Examiner's tip

Almacenes is always plural in Spanish. A department store is singular in English but plural in Spanish.

Reading Test 16

Rellena los espacios con las palabras de la casilla para dar el sentido del mensaje.

MENSAJE TELEFONICO

MENSAJE PARA LA SEÑORITA SUÁREZ

MENSAJE DE LA POLICÍA

Señorita Suárez, la policía llamó a las 10.00 para decirle que han encontrado su coche. Dice que su coche fue robado anoche delante de su casa. No hubo testigos. Esta mañana un granjero lo encontró en un campo al borde de la ciudad. Desgraciadamente el ladrón había prendido fuego al coche y está totalmente destrozado. La policía quiere que Vd. vaya en seguida a la comisaría.

Hubo una .... esta .... de la .... Civil para decir que habían encontrado su .... Nadie vio el .... Esta mañana un granjero lo encontró en los .... de la ciudad. Desafortunadamente el coche fue destruido por .... ¿Puede Vd. .... la comisaría ....?

cama	inmediatamente	misa	vehículo	mañana
camión	robo	madre	alrededores	incendio
deporte	visitar	llamada	Guardia	animal

Examiner's tip

Do not be confused by the two words for 'police' in Spanish – **guardia** and **policía**.

Reading Test 17

He aquí in fragmento de una carta. Lee y contesta a las preguntas.

Al entrar en casa sobre las siete ¡qué ambiente! ¡Cuánta gente! Todos mis amigos, todas mis amigas estaban allí ... todos se reían y cada uno llevaba un regalo para mí. Incluso había un pastel en forma de dieciocho con dieciocho velas encendidas. ¡Me lo pasé bomba!

Luego sobre las nueve de la noche, ocurrió una cosa rara. Alguien llamó a la puerta, un amigo abrió y entró mi hermano. No pude dar crédito a mis ojos. Le vi por última vez hace tres años. Se marchaba a Méjico y dijo que no volvería nunca. Claro que nos abrazamos y los dos llorábamos.

Pero él no fue el último visitante. Sobre las once hubo una llamada a la puerta. ¡Era la Guardia Civil! Entraron y todos teníamos miedo. Los vecinos nos habían denunciado por el ruido. Pues nos amenazaron con multas y se fueron por fin.

Pues bajamos la música y a las doce mis amigos empezaron a marcharse. Mi hermana se tuvo que ir a la cama. Estaba borracha, como es costumbre en ella.

Fue una noche inolvidable. En mi próxima carta te contaré lo enfadado que estaba mi padre al ver la casa al día siguiente.

Con cariño

Laura

1 ¿Qué ocasión celebraban Laura y sus amigos?

2 ¿Cómo era el ambiente en la casa a las siete?
- **(a)** triste ☐
- **(b)** optimista ☐
- **(c)** alegre ☐
- **(d)** miedoso ☐

3 ¿Cómo se sintió Laura cuando llegó su hermano?
- **(a)** decepcionada ☐
- **(b)** sorprendida ☐
- **(c)** miedosa ☐
- **(d)** pesimista ☐

4 ¿Cómo se sintieron todos a las once cuando hubo otra visita?
- **(a)** decepcionados ☐
- **(b)** miedosos ☐
- **(c)** alegres ☐
- **(d)** optimistas ☐

5 ¿Cómo se sintieron los vecinos?
- **(a)** irritados ☐
- **(b)** alegres ☐
- **(c)** miedosos ☐
- **(d)** pesimistas ☐

6 ¿Qué suele hacer su hermana?
- **(a)** beber demasiado ☐
- **(b)** hacer demasiado ruido ☐
- **(c)** bajar la música ☐
- **(d)** marcharse ☐

7 ¿Cómo se sintió el padre de Laura?

(a) contento ☐
(b) triste ☐
(c) orgulloso ☐
(d) enojado ☐

(7)

Examiner's tip

This question tests you on your ability to detect emotions. There is an excellent chance that you will find such a test in your exam. It is particularly important therefore that you spend time learning all the 'emotions' vocabulary that is used in this test.

Reading Test 18

Tu amigo ha hecho este test. ¿Cómo es la personalidad de tu amigo? Pon una señal en la casilla correcta.

ENCUESTA

1 ¿Qué haces los domingos por la mañana?

(a) Salgo con mis amigos. ☐
(b) Hago deporte. ☐
(c) Hago mis deberes. ☐
(d) Voy a misa. ☑
(e) Otra cosa. ☐

Eres deportista ☐
trabajador ☐
valiente ☐
religioso ☐
generoso ☐
sociable ☐
cobarde ☐

2 Si encuentras un perro peligroso ¿qué haces?

(a) No le hago caso. ☑
(b) Le doy algo de comer. ☐
(c) Me marcho. ☐
(d) Tengo miedo. ☐
(e) Le hablo. ☐

Eres deportista ☐
trabajador ☐
valiente ☐
religioso ☐
generoso ☐
sociable ☐
cobarde ☐

3 Has ganado la lotería. ¿Qué haces con el dinero?

(a) Pongo todo el dinero en el banco. ☐

(b) Viajo por todo el mundo. ☐

(c) Invito a todos mis amigos a una gran fiesta. ☑

(d) No digo nada a nadie. ☐

(e) Doy el dinero a mis padres. ☐

Eres	deportista	☐
	trabajador	☐
	valiente	☐
	religioso	☐
	generoso	☐
	sociable	☐
	cobarde	☐

4 ¿Qué tipo de programa te gusta en la tele?

(a) Programas religiosos. ☐

(b) Telenovelas. ☐

(c) Partidos en directo. ☑

(d) Películas. ☐

(e) Actualidad. ☐

Eres	deportista	☐
	trabajador	☐
	valiente	☐
	religioso	☐
	generoso	☐
	sociable	☐
	cobarde	☐

(4)

Examiner's tip

This kind of question requires you to draw conclusions about people's personalities. Be sure to learn the 'personality' vocabulary you meet in this question.

Reading Test 19

Lee esta postal.

> Saludos. Estoy pasando dos semanas aquí en la capital de Francia y hace sol y calor. Los franceses son muy simpáticos y nos encanta la cocina francesa. No queremos volver a España, tanto nos gusta nuestra estancia aquí. Ayer tuvimos un pequeño problema con el coche: los frenos dejaron de funcionar.
>
> Hasta pronto
>
> Angela y familia

> 9 The Street
> Smalltown
> Northshire NT33 6XY
> Gran Bretaña

Rellena los espacios con las palabras de la casilla para dar el sentido del mensaje.

Angela y su familia pasan una .... en .... y el tiempo es .... Les gusta la .... y la .... No tienen .... de volver a España porque se lo pasan .... en Francia. Ayer hubo una .... Se trataba de los frenos .

ganas	puente	bien	estupendo	libro	avería	quincena
París	cocina	gente	barcos	jueves	día	

(8)

Reading Test 20

Tienes que comprar estos artículos. ¿A qué tiendas vas? Pon la letra adecuada en la casilla.

1	ternera	☐
2	suizos	☐
3	merluza	☐
4	piñas	☐
5	guisantes	☐
6	sobres	☐
7	una novela	☐
8	jabón	☐
9	tiritas	☐

(a) frutería
(b) droguería
(c) papelería
(d) librería
(e) pescadería
(f) verdulería
(g) carnicería
(h) panadería
(i) farmacia

(9)

Examiner's tip

Do not be confused by the two meanings of the word **sobre**: 'on' or 'envelope'. Similarly **librería** does not mean 'library'. It means 'book-shop'.

Reading Test 21

Ves este letrero. Contesta a las preguntas.

> **BUSCAMOS A ESTE HOMBRE.**
> **POR ASESINATO.**
> **POR SECUESTRO DE UN NIÑO.**
> **POR ATRACO A UNA JOYERÍA.**
> **SE LLAMA JORGE PEREZ.**
> **ES PERUANO.**
> **TIENE CUARENTA AÑOS.**
> **HA PASADO VEINTE AÑOS EN LA CÁRCEL.**
> **SE ESCAPÓ DE LA CÁRCEL HACE UNA SEMANA.**
> **ES ALTO, DELGADO.**
> **TIENE BIGOTE.**

1 ¿Cuáles son los tres crímenes de Jorge Perez? Pon una señal en las casillas.

(a) Robó dinero de un banco. ☐
(b) Fraude. ☐
(c) Raptó a una persona. ☐
(d) Robó diamantes, oro etc. ☐
(e) Mató a alguien. ☐
(f) Hirió a un guardia. ☐

2 ¿De dónde es?

(a) América del Sur ☐
(b) Australia ☐
(c) Europa ☐
(d) Africa ☐

3 ¿Cuántos años tiene?

(a) 18 ☐
(b) 20 ☐
(c) 25 ☐
(d) 40 ☐

4 ¿Dónde estaba hace ocho días?

(a) En prisión. ☐
(b) En un banco. ☐
(c) En el Perú. ☐
(d) En una joyería. ☐

5 ¿Cuál de estos hombres es Jorge Perez?

(a) ☐

(b) ☐

(c) ☐

(d) ☐

(7)

Examiner's tip

These questions are asking you to draw conclusions. You will have to spend time working things out from the clues. For instance there are clues in the poster but also in the question about the man's age.

Reading Test 22

Lees una revista de jóvenes. Estas personas buscan amigos por correspondencia. ¿Cuáles son sus pasatiempos? Pon unas señales en las casillas correctas. Cada persona menciona dos intereses.

BUSCAMOS AMIGOS

Hola. Me llamo Miguel. Estoy aprendiendo el árabe y el italiano y también compro mucha cerámica de aquellos países. Intento comprar algo de cerámica cada mes. Si te interesa, llámame.
Miguel. 4456734

Me llamo Joselito y tengo 15 años. Pinto retratos y los dibujos también. Los fines de semana voy a la granja de mi tío porque tiene tres caballos. Llámame.
Joselito 2340987

Hola.
Me llamo Teresa y quiero cartearme con alguien que tenga los mismos gustos. Me gustan las películas de amor y también las novelas de amor. Ojalá pudiera encontrar el chico de mis sueños.
Teresa: 2349864

Hola. Me llamo Juana y tengo quince años. Voy a la piscina cuando puedo y tengo una tortuga y una docena de peces dorados. Llámame.
Juana 9876243

Busco amigos que tengan los mismos intereses que yo. Soy miembro de un grupo y toco la batería. También tengo miles de sellos de los países de América del Sur. Llámame:
Ana 9877821

	Música	Animales	Natación	Arte	Idiomas	Coleccionar	Equitación	Cine	Lectura
Miguel	☐	☐	☐	☐	☐	☐	☐	☐	☐
Joselito	☐	☐	☐	☐	☐	☐	☐	☐	☐
Teresa	☐	☐	☐	☐	☐	☐	☐	☐	☐
Juana	☐	☐	☐	☐	☐	☐	☐	☐	☐
Ana	☐	☐	☐	☐	☐	☐	☐	☐	☐

(10)

Examiner's tip

As you read through the adverts underline the key words in the text. (Do not worry about writing on the exam paper.) Underline them as you come to them in the adverts. For instance you know **piscina** is going to be a key word so underline it. In this way you are less likely to miss out one of the points needed in the answer.

Reading Test 23

Lee este artículo sobre el famoso cantante Mark Williams.

10 PUNTOS CLAVES SOBRE LA VIDA DE MARK WILLIAMS

- Nació en Inglaterra el 5 de enero de 1959. Perdió a sus dos padres en un accidente a la edad de un año.
- En el colegio su profesor de música le dijo que se callase porque cantaba muy mal.
- De pequeño quería ser futbolista pero aunque jugaba en un equipo se rompió la pierna en un partido y nunca jugó más.
- La primera chica que le besó fue Antonia Wyles. Esta se casó más tarde con su hermano.
- Trabajó de camarero cuando dejó el colegio pero pronto empezó a tocar en los clubs.
- Un cliente en un club le oyó cantar y tocar, notó su buen parecido y llamó a un amigo que graba canciones.
- En 1979 se le ofreció un contrato por diez millones de pesetas.
- El estreno de su primera película tuvo lugar en Madrid en 1980.
- Se casó con una chica que vivía al lado de su casa en 1981.
- Nunca da dinero ni a su mujer ni a sociedades benéficas. Dice que es una pérdida de tiempo.

1 Subraya tres adjetivos en la lista que describen a Mark.

soltero	pobre	casado	perezoso
guapo	feo	deportivo	orgulloso

2 Di si estas observaciones son verdaderas o falsas.

	verdadero	falso
(a) Mark era huérfano.	☐	☐
(b) De alumno todo el mundo le creía buen cantante.	☐	☐
(c) No quería ser deportista.	☐	☐
(d) Antonia Wyles es su cuñada.	☐	☐
(e) Trabajaba en un bar.	☐	☐
(f) Un desconocido reconoció su talento.	☐	☐
(g) En 1979 ganó un millón de dólares.	☐	☐
(h) Su primera película apareció en Francia.	☐	☐
(i) Una vecina es ahora su mujer.	☐	☐
(j) Es muy generoso.	☐	☐

(10)

Examiner's tip

The adjectives in this Test are very crucial to the understanding of it. Make sure you learn the adjectives in the Vocabulary Chapter of this book, particularly the adjectives which deal with people's personality.

Reading Test 24

¿Dónde van a trabajar?

Lee lo que dicen estos jóvenes y pon el nombre de la persona correcta en el espacio.

Juana
Cuando llega el verano es un gran placer ver la cosecha. El trigo en los campos me encanta. Quiero hacer este tipo de trabajo en el futuro.

Ana
Mis profesores me dicen que no soy muy inteligente y yo creo que tienen razón. Por eso me parece que cuando trabaje es mejor que haga cosas mecánicas, es decir si tengo que hacer la misma cosa repetidas veces no haré errores. También me gusta la idea de trabajar en una empresa y empezar y terminar a la misma hora cada día.

Marco
Cada vez que hay una avería soy yo el experto. Ayer hubo un fallo en la batería, anteayer los frenos no funcionaban. Lo arreglé todo. Ya sé lo que voy a hacer en el futuro.

Sheila
Aquí en España la gente se muere de hambre. Tengo un montón de amigos que trabajan fuera de España y es allí donde voy a trabajar.

Jesús
Mi padre es enfermero y mi madre es ama de casa. Mi hermano es un abogado célebre. Me dice que gana una fortuna pero yo quiero seguir la misma carrera que mi padre.

Rachael
Yo tengo el mejor jardín de esta ciudad. Me encanta estar al aire libre y mis arbustos y plantas me dan mucho placer. En el futuro quiero hacer este tipo de trabajo.

Juan
Toda mi vida he querido ser un payaso. No sé porque pero mis padres me dicen que tengo talento y me gusta la idea de estar con los animales y de viajar de un pueblo a otro.

1 ¿Quién va a trabajar en un circo? ....

2 ¿Quién va a trabajar en el extranjero? ....

3 ¿Quién va a trabajar reparando coches? ....

4 ¿Quién va a trabajar en una granja? ....

5 ¿Quién va a trabajar en un hospital? ....

6 ¿Quién va a trabajar en una fábrica? ....

7 ¿Quién va a trabajar como jardinero? ....

(7)

Examiner's tip

Obviously 'job' vocabulary is crucial in this question. Make sure you know the vocabulary in the 'jobs' section of the Vocabulary Chapter.

Reading Test 25

1 You read this letter from the mother of a teenage girl.

Quiere estudiar, pero necesitamos que trabaje

Una hija mía termina este año el COU y tiene empeño en estudiar una carrera universitaria. Su profesor dice que está muy capacitada. El problema es que en casa tenemos una mala situación económica y necesitamos otro sueldo. Yo quiero que busque un trabajo. ¿Es la mía una proposición egoísta?

OPINION

Su hija podría buscar alguna pequeña ocupación a tiempo parcial, que suelen realizarse fuera del horario de estudios: clases particulares, cuidar algún niño..., así la carrera de su hija no supondría una carga para la economía familiar y realizar estudios superiores le permitiría, en el futuro, acceder a algún puesto de trabajo de mayor categoría.

(a) What does the daughter want to do when she leaves school? (1)
(b) What would her mother prefer her to do? (1)
(c) Why? (1)
(d) Do you think that the answer is biased towards the daughter or the mother or neither? Give a reason for your answer. (2)

NEAB

Reading Test 26

1 Pepe, the perfect tourist, has published a humorous guide for holiday-makers. This is how it begins.

COMO COMPORTARSE EN LA PLAYA

Durante los meses de verano, millones de personas van de vacaciones, abarrotando las piscinas, los lagos, las playas ... ¿Pero, existe algún libro que te diga cómo debes comportarte en esos lugares? ¡No, no lo hay! Aunque no debes preocuparte: las increíbles reglas de comportamiento de 'Pepe, turista modelo', te dirán como hacerlo.

REGLA 1: PEPE conserva la calma cuando en la playa hay niños que no paran de jugar a su alrededor, gritando.
En ningún caso es aconsejable seguir el ejemplo de un ciudadano de Colonia que pasaba sus vacaciones en una isla del Mediterráneo. Le prometió un helado al niño que más aprisa se comiera un pastel de arena que él mismo había hecho … y durante un rato tuvo paz y tranquilidad, pero se dice que algo más tarde mantuvo una ruidosa discusión con los padres del niño.

REGLA 2: PEPE tiene siempre en cuenta que los demás veraneantes también tienen derecho a un ambiente tranquilo y relajado.
Por lo que, con sumo cuidado, Pepe sube el volumen de su equipo de música en el que estaba escuchando un poco de 'heavy metal' sólo con la intención de que no se oiga el rumor de las conversaciones de los demás bañistas, que molesta un tanto …

(a) According to the title, what is the purpose of this guide? (1)
(b) What problem does Rule 1 deal with? (1)
(c) Pepe solved the problem by keeping calm. What exactly did another holiday-maker do? (2)
(d) Why didn't this idea work in the end? (1)
(e) Judging from Rule 2, Pepe is a considerate holiday-maker.
Do you agree? Give a reason for your answer. (2)

NEAB

Examiner's tip

Before reading the text, read through the questions first. It will give you an idea of what to look out for.

Reading Test 27

A Spanish friend shows you this letter. Answer the questions which follow.

Buenos Aires, 5 de junio

Querida Marta:

Espero que al recibir esta carta estés bien, así como toda tu familia. No sé por qué no he recibido ninguna contestación a la carta que te escribí en marzo. ¿Te has equivocado de dirección? Te escribo en un ordenador. Me lo prestó mi cuñado.

Ahora vivimos en Buenos Aires, en la ciudad misma. Antes, vivíamos en una granja pero como mis padres se envejecían y a mi padre le duele la espalda, de mala gana tuvieron que encontrar otra cosa. Yo echo de menos el aire libre.

Mis amigos y yo tenemos bicicletas. Como medio de transporte tiene muchas ventajas. Todos mis amigos trabajan en el centro. Aparte de permitirles llegar temprano a su trabajo, también les permite ahorrar en transporte. Como yo no trabajo, utilizo la mía menos que ellos. Sin embargo, realizo dos o tres paseos por semana y así me mantengo en buen estado físico.

Acabo de leer un libro sobre la historia de la bicicleta. ¡Qué historia! ¿Sabes que las primeras bicicletas eran empujadas con los pies, y que eran totalmente de madera?

Bueno, amiga, no te canso más con mi carta. ¿Por qué no vienes a verme? ¡En Buenos Aires el clima es templado en todas las estaciones!

Recibe un abrazo de tu amigo,

Felipe.

1 What question is Marta asked in the first paragraph? (1)

2 From whom did Felipe borrow his computer? (1)

3 Why did Felipe move house?
Tick one box only.

- His parents wanted to live in the country. ☐
- His parents wanted to be with him. ☐
- His parents wanted to leave their farm. ☐
- His parents were getting old and frail. ☐ (1)

4 What regrets does Felipe have about moving house? (1)
5 What *two* advantages does cycling have, according to Felipe's friends? (2)
6 What specific advantage does cycling have for Felipe? (1)
7 What *two* surprising facts has Felipe learnt about the first bicycles? (2)
8 Why might a tourist be attracted to Buenos Aires? (1)

MEG

Examiner's tip

Examiners often use the word 'advantage' (**ventaja**) in the text to indicate that the question is testing your ability to draw a conclusion. This means that you have to work something out for yourself: it is not spelt out for you in the text. Sometimes you will see the word **ventaja** in the text (question 5) but sometimes (question 6) you have to work out the advantage yourself.

7.7 Suggested answers to examination questions

Reading Test 13

1 (h)
2 (d)
3 (c)
4 (a)
5 (i)
6 (f)
7 (g)
8 (b)
9 (e)

Reading Test 14

1 (d)
2 (a)
3 (f)
4 (i)
5 (b)
6 (c)
7 (e)
8 (g)
9 (h)

Reading Test 15

1 rebaja
2 cuero
3 guante
4 pareja
5 hoja

Reading Test 16

llamada	mañana	Guardia	vehículo	robo
alrededores	incendio	visitar	inmediatamente	

Reading Test 17

1 Laura cumple los 18.
2 (c)
3 (b)
4 (b)
5 (a)
6 (a)
7 (d)

Reading Test 18

1 Religioso
2 Valiente
3 Sociable
4 Deportista

Reading Test 19

quincena	París	estupendo	gente
cocina	ganas	bien	avería

Reading Test 20

1 (g)
2 (h)
3 (e)
4 (a)
5 (f)
6 (c)
7 (d)
8 (b)
9 (i)

Reading Test 21

1 (c) (d) (e)
2 (a)
3 (d)
4 (a)
5 (d)

Reading Test 22

	Música	**Animales**	**Natación**	**Arte**	**Idiomas**	**Coleccionar**	**Equitación**	**Cine**	**Lectura**
Miguel	☐	☐	☐	☐	☒	☒	☐	☐	☐
Joselito	☐	☐	☐	☒	☐	☐	☒	☐	☐
Teresa	☐	☐	☐	☐	☐	☐	☐	☒	☒
Juana	☐	☒	☒	☐	☐	☐	☐	☐	☐
Ana	☒	☐	☐	☐	☐	☒	☐	☐	☐

Reading Test 23

1 casado guapo deportivo
2
- **(a)** v
- **(b)** f
- **(c)** f
- **(d)** v
- **(e)** v
- **(f)** v
- **(g)** f
- **(h)** f
- **(i)** v
- **(j)** f

Reading Test 24

1 Juan
2 Sheila
3 Marco
4 Juana
5 Jesús
6 Ana
7 Rachael

Reading Test 25

1 **(a)** Study at University.
(b) She wants her to work.
(c) The family needs the money.
(d) No because it suggests a way that both family and daughter can benefit.

Reading Test 26

1 **(a)** How to behave on the beach.
(b) Children who constantly play and shout on the beach.
(c) Told a child to eat a sand-cake.
(d) There was a row with the parents.
(e) No because he turns up the volume of his music to drown other noises.

Reading Test 27

1 Has she got his address wrong?

2 Brother-in-law.

3 His parents were getting old and frail.

4 He misses the fresh air.

5 They arrive early for work and they save money.

6 Keeps fit.

7 They were pushed along by your feet and they were made entirely of wood.

8 The climate was temperate all year round.

Chapter 8
Writing

8.1 Introduction to Foundation Tier

This is what you need to know about the exam:

- Most of the Boards set the questions in Spanish.
- There is an overlap in the questions between Foundation and Higher Tier questions. That means that the last question in the Foundation Tier is the first question in the Higher Tier.
- It is very possible that the last question you will have to do in the Foundation Tier is to write a letter. If you attempt Higher Tier this same letter will be your first question.
- Some Boards (e.g. NEAB) set two of the Foundation questions in English and the rest in Spanish.
- In the Foundation Tier your work will be mainly assessed on your ability to communicate. If you get the message across to a sympathetic native speaker then you score. The quality of your language is also taken into consideration but not as much as in the Higher Tier.
- A lot of marks are lost in Foundation and Higher Tier Writing by candidates who misread or ignore the instructions. There are certain tasks to be completed and marks are allocated to each of these tasks. If you omit a task, you lose those marks no matter how brilliant your Spanish is!
- Your handwriting is all-important. Your paper may be marked by a very tired examiner with a hundred or so papers to mark after yours. He/she does not have time to decipher your handwriting. If what you write is not immediately readable it may well be presumed to be wrong.
- The day of your GCSE exam is not the day to experiment. You must build up a stock of Spanish that you know is correct and on the day select from your stock.

8.2 The tasks you have to complete for Foundation Tier

- Writing a list
- Messages and notes
- Postcards
- Form-filling
- Diary entries
- Writing a letter

Writing a list

This is one of the easiest of the tasks. The kind of questions asked are predictable. You may be asked for:

- a list of items of food and drink for a party or picnic
- a list of presents to take home from Spain
- a list of relatives and family members
- a list of clothes
- a list of contents in a bag
- a list of activities to be undertaken with a friend
- a list of colours
- a list of animals

Note that a one-word answer is enough to score. For instance on a shopping list you do not have to say **un kilo de manzanas**. **Manzanas** by itself is sufficient to score. In the same way, if you have to write a list of family members, **hermano** is enough to get the score. You do not have to write **mi hermano**.

- Make sure you do not repeat the same article.
- Make sure you do not write English words. **Sandwich** and **hockey** may be acceptable Spanish words in other contexts but not here!
- Make sure you know the vocabulary for the above 'list' suggestions.

Messages and notes

These are examples of typical questions, followed by suggested answers:

(a) Di dónde estás y a qué hora y cómo volverás.
He salido. Voy a la discoteca con Juan. Volveré a las ocho en el autobús.

(b) Explica por qué te acostaste y di algo de tus planes para mañana.
Estoy en la cama. Estoy cansado/a. Quiero levantarme mañana a las ocho. Voy a la playa con Juan.

(c) Da direcciones a la casa de un amigo.
Toma el autobús número ocho hasta la catedral. Cruza la plaza, y toma la segunda calle a la derecha.

(d) Invita a un amigo/una amiga y dile dónde está la discoteca.
¿Quieres venir? Estoy en una discoteca que se llama 'La Mariposa' en la plaza mayor.

(e) Dile que tiene que llamar a una amiga. Di la hora.
¿Puedes llamar a Juana a las ocho?

(f) Explica dónde has ido.
He ido a la playa/la discoteca/la casa de Juana.

(g) Explica cómo te sientes después del viaje.
Tengo hambre/sed.

(h) Explica lo que dijo Juan. Di dónde estará y por qué su hermana no viene.
Juan llamó a las seis. Estará delante del cine a las ocho. Su hermana no puede ir. Está enferma.

Examiner's tip

Candidates lose marks on these tasks because they do not indicate *who* is doing what and *whether it is in the past, present or future*. So the endings to your verbs are all-important.

Postcards

Usually a blank postcard is printed on the exam paper and you have to fill it in. You are given a set of tasks to complete. These tasks are often fairly predictable. Here are some typical tasks followed by suggested answers:

(a) Di dónde estás y con quién.
Estoy en Málaga con mi hermano.

(b) Describe el tiempo.
Hace calor todos los días.

(c) Describe tu hotel.
Mi hotel es moderno y cómodo. Hay dos piscinas.

(d) Describe tu camping.
El camping es muy grande. Hay dos piscinas.

(e) Describe tu albergue juvenil.
El albergue juvenil es muy limpio y cómodo.

(f) Da información sobre tu llegada.
Llegué aquí ayer. Llegaré a Madrid mañana.

(g) Da información sobre tu salida.
Me marché de Madrid ayer. Me marcharé de aquí mañana.

(h) Di cuándo te marcharás.
Estaré aquí hasta el domingo.

(i) Explica lo que has hecho.
He visitado los monumentos históricos, he hablado mucho español, he comido mucho, he bailado en las discotecas.

(j) Explica lo que haces durante el día.
Visito los monumentos históricos, hablo mucho español, como mucho, bailo en las discotecas.

(k) Describe lo que harás mañana.
Voy a ver los monumentos históricos, voy a hablar mucho español, voy a comer mucho y voy a bailar en las discotecas.

(l) Di si te gusta España o no. Da razones.
Me gusta España mucho. Me gusta el sol, la playa y la gente.

(m) Da tu opinión de la comida.
Me gusta la comida, sobre todo las tortillas y los mariscos.

(n) Describe a una persona que conociste.
En la discoteca, conocí a un(a) español(a). Es muy guapo(a) y tiene el pelo largo y moreno.

(o) Describe tus compras.
He comprado una guitarra y muchos discos y perfume para mi madre.

(p) Explica lo de tu amigo/a.
Espero visitar a un(a) amigo(a).

Form-filling

You should always look at the mark distribution for this question. For some of the easy entries, no marks at all are awarded. On the other hand, some of the entries attract two marks so you should make sure you give two details in these questions.

The questions asked are usually fairly predictable. You should know the following vocabulary:

nombre	first name
apellido	surname
edad	age
dirección	address
fecha	date
fecha de nacimiento	date of birth
fecha de llegada	date of arrival
fecha de salida	date of departure
firma	signature

Be prepared to answer questions like the following (suggested answers in brackets):

Nacionalidad	(británica)
Profesión	(estudiante)
Asignatura preferida	(español)
Asignatura que no te gusta	(inglés)
Pasatiempo favorito	(tenis)
Comida favorita	(patatas)
Comida que no te gusta	(pescado)
Animales en casa	(perro y gato)

Examiner's tip

Notice that **británica** always here has an **-a** ending even if it refers to a boy because it agrees with **nacionalidad** which is feminine.

Diary entries

Again the questions asked tend to be very predictable. You will have to give a list of things you plan to do on certain days or a list of things you did on certain days. Make sure you can muster ten things that you either did or will do. For example:

fui/iré al campo
fui/iré a un concierto
fui/iré a un museo
fui/iré de compras
fui/iré a un restaurante
fui/iré al cine
fui/iré al teatro
fui/iré a ver a mi amigo
fui/iré al parque
fui/iré a una discoteca

Writing a letter

- You must double-check and triple-check that you do not leave out a communication point. You may have to reply to a letter. If so, make a careful list of the points you have to communicate. If the question sets out which points to make, be sure to include them all. Make a list and tick them off once you have completed the task.
- Your letter will be either formal (i.e. to a person that you do not know) or informal (i.e. to a Spanish friend). For formal letters, use **Usted**. For informal letters, use **tú**. Make sure you know how to change vocabulary accordingly:

	FORMAL LETTER	INFORMAL LETTER
Beginning:	**Muy señor mío**	**Querido Juan/Querida Juana**
	(Dear Sir)	(Dear Juan/Juana)
Ending:	**Le saluda atentamente**	**Un abrazo de ...**
	(Yours faithfully)	(A hug from ...)
Can you send me ...?	**¿Puede Vd. mandarme ...?**	**¿ Puedes mandarme ...?**
your	**su/sus**	**tu/tus**
I am sending you ...	**Le mando ...**	**Te mando ...**

Informal letters

You should be able to predict at least some of the things you will have to write about. Make sure you have answers ready to the following:

(a) Da unos datos personales.
Me llamo ... Tengo dieciséis años. Vivo en Birmingham. Me gusta tocar la guitarra y leer novelas. Voy a una discoteca con mis amigos los sábados.

(b) Describe tu familia.
Mi padre es mecánico y mi madre es dentista. Tengo una hermana de diez años. También tenemos un perro. Los domingos damos un paseo juntos cuando hace buen tiempo.

(c) Describe tu casa.
En mi casa hay tres dormitorios, una cocina, un comedor y una sala de estar. También tenemos un pequeño jardín detras de la casa. Desafortunadamente no tenemos garaje.

(d) Describe tu colegio.
Mi colegio es bastante grande. Hay quinientos alumnos más o menos y cuarenta profesores. Hay tres laboratorios, un campo de deportes, dos pistas de tenis pero desafortunadamente no hay piscina.

(e) Describe tu región.
Cerca de mi casa hay cines, parques y un club de jóvenes. También hay fábricas y mucho tráfico. El campo no está lejos y me gusta dar paseos por el campo con mi familia.

(f) Describe una ocasión especial.
Ayer era el cumpleaños de mi madre y fuimos a un restaurante. La comida era excelente. Tomé sopa de verduras, luego bistec con patatas y luego un helado enorme. Después fuimos todos juntos al cine a ver una película americana. ¡Lo pasé bomba!

(g) Describe un incidente en el colegio.
Ayer hubo un incendio en mi colegio. Todos los alumnos tuvimos que salir y fuimos al campo de deportes. Los bomberos llegaron diez minutos más tarde y apagaron el fuego. El laboratorio de química quedó destrozada.

(h) Describe un incidente con tu familia.
Ayer fuimos a la playa en el coche de mi padre. Durante el día mi padre perdió las llaves del coche. Tuvimos que dejar el coche allí y volver en autobús.

(i) Invita tu amigo a Inglaterra.
¿Por qué no vienes a Inglaterra en verano? Mi madre dice que puedes venir. Tenemos un dormitorio libre o quizás prefieres compartir conmigo? ¡Lo pasaremos bomba!

(j) Acepta una invitación.
Muchísimas gracias por tu carta y gracias por haberme invitado a España. Sí, mis padres dicen que puedo ir. ¡Lo pasaremos bomba! Llegaré en avión el tres de julio.

(k) Di no a una invitación.
Muchísimas gracias por tu carta y gracias por haberme invitado a España. Lo siento pero no puedo ir porque mis padres no tienen dinero y además tengo exámenes y tengo mucho que hacer.

(l) Da las gracias.
Muchas gracias por el regalo. ¡Qué camiseta más bonita! Cuando lo abrí ¡qué sorpresa! Voy a llevarla esta tarde a la discoteca.

(m) Da las gracias por su hospitalidad.
Muchas gracias por todo lo que hiciste para mí durante mi estancia contigo. Gracias a tus padres también. Todo era excelente: la comida, mi habitacíon, las excursiones.

(n) Describe el viaje de regreso.
El viaje de regreso fue muy agradable. No hubo retrasos y en el avión me dieron una comida excelente. Mis padres me esperaban en el aeropuerto de Londres.

(o) Describe tus planes para la visita.
¡Lo pasaremos bomba! Iremos al campo, iremos a discotecas, veremos los museos, iremos al cine, conocerás a mis amigos, nadaremos en la piscina.

Formal letters

Again you should be able to predict at least some of the tasks you will be set. For example:

(a) Di que no estabas contento/a con tu alojamiento y di una razón.
Quiero quejarme. No me gustaba el hotel/camping/albergue juvenil. Los servicios estaban muy sucios.

(b) Pide información sobre actividades en la ciudad.
¿Qué se puede hacer en la ciudad?

(c) Reserva alojamiento para la familia.
Quiero reservar dormitorios/camas para toda la familia.

(d) Pide información sobre el hotel.
¿Qué facilidades hay en el hotel? ¿Hay una piscina?

(e) Describe un incidente cuando estabas allí.
Mientras estaba en su hotel, perdí mi reloj.

(f) Da las fechas de tu llegada y salida.
Llegaré el dos de mayo y me marcharé el cinco de mayo.

8.3 Foundation Tier examination questions

Writing Test 1

Lola te invita a su fiesta. Escribe una contestación. Menciona estos puntos:
– que no puedes ir
– lo triste que estás
– una excusa
– menciona un concierto aquel día
– dile que llamarás

Student's answers

Quiero venir a la fiesta.
No puedo.
Voy a Granada el sábado.
Quiero ver un concert.
Compra los billetes mañana.
Voy a llamar desde Granada.

Examiner's comments

On line 2, you have left out the regret element. You should have included **lo siento.**

On line 4, **concert** is French! You should have written **quiero ver un concierto allí**.

On line 5, **compra** is wrong. That means you want someone else to buy the tickets. You need to know the endings of the verbs, even for Foundation Tier. **Billetes** is used for transport tickets and **entradas** for entertainment tickets. **Mañana** by itself means 'tomorrow'. You should have written **Compré las entradas esta mañana**.

Writing Test 2

Quieres comprar ropa. Haz una lista de la ropa que quieres comprar. También el color.

	Ropa	Color
Ejemplo:	bañador	marrón
	(a)	**(f)**
	(b)	**(g)**
	(c)	**(h)**
	(d)	**(i)**
	(e)	**(j)**

(10)

Student's answers

(a)	zapatos	**(f)**	negro
(b)	abrigo	**(g)**	blanco
(c)	sombrero	**(h)**	azul
(d)	T-shirt	**(i)**	amarillo
(e)	jupe	**(j)**	negro

Examiner's comments

For the fourth item you have used an English word. Although this word is used extensively in Spain, you would be wise to steer clear of English words here and in other parts of the Spanish GCSE.

For the fifth entry you have given a French word. You should have written **falda**. You have also thrown away a mark for using the same word twice. You have written **negro** twice.

Writing Test 3

Escribe una carta a tu amiga Marisa describiendo tu fin de semana. Menciona estos puntos:
– cuánto duermes
– tu almuerzo

– tres cosas que haces
– tus deberes
– pide información sobre el sábado de Marisa
– pide información sobre sus vacaciones

Student's answers

Me lavo a las nueve.
Como bocadillos para la cena.
Salgo al cine y a discotecas los finales de semana.
Tengo muchos deberes los finales de semana.
¿Vas al colegio los sábados?
¿Cuándo empiezan tus vacaciones?

Examiner's comments

You have not written your reply in the form of a letter. You should write an opening and a closing expression.
On the first line **me lavo** means 'I wash'.
On the second line **la cena** means 'the evening meal'.
Finales is wrong for a week-end.

8.4 Suggested answers to examination questions

Writing Test 1

Lola:
Quiero venir a la fiesta.
Lo siento pero no puedo.
Voy a Granada el sábado.
Quiero ver un concierto allí.
Compré los billetes esta mañana.
Voy a llamar desde Granada.

Writing Test 2

(a) zapatos
(b) abrigo
(c) sombrero
(d) camisetsa
(e) falda
(f) negros
(g) blanco
(h) azul
(i) amarilla
(j) negra

Writing test 3

Querida Marisa:
Gracias por tu mensaje. Voy a contestarte:
Me levanto a las nueve.
Como bocadillos para el almuerzo.
Salgo al cine, al teatro y a discotecas los fines de semana.
Tengo muchos deberes los fines de semana.
¿Vas al colegio los sábados?
¿Cuándo empiezan tus vacaciones?
Un abrazo
Tu amigo inglés/amiga inglesa

8.5 Foundation Tier practice examination questions

Here are some more past questions for you to practise on. Suggested answers are given at the end.

Writing Test 4

Rellena esta hoja.

Nombre................................Apellido...
Edad............años................meses. Fecha de nacimiento.......................
Familia...
....(1)
¿Qué animales tienes en casa? ....
....(1)
¿Cómo eres tú? ....
....(2)
Estudios y trabajo:
La asignatura que prefieres:...(1)
La asignatura que no te gusta:..(1)
¿Qué haces para ayudar en casa? ....
....(2)
Intereses y pasatiempos
Me gusta más:..(1)
Me gusta bastante:...(1)
Firma.....................................Fecha..

Writing Test 5

Buscas un hotel. Estás en la oficina de turismo. Rellena esta ficha.

Nombre................................Apellido...
Dirección ....
....
Nacionalidad..(1)
Preferimos un hotel situado en...
....(2)
Tipo de habitaciones que queremos..
....(2)
Comidas que vamos a tomar en el hotel:
(a)...(1)
(b)...(1)
(c)...(1)
Fecha de llegada...(1)
Fecha de salida...(1)
Firma.....................................Fecha..

Writing Test 6

Escribe una carta a tu amiga Isabel. Menciona estos puntos:
– tus asignaturas
– el fin de tus exámenes
– tus planes para las vacaciones
– Pide información sobre el colegio de Isabel y sobre las vacaciones de Isabel

Writing Test 7

Tu amigo te ha invitado a España. Tienes que cambiar la fecha de tu viaje. Manda un telegrama. Menciona estos puntos:
– tu problema con la fecha original
– la razón
– menciona una persona que te acompañará
– detalles de tu llegada
– detalles de tu viaje de vuelta

Writing Test 8

Tu amiga va de compras. Escríbele un mensaje. Menciona estos puntos:
– transporte a las tiendas
– dos cosas que ella puede comprar para ti
– dile dónde está el supermercado
– dile dónde la encontrarás más tarde

Writing Test 9

Rellena esta hoja con las actividades que haces.

Día	**Actividad**
Lunes	limpiar mi dormitorio
Martes	
Miércoles	
Jueves	
Viernes	
Sábado	
Domingo	

Examiner's tip

For this kind of writing test, you do not need to use complete sentences so long as the essential information is conveyed.

Writing Test 10

Has alquilado una casa para el verano. Escribe una carta a tu amiga española. Menciona estos puntos:
– lo que haces en el verano
– la situación de la casa
– la duración de tu estancia
– el precio
– describe la casa
– menciona sitios cercanos

Writing Test 11

Escribe una carta a tu amigo español describiendo tu rutina diaria. Menciona estos puntos:
– cuánto tiempo duermes
– detalles de dos de tus comidas
– dos cosas que te gustan hacer
– dos quehaceres que haces en casa

Examiner's tip

Always try to give yourself plenty of time at the end of the exam to check your work. *Never* finish your exam early. You should use every minute in the exam.

Writing Test 12

Vas a hacer camping en España. Escribe una carta a una oficina de turismo. Menciona estos puntos:
– la duración de tu estancia
– cuántos seréis
– pide información sobre los campings
– las cosas que vas a hacer

Writing Test 13

Tu amiga española te ha escrito pidiendo información sobre estos puntos. Escribe una contestación:
– detalles de tu familia
– detalles de tu colegio
– transporte al colegio
– tus planes para el verano

Examiner's tip

Informal letters at GCSE level are usually about yourself/family and friends/your home and the area where you live/school/leisure activities and holidays. Revise all the vocabulary in this book on these topics and prepare in advance some of the things you might want to write in Spanish in a letter on these topics.

8.6 Suggested answers to practice examination questions

Writing Test 4

The following are suggested answers to those questions which attract a mark.

1 Vivo con mi padre y mi madre y mi hermana.
2 Un gato y un perro.
3 Soy alto/a, tengo el pelo negro.
4 Español.
5 Química.
6 Lavo los platos y hago las camas.
7 El baloncesto.
8 Jugar a las cartas.

Writing Test 5

The following are suggested answers to those questions which attract a mark.

1 británica
2 la costa cerca de la playa
3 una habitación doble y dos habitaciones individuales
4 **(a)** pollo con patatas
(b) pescado con guisantes
(c) bistec con zanahorias
5 el dos de mayo
6 el dieciséis de mayo

Writing Test 6

Manchester
2 de mayo

Querida Isabel:

Gracias por tu tarjeta. Eres muy amable. Ya sabes que estoy estudiando el inglés, las matemáticas, la geografía, la historia, el francés y la religión. Terminaré mis exámenes el veinte de junio y quiero ir a Francia y luego iré a España a broncearme. Después de las vacaciones volveré al colegio a estudiar el español, el francés y el inglés. Quiero también aprender a tocar la guitarra.

¿Qué estudias en tu colegio?
¿Vas al extranjero este verano?
Un abrazo
Paula

Writing Test 7

No puedo venir mañana. Mi amigo está enfermo.
Mi hermana viene conmigo. Llego el lunes por la mañana.
Vuelvo a Madrid el viernes.
John

Writing Test 8

No cuesta mucho ir en autobús. Necesito un carrete para mi máquina fotográfica. También necesito un bolígrafo azul. El supermercado no está lejos de mi colegio. ¿Puedes encontrarme al final de mis clases?

Writing Test 9

hacer mis deberes
escuchar música
visitar a amigos
ir a la piscina
leer mi libro
salir a la discoteca

Writing Test 10

Belfast
3 de mayo
Querida Isabel:

Voy a decirte lo que hago en verano. Voy con mi club de jóvenes a una casa en la costa. Está a sesenta kilómetros al norte de Belfast. Nos quedamos dos semanas y cuesta solamente sesenta libras. La casa es cómoda y tiene dos pisos y un jardín. Hay un cine y un teatro cerca.

Un abrazo
Mary

Writing Test 11

Lurgan
12 de octubre

Querido Miguel:

Voy a contarte algo de mi vida. Me levanto a las ocho y me acuesto a las once. Desayuno a las ocho y diez y tomo un café solamente. A la una como mis bocadillos con mis amigos. Me gusta el fútbol. Juego los domingos y veo partidos en la televisión. Juego al ajedrez con mi padre por la tarde.

Limpio mi habitación los lunes a las ocho y paso la aspiradora los sábados cuando mis padres trabajan.

Un abrazo

Paul

Writing Test 12

Liverpool

el 24 de mayo

Muy señor mío:

Espero ir a la Costa Brava y quiero pasar dos semanas allí. Vamos a acampar y seremos cuatro. Haga el favor de enviarme información sobre un camping de primera clase. El camping ideal estaría en la costa. Vamos a dormir en una tienda. Esperamos tomar el sol, ir a la playa y conocer a muchos españoles.

Le saluda atentamente

D. Ferguson

Writing Test 13

Stoke

30 de mayo

Querida Marisol:

Muchas gracias por tu carta. Voy a contestar las preguntas que me haces.

Tengo un hermano y se llama John. Mi madre se llama Sue. Tenemos un perro que se llama Toby. Es enorme y come muchísimo. Mi colegio es bastante tranquilo. Hay quinientos alumnos y es mixto. Hay campos de deporte y ordenadores en todas partes. Llego al colegio a pie porque está a dos minutos de aquí. Este verano espero ir a Francia con mi familia. Vamos a tomar el sol y comer y beber muchísimo. Me gusta la cocina francesa.

Un abrazo

Paula

8.7 Introduction to Higher Tier

This is what you need to know about the Higher Tier exam:

- The questions will be set in Spanish.
- There is an overlap between the questions you do if you enter for Foundation Tier and the questions you do if you enter for Higher Tier.
- Writing Tests 11, 12 and 13 would be considered overlap questions so attempt those before you go on to Writing Test 14.
- You need to know the number of words to write for your Board. Look in the Analysis of Syllabuses section at the front of this book.

Number of Words

- Do not write less than the number stipulated.
- Do not go over the number stipulated more than you need, to make the last sentence make sense.
- The Exam Boards say a word is 'a group of letters with a space either side'. Count your words as you go and note the number.

Mark Allocation

Marks for Higher Tier Writing are allocated for:
- Communication (getting the message across).
- Accuracy. (The fewer mistakes the more marks you get. But remember that your work will be marked positively. Your mistakes are not counted.)
- Richness of your vocabulary and expressions.

The type of question you will have to answer

Check with the list above for the requirements of your Board. Also check with your teacher. You will probably have to write a letter. If so, work through the advice given earlier in the chapter. It is very likely that you will have to write an account. It could be a description of an event or an accident, it could be a report destined for the police or for your school magazine. Sometimes the instructions ask you to write an account as part of a letter. If this is the case, do not write the beginning or end of the letter or include letter-material expressions like ¿cómo estás? but go straight into the account that you have to write.

8.8 Preparing for the examination

For letter-writing, see the advice given earlier in the chapter.

For account or compositions, you need to build up a stock of Spanish that you know is correct and that you can use with just about any task you are set. You can call this stock of Spanish your *Survival kit*.

8.9 Survival kit

You will find this list of preterites useful:

bebí	I drank
comí	I ate
compré	I bought
decidí (+ inf.)	I decided
di un paseo	I went for a walk
empecé a (+ inf.)	I started to
encontré	I found
encontré a	I met
entré en	I went in
fui	I went
llegué	I arrived
perdí	I lost
tomé	I took
vi	I saw
viajé	I travelled
visité	I visited
volví	I returned

Try and introduce an imperfect tense into your work. If you find this difficult, just mention the weather or what you were wearing.

Hacía buen tiempo.	It was nice weather.
Hacía sol.	It was sunny.
Llovía a cántaros y estábamos mojados hasta los huesos.	It was pouring and we were soaked to the skin.
Llevaba mi jersey nuevo.	I was wearing my new jersey.

Try to build up a collection of mark-winning phrases:

al + inf.	
e.g. **al llegar**	on arriving
antes de + inf.	
e.g. **antes de comer**	before eating
después de + inf.	
e.g. **después de comer**	after eating
para + inf.	
e.g. **para reservar un billete**	in order to book a ticket
sin perder un momento	without wasting a moment
¡Qué día!	What a day!
¡Qué barbaridad!	How awful!
desgraciadamente	unfortunately
afortunadamente	fortunately
luego	then
al día siguiente	on the following day
como estaba cansado/a	as I was tired
con mucho cuidado	with great care
dos minutos más tarde	two minutes later

Look through the questions in 8.11 and 8.12. After the questions there are suggested answers. These are not at a level that you cannot possibly hope to achieve, but they are at a level that can be reasonably expected of a student who has studied Spanish for two or three years and, though they may not gain full marks, they are of good enough quality to earn the full points available for the questions.

8.10 During the examination

Just before the examination, check the present, imperfect and preterite tenses of **mirar**, **comer** and **vivir**. As soon as you can after going into the examination room, after you have been given the signal to start, write them out on rough paper or on the actual examination paper. Then write out the expressions that you have learnt, i.e. **antes de comer**, **al llegar**, **llovía a cántaros** etc. During the exam, *tick them off as you use them!* Read through the questions carefully. Make a list of points you have to communicate or if you think that is too time-consuming underline them as they appear on the exam paper. *Tick them off as you answer them.*

In your mock exam, you should have made a note of how long each question took you. You should have worked on this in the weeks before the exam. Now set yourself a schedule that will give you time to check what you have written. *Remember:* once you have written something it is very difficult to spot the error. Once it is down on paper, somehow it looks right! *Think* carefully before you write. *Check* each verb with the lists you have written for *tense* and *ending* before you write it down.

Remember that what you write must be relevant to the question. Any material you have pre-learnt will not score any marks unless it is used in a question that is relevant to that material.

It is a good idea to work through the suggested answers that follow and see if you can learn parts of them off by heart. But remember if you do use these selections, they must be relevant to the question.

8.11 Higher Tier examination questions

Writing Test 14

Acabas de volver de una visita a España. Durante tu visita tuviste tres problemas. Tu amigo Pablo te ayudó en los tres casos. Escríbele.

- menciona los tres problemas
- menciona la ayuda que te prestó en cada caso
- da la gracias
- menciona el regalo que acompaña la carta
- menciona el resto de sus vacaciones

Student's answer

Estimado Pablo:

¿Cómo estás? Volví a Inglaterra sin incidente pero aquí hace muy mal tiempo.

Lo pasé muy bien en España; fui a discotecas, tomé el sol y bebí demasiado.

Estoy escribiendo para decirte gracias por todo lo que hiciste para mí. El primer desastre ocurrió cuando perdí mí dinero en la playa. Luego estuve enfermo y no podía hacer nada. Llamaste al médico.

Más tarde pude ir a la playa donde encontré a mucha gente interesante.

Te doy las gracias sinceramente por todo. Espero que os guste el regalo. Espero que pases bien el resto de tus vacaciones.

Te saluda atentamente

A. Whittle

Examiner's comment

The candidate must realise that there are nine items which he/she has to communicate. It is spelt out on the question paper. Yet only two problems are mentioned and for the first problem the help you received is not mentioned. So the maximum content mark is 6 out of 9. Moreover, the introduction and the end of the letter are more like a business letter than a letter to a friend. You would lose more marks here.

Some of the Spanish you introduce is perfectly correct but it is not relevant to the question. It is obvious padding. If the question had been to describe what you did in Spain this material would be perfectly acceptable. There is no date or town at the beginning.

Please see the suggested version later.

Writing Test 15

Durante tus vacaciones en España, tienes un accidente. Un coche te atropella. Tienes que escribir un informe para la policía.
Menciona:

- adónde ibas
- cómo era el coche
- cómo era el conductor
- tus heridas
- el tratamiento
- el efecto de tu accidente en tus vacaciones

Student's answer

Voy describir lo que ocurrió esta manaña. Estoy turista británica y mi hotel se llama el Hotel Sol. Mi madre me mandó al supermercado a comprar loción bronceadora. Para ir al supermercado tuve que cruzar la calle. Encontré un paso de peatones y crucé. Un Ford Escort negro no paró. Frenó fuertemente pero el coche me hizo caer.

El conductor era joven, llevaba gafas de sol, tenía unos veinticinco años y tenía pelo largo y negro.

Al caerme, perdí dos dientes y me hice una herida en la cara. Afortunadamente no tenía huesos rotos. Una ambulancia me llévo al hospital pero salí a las dos horas.

El médico ha dicho que tendré que guardar cama durante dos días.

Examiner's comment

On line 1, there should be 'a' between 'voy' and 'describir'. 'Estoy' should be 'Soy'. The candidate has obviously built up a survival kit of preterites, imperfects and expressions and I have underlined them in the text.

He/she has done well to do this: the expressions are all relevant to the question and so will score marks.

Perhaps the candidate could have written 'sin perder un momento' before 'encontré', 'desgraciadamente' before 'un Ford Escort', and 'Después de examinarme' before 'el médico'. All these are expressions from the Survival kit mentioned above.

Writing Test 16

Escribe una carta a un hotel para reservar habitaciones. Menciona estos puntos:

- las fechas de tu estancia
- la persona que te acompañará
- el tipo de habitaciones que quieres
- el precio
- menciona otros dos puntos sobre las habitaciones
- pide información sobre los sitios de interés
- tu medio de transporte en España

Student's answer

Carlisle
20 de mayo

Querido señor:

Quiero reservar una habitación el treinta de mayo hasta el cinco de junio. Seremos dos, mi hermana y yo. Quiero una habitación con dos camas individuales y un cuarto de baño. ¿Puede decirme cuánto cuesta? También quiero una habitación con vistas al mar y en el primer piso. ¿A qué distancia está el Parador del centro de Toledo? ¿Hay parking? Queremos visitar Madrid. ¿Vale la pena? ¿Tiene Vd. Información sobre Madrid?

Adiós

P. Reid

Examiner's comment

'Querido señor' and 'Adiós' are not the best ways to start and finish a formal letter. See the suggested versions for better versions. The candidate has used 'quiero' three times. He/she would attract more marks if he/she used 'quisiera' and 'me gustaría' on the second and third occasion. You are asked to say how you will be travelling: you have asked if there is a car-park. This is relying a lot on the examiner's good will. You could be travelling by train and thinking of hiring a car once you have arrived. It is much better to spell out what you are asked to communicate. See the suggested answer.

Apart from that the level of Spanish is excellent and should score full points.

8.12 Higher Tier practice examination questions

Here are some questions for you to practise on. Suggested answers are given at the end.

Writing Test 17

Escribe un artículo sobre tu colegio anterior. Menciona estos puntos:

- una descripción del colegio

- un suceso inolvidable
- un profesor
- la razón por la cual te marchaste
- tus impresiones de tu colegio actual

Writing Test 18

Ganaste un concurso y el premio es una tarde con una superestrella. Después tienes que escribir un informe. Menciona estos puntos:

- cómo ganaste el premio
- cómo te preparaste para tu tarde
- dónde fuisteis y qué hicisteis
- una descripción de la superestrella
- tus planes para ver a la superestrella otra vez

Writing Test 19

Quieres trabajar en España. Escribe una carta a un hotel. Menciona estos puntos:

- por qué quieres ir a España
- el tipo de trabajo que te gusta
- tu experiencia
- tus idiomas
- te gusta trabajar con gente
- la duración de tu estancia
- el dinero
- comida y alojamiento

Writing Test 20

Lees una revista española y ves un concurso. El premio es un viaje por todo el mundo. Decides participar en el concurso. Tienes que escribir un artículo. En el artículo menciona estos puntos:

- por qué te gusta la revista
- por qué quieres viajar
- la persona que te acompañará
- adónde irás y cuándo
- por qué mereces ganar el premio

Writing Test 21

Tu amiga María quiere hacer un curso de inglés en los Estados Unidos. Escríbele una carta. Menciona estos puntos:

- dile que los cursos en Inglaterra son mejores
- que quieres verla
- invítala a visitarte en Inglaterra
- las cosas que podríais hacer en Inglaterra
- una persona especial que quiere verla

Writing Test 22

Al volver de una visita a España descubres que has dejado algo en tu hotel. Escribe una carta a tu hotel mencionando estos puntos:

- el número de tu habitación
- las fechas de tu visita
- lo que perdiste
- lo que el hotel debe hacer si encuentran la cosa perdida
- una queja contra el hotel

Writing Test 23

Durante una visita a España pierdes algo y un español te ayuda a recuperar lo que perdiste. Describe el incidente. Menciona estos puntos:

- dónde estuviste
- lo que hacías
- cómo perdiste el artículo

- la persona que te ayudó
- lo que hizo

Writing Test 24

Acabas de volver de España. Escribe una carta a tu amiga española describiendo el viaje de regreso. Menciona estos puntos:

- un problema antes de llegar al aeropuerto
- un retraso
- lo que hacías para divertirte
- una persona a quien encontraste
- el resto del viaje

Writing Test 25

Tus padres van a intercambiar tu casa con una familia española durante las vacaciones. Escribe una descripción de tu casa. Menciona estos puntos:

- las habitaciones
- los muebles
- el jardín
- cosas de interés cerca de tu casa
- transporte público

Examiner's tip

Always try to give yourself plenty of time at the end of the exam to check your work. *Never* finish your exam early. You should use every minute in the exam.

Writing Test 26

Vas a pasar unos días en un albergue juvenil en España. Escribe una carta al albergue. Menciona estos puntos:

- tus visitas a España en el pasado
- detalles de tu llegada y salida
- por qué vas a España
- pide información sobre los alrededores
- pide información sobre el albergue y su situación

8.13 Suggested answers to examination questions

Writing Test 14

Uttoxeter
9 de junio

Querido Pablo:

¿Cómo estás? Volví a Inglaterra sin incidente pero aquí hace muy mal tiempo.

Estoy escribiendo para darte las gracias por todo lo que hiciste por mí. El primer desastre ocurrió cuando perdí mi dinero en la playa. Afortunadamente me prestaste dinero. Luego estuve enfermo y no podía hacer nada. Llamaste al médico. Luego hubo un retraso con el vuelo de regreso y me dejaste quedarme una noche más.

Te doy las gracias sinceramente por todo. Espero que te guste el regalo que mando como agradecimiento.

Espero que pases bien el resto de tus vacaciones.

Un abrazo

A Whittle

Writing Test 15

Voy a describir lo que ocurrió esta mañana. Soy turista británica y mi hotel se llama el Hotel Sol. Mi madre me mandó al supermercado a comprar loción bronceadora. Para ir al supermercado tuve que cruzar la calle. Encontré un paso de peatones y crucé. Un Ford Escort negró no paró. Frenó fuertemente pero el coche me hizo caer.

El conductor era joven, llevaba gafas de sol, tenía unos veinticinco años y tenía pelo largo y negro.

Al caerme, perdí dos dientes y me hice una herida en la cara. Afortunadamente no tenía huesos rotos. Una ambulancia me llevó al hospital pero salí a las dos horas.

El médico ha dicho que tendré que guardar cama durante dos días.

Writing Test 16

Carlisle
20 de mayo

Muy señor mío:

Quiero reservar una habitación el treinta de mayo hasta el cinco de junio. Seremos dos, mi hermana y yo. Quisiera una habitación con dos camas individuales y un cuarto de baño. ¿Puede decirme cuánto cuesta? También me gustaría una habitación con vistas al mar y en el primer piso.

¿A qué distancia está el Parador del centro de Toledo? Vamos a llegar allí en coche. ¿Hay parking? Queremos visitar Madrid. ¿Vale la pena? Tiene vd. información sobre Madrid?

Le saluda atentamente

P. Reid

Writing Test 17

Mi primer colegio era bastante viejo. Había laboratorios, un laboratorio de lenguas pero desafortunadamente no había una piscina. El colegio se encontraba en el campo y había vistas maravillosas.

Un día ¡hubo un incendio! El incendio tuvo lugar en el laboratorio de química y tuvimos que salir al campo de deportes. Había mucho humo. Los profesores pasaron lista y cinco minutos más tarde los bomberos llegaron y apagaron el fuego sin perder un momento.

No olvidaré nunca a mi profesor de español. Era muy simpático e hizo mucho por nosotros. Organizó un intercambio con España y fuimos todos a Granada. ¡Lo pasé bomba! Nuestro profesor de español nos acompañó y nos compró helados todos los días.

Desgraciadamente tuve que cambiar de colegio. Mi padre cambió de trabajo y tuvimos que mudarnos de casa.

Me encanta este colegio y tengo muchos amigos aquí. Las facilidades son muy buenas pero echo de menos a mis amigos de allí … y a mi profesor de español.

Writing Test 18

Cuando estuve en España, gané un concurso de tenis y el premio era una tarde con Anita Suárez. ¡No podía creerlo! Para prepararme para la tarde con Anita, fui a las tiendas y compré mucha ropa nueva. Fui a la peluquería y también le compré flores. Nos encontramos en El Tulipán, restaurante muy famoso en Madrid. No tuve que pagar nada. Anita era muy simpática y estaba con su novio. Ninguno de los dos habla inglés así que tuve que hablar en español toda la tarde. La cena era riquísima. Comí sopa de verduras, filete de pescado con patatas y huevo y después comí un helado enorme.

Anita llevaba una falda gris de seda y una blusa blanca. Era muy guapa. Llevaba gafas de sol todo el tiempo. Hablaba de sus planes para el futuro: va a casarse y quizás irá a los Estados Unidos a jugar allí.

Después de cenar, Anita me dio dos entradas para un gran campeonato de tenis así que podré ver a Anita en Londres el mes que viene. ¡Qué suerte!

Writing Test 19

Blackpool
23 de marzo

Estimado Señor:

He visto su anuncio en el periódico y me gustaría trabajar en su hotel. Quiero trabajar en España porque estoy aprendiendo español y quiero conocer las costumbres de España. Podría trabajar en el bar lavando los vasos porque he hecho este trabajo ya en Inglaterra durante un período de experiencia de trabajo. También he trabajado en una tienda vendiendo ropa. Llevo cuatro años aprendiendo español y francés y hablo las dos lenguas casi perfectamente. También me gusta conocer gente y me gustó muchísimo mi trabajo en un hotel.

¿Puedo trabajar seis semanas durante julio y agosto? ¿Cuánto ganaré? ¿Tendré que pagar mis comidas y mi alojamiento?

Le saluda atentamente

Alex Young

Writing Test 20

Acabo de comprar la revista y estoy seguro que es la mejor revista que he leído. Me interesan los artículos sobre la moda y el deporte. También los artículos sobre los problemas de los jóvenes en España son interesantes.

Me gusta viajar porque quiero conocer otros países del mundo y quiero hacer amigos en todas partes. Viajaría con mi hermano y mi hermana porque aparte de ser miembros de mi familia son mis mejores amigos.

Los dos sitios que me interesan más son Nueva York porque he visto la ciudad tantas veces en la televisión y Honolulú porque me han dicho que el clima allí es perfecto. Me gustaría hacer el viaje durante las vacaciones de verano porque quiero volver antes del cinco de setiembre.

Yo creo que deberían darme el premio porque nunca he ido en el extranjero. Mis padres son muy pobres y si no gano quizás nunca podré ir al extranjero.

Writing Test 21

Londres
12 de marzo

Querida María:

Gracias por la carta que me mandaste. Estoy muy decepcionada. ¿Por qué no vienes aquí para aprender inglés? Yo creo que tus planes son una pérdida de dinero. Hay cursos similares en Inglaterra y probablemente son mejores. ¿Por qué no vienes a quedarte conmigo y con mi familia? Es la mejor manera de aprender inglés. Si vienes, podemos ir a conciertos y visitar los sitios interesantes de Londres. Hay otra razón: Peter, el chico a quien conociste el año pasado quiere verte.

Un abrazo

Margaret

Writing Test 22

Londres
18 de junio

Estimado Señor:

Acabo de pasar una semana en su hotel en la habitación número trece. Llegué el dos de junio y me marché el nueve de junio. Dejé algo de valor en mi habitación. Era un reloj de oro que me regaló mi padre. ¿Puede Vd. buscarlo? Si lo encuentra, haga el favor de mandarlo a mi dirección.

Acabo de descubrir que mi traje nuevo ha sido estropeado. No me lo puse nunca durante mi estancia así que los daños ocurrieron en mi habitación. Quiero que Vd. haga algo para solucionar este problema.

Le saluda atentamente

D Ferguson

Writing Test 23

Mi novio y yo estábamos pasando las vacaciones a orillas del mar y un día decidimos comer un helado porque hacía buen tiempo. Nos sentamos en un muro al lado del puerto. Detrás de nosotros un pescador pescaba con una caña de pescar. Al terminar los helados decidimos volver al hotel y nos marchamos en bicicleta. Desafortunadamente nos habíamos dejado una bolsa en el muro y había una cámera fotográfica dentro. No notamos lo que habíamos hecho hasta el momento que llegamos a nuestro hotel. Afortunadamente el pescador había visto lo que había pasado y vino a nuestro hotel con la bolsa.

Writing Test 24

Bedford
12 de mayo

Querida Marta:

¿Cómo estás? Espero que todo vaya bien. El viaje de regreso fue muy interesante. Al salir de tu casa, tomé un taxi. Cuando estuve a cinco kilómetros del aeropuerto el taxi tuvo un pinchazo per afortunadamente el taxista lo reparó en cinco minutos.

Después de llegar al aeropuerto fui a la oficina de Iberia y me dijeron que había un retraso de cinco horas porque había niebla en el aeropuerto de Londres. ¡Cinco horas! ¡Qué barbaridad!

Afortunadamente tenía una novela conmigo y me senté en un banco. Escuché música en mi estéreo personal y comí mis bocadillos. Un español vino a hablar conmigo y luego me invitó a tomar algo con él. Fui al café con él y bebí una limonada. Hablamos en español todo el tiempo y aprendí mucho. Finalmente Iberia dijo que el vuelo iba a salir y dije adiós tristemente a mi nuevo amigo y fui a bordo. El vuelo transcurrió sin incidente y la comida durante el vuelo fue excelente. Al llegar a Belfast, estaba lloviendo a cántaros como siempre. Me sentía bastante cansada y tenía hambre. Mis padres estaban allí y no fui directamente a casa. Fuimos a comer una hamburguesa antes de volver a casa.

Un abrazo

Lizzie

Writing Test 25

Descripción de mi casa:

Nuestra casa es bastante grande y tiene dos pisos y un total de ocho habitaciones. En la planta baja hay una cocina, un comedor y una sala de estar. En el primer piso hay cuatro dormitorios y un cuarto de baño.

Los muebles en la casa son todos nuevos. En los dormitorios hay una cama individual en cada dormitorio salvo en un dormitorio donde hay una cama doble. En la cocina hay una nevera, un lavaplatos y una lavadora.

Hay un pequeño jardín y hay muchas tiendas en la localidad. Hay también un cine y un teatro muy cerca. Se puede tomar un autobús de enfrente de la casa al centro de la ciudad.

Writing Test 26

Preston
5 de mayo

Muy señor mío:

Le escribo porque quiero pasar unos días en su albergue durante el verano. He visitado España muchas veces pero me hospedé en hoteles y campings solamente.

Llego el dos de junio y me marcho el nueve de junio. Quiero pasar tiempo en España porque estoy aprendiendo español y tengo amigos en la ciudad.

¿Puede Vd. mandarme detalles sobre el albergue y los sitios de interés en la región?

¿Puede decirme cómo puedo encontrar el albergue? Está en el centro de la ciudad?

Le saluda atentamente

J Harris

8.14 Coursework

Writing coursework

Instead of doing what is called a terminal exam in Writing, you might decide to offer coursework as an alternative.

This is what you need to know:

- The requirements vary slightly from Board to Board. Your teacher has a copy of all the regulations. First read the Exam Board analysis at the beginning of this book.
- You will probably have to offer about three pieces of work chosen from the Areas of Experience.
- You can use materials to help you with your work, e.g. articles from a magazine.
- You cannot copy directly from these articles.
- Your teacher can give you guidance before you start writing but not after.
- You may be allowed to do some of the work at home or in the computer room. But at least one piece of work will have to be done under controlled conditions, i.e. under examination conditions in your classroom.
- You can use a dictionary at all times.
- Your teacher will give you guidance as to how long each piece of work should be. MEG requires 150 words for each piece of work if you are aiming for B–A*. Edexcel (London) requires a total of 500–600 words over the three pieces. NEAB requires between 300–500 words over the three pieces.
- Your teacher will have a long list of possible topics that you might like to choose from. The kind of things the Exam Boards suggest are:

  – tell the story of a film you have seen

– read Spanish materials and English materials on a topic and then write in Spanish about the difference in points of view
– write a diary of a person involved in an adventure
– write a poem, short story or a sketch
– describe a town
– write about your uniform
– write about a character in a film or a book
– your ideal school
– use of new technology
– your life-style and exercise and eating habits
– an article on a famous person
– an account of something that happened to you
– a letter to an agony aunt
– your reaction to a Spanish song
– Spanish TV
– description of your area or a Spanish region/town
– transport between Spain and England
– special occasions in the UK, e.g. Christmas
– an account of work experience
– your ideal job
– an advert to promote, e.g. anti-smoking
– event(s) in Spain
– an environmental issue
– planning a holiday in Spain

What happens to your coursework?

Your teacher will give your work a mark and the Exam Board will look at a sample of work from your school to see if your teacher has been too lenient or too severe. This is called moderation. When your teacher is allocating a mark to your work, he/she will be looking for:

- the length
- the content
- the accuracy
- the quality of the language

Tips for writing coursework

Here are some tips for writing a good piece of coursework:

- Build up a collection of phrases and sentences in Spanish that you know are correct. Do not experiment when it comes to writing your coursework pieces.
- Try to express an opinion about what you are writing about: say whether you think it is good or bad and give reasons.
- Try to use a variety of tenses in your work.
- Try to use adverbs and adjectives.
- Find an article on which to base your writing.

Example

Here is an example of a piece of Spanish which could have been offered for coursework. *You must not use this as it is against the regulations to copy other people's work.* However it may give you ideas.

It is a diary of someone who has experienced an exciting incident. It is a good topic to choose because you can use past, present and future tenses and as the incident is imaginary you can use the adjectives and adverbs that you like.

Notice the use of past, present and future tenses, the **tener** constructions, the adjectives **enorme**, **suculento**, **lejano**, the adverbs **desgraciadamente**, **quizás**, **profundamente**.

Dos días en una isla desierta

Lunes 3 de mayo

11.00 ¿Qué voy a hacer? Esta mañana mi barco de vela se hundió (*sank*) y desgraciadamente (*unfortunately*) mis dos compañeros murieron ahogados (*drowned*). Me encuentro aquí sin comida, sin agua en una isla desierta. Iré a buscar agua.

14.00 ¡Por fin! He encontrado un arroyo (*stream*) con agua limpia. Ahora no tengo sed pero tengo mucha hambre. Intentaré encontrar fruta.

16.00 Tengo suerte. He encontrado fruta y también cogí unos peces suculentos. Voy a hacer un fuego para poder cocinar los peces.

19.00 Hice un fuego con madera (*wood*) y hojas (*leaves*) y comí bien. Voy a dormir en esta caverna (*cave*) seca. ¡Ojalá (*I hope*) vengan a rescatarme (*rescue me*) mañana!

Martes 4 de mayo

15.00 Dormí profundamente (*deeply*) pero sigo esperando rescate. Vi un avión lejano esta mañana pero el piloto no me vio. En seguida construiré un fuego enorme con mucho humo (*smoke*) como señal (*signal*).

19.00 Tengo miedo. Quizás (*perhaps*) haya animales en esta isla. Voy a dormir pronto cerca del fuego. Menos mal (*thank goodness*) que hace buen tiempo.

Miércoles 5 de mayo

¡Un helicóptero ha llegado hace unos momentos! ¡La pesadilla (*nightmare*) está terminada!

Complete GCSE paper

Introduction

In this chapter you have a complete Foundation and Higher Tier GCSE paper written by a Chief Examiner. Probably the best time to attempt it is a week or two before your Spanish exams start. The recordings for the Listening and Speaking tests are on the CD accompanying this book. The transcripts of the recordings and the suggested answers are also given later in the book.

- Try to do the papers under exam conditions.
- Try to adhere to the times that your Board allows for each paper.
- Ask your teacher to mark your work for the writing paper.

The examination paper

LETTS SCHOOL EXAMINATIONS BOARD

General Certificate of Education Examination

SPANISH

Answer all four papers (Listening, Speaking, Reading, Writing).

Answer all the questions relating to your Tier (Foundation or Higher).

Listening

Instructions for candidates:

Foundation Tier: attempt sections 1 and 2
Higher Tier: attempt sections 2 and 3
You may use a dictionary during the preparation period before the exam.

Section 1 (Foundation Tier)

Recording 21

Valencia

A Spaniard is talking about Valencia. Answer these questions about the city.

(a) Where in Spain is Valencia? .... (1)
(b) Why is it an important city? .... (1)
(c) Why do many English people like to live there? .... (1)
(d) In which month are the famous festivals? .... (1)

(4)

Recording 22

Estás en un café. Cada cliente pide algo de comer y una bebida. ¿Qué piden los cinco clientes?

Cliente 1

De comer

(a) ☐ **(b)** ☐ **(c)** ☐ **(d)** ☐ **(e)** ☐ **(f)** ☐

De beber

(a) ☐ **(b)** ☐ **(c)** ☐ **(d)** ☐ **(e)** ☐ **(f)** ☐

Cliente 2

De comer

(a) ☐ **(b)** ☐ **(c)** ☐ **(d)** ☐ **(e)** ☐ **(f)** ☐

De beber

(a) ☐ **(b)** ☐ **(c)** ☐ **(d)** ☐ **(e)** ☐ **(f)** ☐

Cliente 3

De comer

(a) ☐ **(b)** ☐ **(c)** ☐ **(d)** ☐ **(e)** ☐ **(f)** ☐

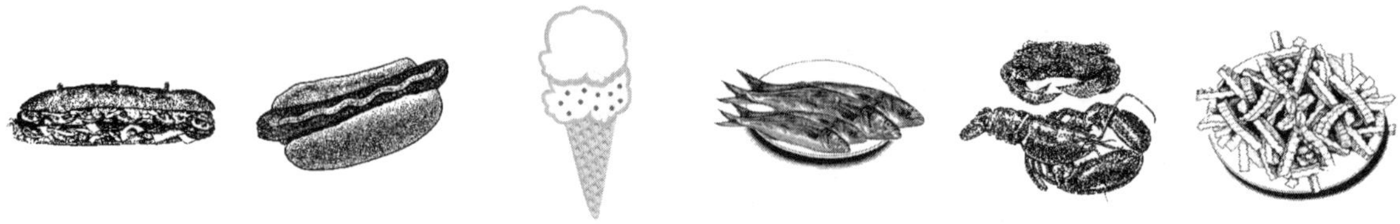

De beber

(a) ☐ **(b)** ☐ **(c)** ☐ **(d)** ☐ **(e)** ☐ **(f)** ☐

Cliente 4

De comer

(a) ☐ **(b)** ☐ **(c)** ☐ **(d)** ☐ **(e)** ☐ **(f)** ☐

De beber

(a) ☐ **(b)** ☐ **(c)** ☐ **(d)** ☐ **(e)** ☐ **(f)** ☐

Cliente 5

De comer

(a) ☐ **(b)** ☐ **(c)** ☐ **(d)** ☐ **(e)** ☐ **(f)** ☐

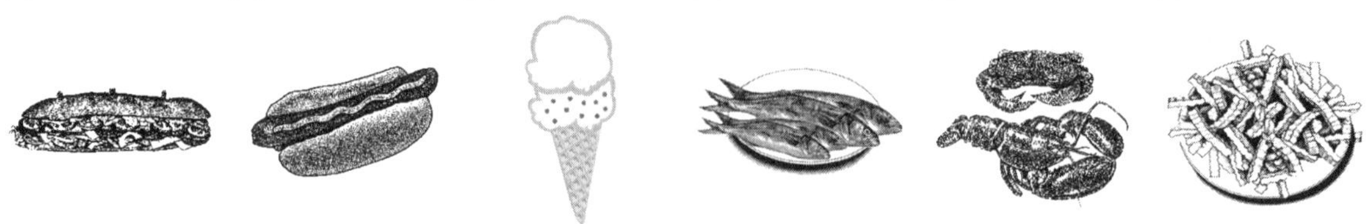

De beber

(a) ☐ **(b)** ☐ **(c)** ☐ **(d)** ☐ **(e)** ☐ **(f)** ☐

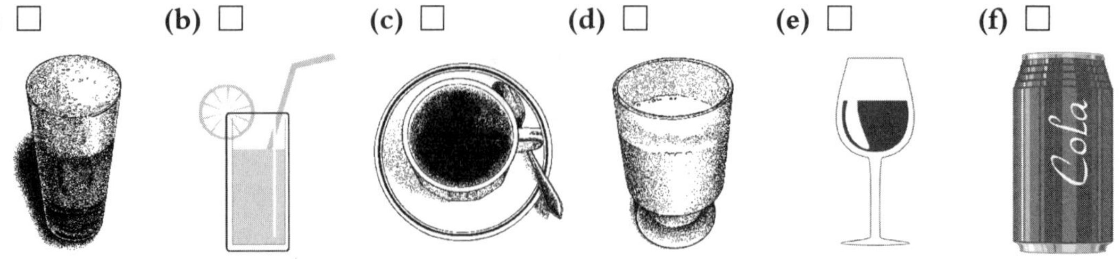

(10)

Recording 23

De compras

Estás en el Corte Inglés. Quieres comprar una blusa, una maleta, unos plátanos y una corbata.

1 ¿A qué planta vas para la blusa?

- **(a)** 3a planta ☐
- **(b)** 2a planta ☐
- **(c)** 1a planta ☐
- **(d)** planta baja ☐

2 ¿A qué planta vas para la maleta?

- **(a)** 3a planta ☐
- **(b)** 2a planta ☐
- **(c)** 1a planta ☐
- **(d)** planta baja ☐

3 ¿A qué planta vas para los plátanos?

- **(a)** 3a planta ☐
- **(b)** 2a planta ☐
- **(c)** 1a planta ☐
- **(d)** planta baja ☐

4 ¿A qué planta vas para la corbata?

- **(a)** 3a planta ☐
- **(b)** 2a planta ☐
- **(c)** 1a planta ☐
- **(d)** planta baja ☐

(4)

Section 2 (Foundation and Higher Tiers)

Recording 24

El futuro

Escucha lo que dice José y después Lolita sobre sus asignaturas, sus ambiciones y sus pasatiempos. Las asignaturas que no les gustan ya están escritas. Rellena los huecos.

José

Asignatura que no le gusta ......los idiomas..

1 Asignatura preferida .... (1)

2 Ambición .... (1)

3 Pasatiempo preferido .... (1)

Lolita

Asignatura que no le gusta .....la historia..

4 Asignatura preferida .... (1)

5 Ambición .... (1)

6 Pasatiempo preferido .... (1)

(6)

Recording 25

El médico

Estás enfermo/a y vas al médico. ¿Cuáles son las causas de tu enfermedad? Pon una x en las dos casillas correctas.

(a) ☐ **(b)** ☐ **(c)** ☐ **(d)** ☐

(2)

Section 3 (Higher Tier)

Recording 26

El cine Astoria

Llamas al cine y escuchas un mensaje automático. Di si las observaciones son verdaderas o falsas.

	verdadero	**falso**
Ponen *Corazón de acero* durante tres días	☐	☐
Corazón de acero es una película de amor	☐	☐
Corazón de acero es subtitulado	☐	☐
Los muertos es una película de miedo	☐	☐
Ponen *Los muertos* durante una semana	☐	☐
Los muertos tiene lugar en Gran Bretaña	☐	☐
No me toques es una película de risa	☐	☐
No me toques ha ganado un premio	☐	☐
Se pone cada película tres veces al día	☐	☐
La última sesión es a medianoche	☐	☐

(10)

Recording 27

El tiempo

Quieres ir a la playa hoy lunes, mañana o pasado mañana. Escuchas el pronóstico del tiempo. ¿Qué día escoges? Pon una x en la casilla correcta.

(a) lunes ☐
(b) martes ☐
(c) miércoles ☐

(1)

Recording 28

Un señor

¿Qué tipo de persona es este señor? Pon una x en la casilla correcta.

(a) Su vida social le es muy importante. ☐
(b) Quiere mantenerse en buena condición física. ☐
(c) Su trabajo es la cosa más importante de su vida. ☐

(1)

Recording 29

Un empleo

Oyes un anuncio en la radio. ¿Cuáles son las dos ventajas de este empleo?

....

....

(2)

Recording 30

Conversación de novios

Escucha a Conchita y a Ramón. ¿Cómo se sienten? Pon una x ena la casilla correcta.

Conchita
(a) contenta ☐
(b) orgullosa ☐
(c) enfadada ☐
(d) avergonzada ☐

Ramón
(a) contento ☐
(b) orgulloso ☐
(c) enfadado ☐
(d) avergonzado ☐

(2)

Recording 31

María

Escucha lo que dice María. Pon una x en las casillas correctas.

1 María habla de

(a) sus vacaciones ☐
(b) una enfermedad ☐
(c) un regalo ☐
(d) un crimen ☐

2 Se siente

(a) agradecida ☐
(b) enfadada ☐
(c) celosa ☐
(d) sospechosa ☐

(2)

Speaking (Foundation and Higher Tiers)

Instructions to candidates:
Foundation Tier: attempt Role-plays 1 and 2
Higher Tier: attempt Role-plays 2 and 3
You must carry out the tasks specified.
You must assume that the Examiner speaks no English.
Information for Candidates:
You may use a bilingual dictionary in the preparation period before the exam.

Role-play 1

You are in a Madrid railway station and you want a second class return ticket to Oviedo. Your teacher will play the part of the ticket-office clerk.

1

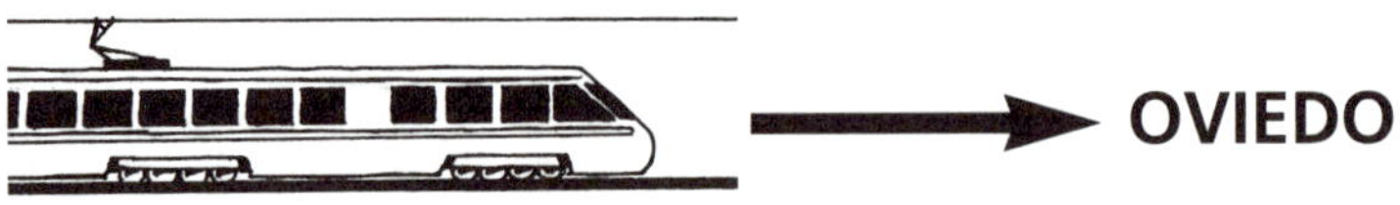

2

3

4

5

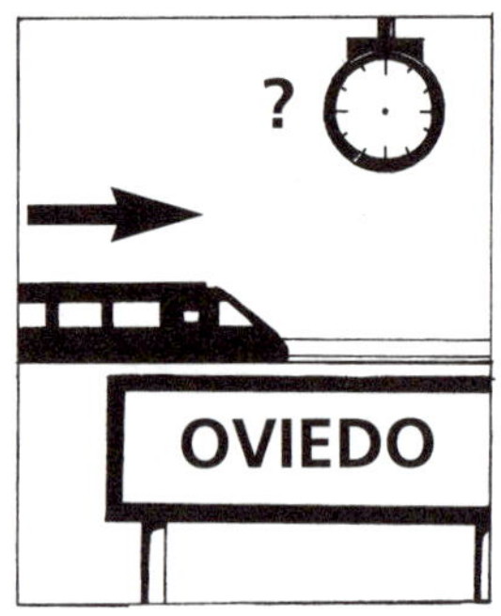

Role-play 2

Your English friend who speaks no Spanish has a headache after sun-bathing on the beach. You go to see the doctor. Your teacher will play the part of the Spanish doctor.

1 Describe los síntomas de tu amigo/a.
2 Explica por qué tu amigo/a no habla.
3 Describe la causa de los síntomas.
4 Contesta a la pregunta.
5 Da detalles de vuestra vuelta a Inglaterra.

Role-play 3

Your Spanish friend`s parent has made some suggestions for the day. The suggestions are: either the beach, the cinema, fishing, a disco or a football match. You need to choose an activity, discuss when to go and how to get there. Your teacher will play the part of the Spanish friend and may well disagree with your preferences.

1 Propon una actividad.
2 Cuando tu amigo/a dice que no, insiste y da una razón.
3 Propon una hora para la actividad.
4 Cuando tu amigo/a no esté de acuerdo, propon otra hora.
5 Propon un sitio donde podéis encontraros y un medio de transporte.

Reading

Instructions to candidates:
Foundation Tier: attempt sections 1 and 2
Higher Tier: attempt sections 2 and 3
You may use a dictionary throughout.

Section 1 (Foundation Tier)

1

EL CORTE INGLES

TODO PARA TUS NIÑOS

ABRIGOS	8500
CALCETINES	450
BLUSAS	925
ZAPATOS	5300
GUANTES	975

Especialistas en ropa de invierno

1 You see a leaflet advertising a store that sells children's clothes.

(a) How much are gloves? (1)

(b) What kind of children's clothes does the store specialise in? (1)

2 You are about to go onto the beach. You see this sign. What is forbidden apart from camping? (2)

3 While on holiday, you want to enrol on a tennis course run by your hotel.

HOTEL SOL
CLASES DE TENIS

¡GRATUITO! ________________
NOMBRE ________________
NACIONALIDAD ________________
NUMERO DE HABITACION ________________
¿Desde hace cuántos años juegas al tenis?
____
¿Juegas en un equipo?
____

Apart from name, nationality and room number, what other information are you asked for? (2)

4 You are expecting your Spanish friend and all his family to visit you in England. You receive a letter from your friend's father.

Sevilla 19 de mayo de 1994

Querido amigo:

Esperamos nuestra visita con mucha impaciencia. En sólo veinte días estaremos en Inglaterra. ¡Qué bien!

¿Me puedes hacer un favor? ¿Puedes ir a la oficina de turismo de tu pueblo a buscar información sobre la región?

Mi esposa se interesa por los muebles antiguos y a mí me gustan las iglesias viejas. A mi hijo le gusta el deporte, sobre todo el baloncesto. A mi hija no le gustan los deportes. Ella prefiere bailar.

¿Puedes buscar información sobre estas cuatro cosas?

Sin más

Juliano

el padre de tu amigo español

(a) What is the chief interest of the mother? (1)
(b) What is the father interested in? (1)
(c) What is the favourite sport of the son? (1)
(d) What is the favourite activity of the daughter? (1)

MEG

2 En tu hotel hay este aviso en la puerta de tu habitación:

Estimado Cliente

Bienvenido a nuestro hotel. Esperamos que su estancia con nosotros sea agradable. He aquí información sobre el hotel.

El desayuno se sirve entre las 7 y las 9.30. Está incluido en el precio de su habitación. No se sirve el almuerzo en el hotel. Hay un restaurante enfrente llamado 'El Stop'. Su especialidad: boquerones, langosta, mejillones, calamares, gambas.

Por la tarde la cena se sirve de las 9.00 hasta las 10.30. El hotel está abierto hasta las 11.30. A partir de esa hora nuestros clientes necesitarán la llave de su habitación: esa llave abrirá la puerta de entrada.

El teléfono en su habitación es fácil de usar. Bomberos 334455, Policía 666666, Portería 2343, Servicios Médicos de Urgencia 342573, Taxis 348239.

En la recepción tenemos juegos y juguetes a disposición de nuestros clientes. Para mayores tenemos cartas.

Haga el favor de dejar sus joyas, etc en la caja fuerte en la recepción.

Le deseamos una feliz estancia.

La dirección

1 ¿Cuál es la especialidad de 'El Stop'?

(a) aves ☐
(b) carnes ☐
(c) pescado ☐
(d) mariscos ☐ (1)

2 Si sales hasta muy tarde, ¿qué debes llevar contigo?

.... (1)

3 Si estás enfermo/a, ¿a qué número debes llamar?

.... (1)

4 ¿Qué juego se ofrece para los adultos?

.... (1)

5 ¿Qué servicio hay para tus objetos de valor?

.... (1)

(5)

3 Tus amigos son estudiantes y buscan trabajo. ¿Deben buscar trabajo en qué empresa?

(a)

Tradiciones

– nuestra especialidad – los platos típicos
– abierto todos los días del año
– nuestro personal es experto
– aire acondicionado
c/ Buenos Aires 12 Tel: 2324903

(b)

ROVI

– ordenadores de toda clase
– servicio excelente
– todo nuestro equipo garantizado
– entregamos el mismo día
c/ Hermanos Miralles 13 Tel: 6738493

(c)

Hermanos Teruel

– abogados
– mucha experiencia
– satisfacción garantizada
– servicio rápido
c/ Italia 34 Tel: 3458239

(d)

Herraiz

– servicio de traducción
– muy rápido
– muy barato
– todo nuestro personal es nativo
c/ Salamanca 45 Tel: 2346234

(e)

Díaz y Díaz

– ingenieros y constructores de edicificos nuevos
– llama para hablarnos
– el nombre más conocido de España
c/ Echegarray 23 Tel: 9349235

(f)

Alonso Pérez

– mudanzas
– España o el extranjero
– el más barato
c/ Iglesia 566 Tel: 9345265

¿**(a) (b) (c) (d) (e)** o **(f)**?

1 Pablo estudia arquitectura ☐
2 Ana estudia idiomas ☐
3 Cristina estudia informática ☐
4 Pedro estudia derecho ☐
5 Enrique estudia hostelería ☐

(5)

Section 2 (Foundation and Higher Tiers)

1 Lee esta carta.

Madrid, 16 de junio

Estimado Señor Gómez:

Le escribo porque me encuentro en paro. Tengo cinco hijos y mi esposa no trabaja tampoco.
¿Hay puestos disponibles en su fábrica? He trabajado hasta recientemente como mecánico pero puedo hacer de todo salvo levantar cosas porque me duele el hombro. Me gustaría trabajar en la producción de coches. Puedo trabajar los fines de semana pero las noches no, porque tengo que ayudar a mi esposa con los niños.

En espera de su contestación
Le saluda atentamente

Pablo Blanco

1 ¿Por qué escribe Pablo esta carta?

.... (1)

2 ¿Cuántos son en total en la familia de Pablo?

(a) 4 ☐ **(c)** 6 ☐

(b) 5 ☐ **(d)** 7 ☐

3 ¿Cuál es el trabajo normal de Pablo?

(a) ☐ **(b)** ☐ **(c)** ☐ **(d)** ☐

4 ¿Pablo tiene problema en qué parte del cuerpo?

(a) ☐ **(b)** ☐ **(c)** ☐ **(d)** ☐

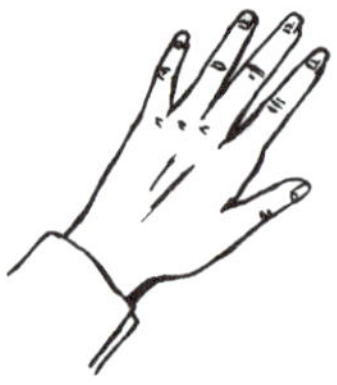

5 ¿Qué producto produce el Señor Gómez?

(a) ☐ **(b)** ☐ **(c)** ☐ **(d)** ☐

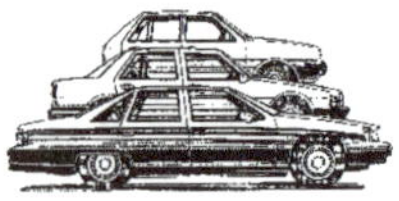

(5)

2 Lee este folleto que ofrece transporte barato.

Red Nacional de Ferrocarriles Españoles

RENFE 'OFERTA OTOÑO'

OFERTA ESPECIAL PARA OTOÑO SOLO

REBAJAS REBAJAS REBAJAS

No sólo para los jóvenes sino para toda la familia

Descuento del 50% para familias

Parejas sin hijos pueden aprovechar la oferta

Los niños deben vivir con sus padres para poder aprovechar la oferta.

Los niños deben ser menores de 18 años

La oferta es para viajes de ida y vuelta solamente

Billetes 'oferta otoño' están a la venta en estancos, estaciones y en el Corte Inglés

Para los trenes Talgo el descuento se reduce al 25%

	verdadero	falso	no se sabe
Ejemplo:			
El folleto habla de transporte barato en tren.	×		
1 La oferta es para el verano.			
2 Los adultos también pueden aprovechar la oferta.			
3 Se ofrecen billetes a mitad de precio.			
4 Hay que tener hijos para aprovechar la oferta.			
5 Los niños deben tener la misma dirección que sus padres.			
6 No hay descuento para niños de 19 años.			
7 La oferta no vale para viajes de ida.			
8 Hay que ir a la estación para sacar estos billetes.			
9 Esta oferta tuvo lugar el otoño pasado también.			
10 Los viajes en Talgo son más caros.			

(10)

Section 3 (Higher Tier)

1 Lee unos anuncios en el periódico.

Busco propiedad en la costa para un aparcamiento. Llámame. Rafael 2456432

El Señor Don Inocencio Salazar Donate ha fallecido en el día de ayer a los 86 años de edad. Mañana una misa se celebrará.

Querida Josefina. Discúlpame. Lo siento mucho. Llámame. Pedro

Enhorabuena. El Señor Don Juan Nobles Guerra ha cumplido los 75 años hoy.

Muchas gracias a todos nuestros parientes y amigos por los regalos que recibimos el día de nuestra boda.
José y María Alonso

Quiero comprar apartamento en el barrio de Salamanca – tres dormitorios. Llama 1237273 Ramón

	Rafael	Pedro	Inocencio	José	Ramón	Juan Nobles
1 ¿Quién pide perdón?	☐	☐	☐	☐	☐	☐
2 ¿Quién se ha muerto?	☐	☐	☐	☐	☐	☐
3 ¿Quién quiere mudarse de piso?	☐	☐	☐	☐	☐	☐
4 ¿Quién acaba de casarse?	☐	☐	☐	☐	☐	☐
5 ¿Quién celebra un cumpleaños?	☐	☐	☐	☐	☐	☐

(5)

2 Empareja cada situación con una solución. Pon la letra correcta en la casilla.

Las situaciones

Ejemplo : Quieres comer carne. [1]

1 Quieres comer merluza. ☐
2 Quieres salir y está lloviendo. ☐
3 Estás cansado/a. ☐
4 Estás en la autopista y tienes una avería. ☐
5 Te aburres en casa. ☐
6 Quieres decir 'lo siento' a una amiga. ☐
7 Quieres aprender a conducir. ☐
8 Ves un accidente en la calle. ☐
9 Quieres cruzar la calle mayor. ☐
10 Quieres escribir una carta. ☐

Las soluciones

(a) Llamas a un mecánico.

(b) Le regalas flores.

(c) Buscas un paraguas.

(d) Vas a un paso de peatones.

(e) Buscas un bolígrafo.

(f) Buscas una pescadería.

(g) Sales con una amiga.

(h) Te acuestas.

(i) Llamas a una autoescuela.

(j) Compras una alfombra nueva.

(k) Llamas a los servicios de urgencia.

(l) Vas a la carnicería.

(10)

3 Here is an article about the Spanish golfer Jose Maria Olazabal ('Chema').

JOSE MARIA OLAZABAL

TERCERO DEL MUNDO

Para muchos es el rival y la amenaza de Severiano Ballesteros, cuando lo cierto es que son amigos tanto fuera como dentro del campo. Este año, Chema se ha situado en el tercer puesto en el podio de las grandes figuras, y ni siquiera una mujer — palabras del campeón — podría quitarle esta idea de la cabeza: ser el número uno, el mejor del mundo. Para esta temporada, de momento tiene puestas las ilusiones en Inglaterra: ha dicho que quiere ganar el Open británico.

(a) Read the four statements about the relationship between José María Olazabal and Severiano Ballesteros and place a tick in the box beside the statement which is most accurate according to the article.

(i) They are rivals on the golf course. ☐

(ii) They are rivals except on the golf course. ☐

(iii) They are friends on and off the golf course. ☐

(iv) They are friends only off the golf course. ☐

(1)

(b) What is his overall ambition? (1)

(c) What is his ambition for *this* season? (1)

WJEC

4 Here is an article about the death of John Lennon.

1980 JOHN LENNON MUERE ASESINADO

"¡Mister Lennon!". Ni siquiera tuvo tiempo de contestar. Mark David Chapman disparó contra el "beatle" un revólver calibre 38. Todo el cargador. Eran las diez de la noche de un martes ocho de diciembre. Y acababan de matar a John Lennon. Mark Chapman no intentó escapar. Dejó caer el arma y, según algunos, murmuró "he matado a un 'beatle'". Al lado, abrazada al cuerpo de su marido, Yoko Ono se repetía desconsolada "no puede ser, no puede ser", mientras la gente y la policía llegaban a la calle 72, a la puerta de los apartmentos "Dakota", donde residía el cantante.

La noticia recorrió el mundo como un latigazo. Incluso la agencia soviética "Tass" informó a los países del Este del acontecimiento.

El cuerpo acribillado de John Lennon fue conducido al hospital Roosevelt, donde aún llegó con vida. Pero todos los intentos del doctor Stephen Lynn fueron inútiles: las heridas en pecho y espalda eran mortales. Lennon falleció antes de la medianoche.

Chapman se convirtió en el centro de atención. El criminal, un desequilibrado, había rondado toda la semana el domicilio de la estrella de la canción. Dicho martes, cuando la pareja salía de paseo, el asesino abordó al cantante pidiéndole un autógrafo. No se lo dio. La negativa, quizá, le costó la vida.

Mientras en Nueva York alguien cubría con pétalos de rosa la sangre sobre el pavimento, Londres quedaba conmocionado. La esperanza secreta de volver a escuchar a los "Beatles" reunidos ya no podría cumplirse.

Chapman fue condenado. Pero, como podrían decirle millones de personas, nadie lo condenó por habernos arrancado parte de nuestro pasado.

(a) When was John Lennon shot? (2)
(b) How did his killer react? (2)
(c) What information does the article give to illustrate the world-wide interest in the tragedy?(1)
(d) What possible motive is suggested? (1)
(e) What secret hopes were dashed as a result of his death? (1)

WJEC

Writing (Foundation and Higher Tiers)

Instructions to candidates
Foundation Tier: attempt questions 1, 2 and 3
Higher Tier: attempt questions 3 and 4
You may use a dictionary throughout.

1 Vas de compras. Haz una lista de las tiendas que vas a visitar.
Ejemplo: la carnicería

1 ....
2 ....
3 ....
4 ....
5 ....

2 Escribe una postal de unas 40 palabras describiendo tus vacaciones del año pasado. Menciona estos puntos:

– las fechas de tus vacaciones

					1	2
3	4	5	6	7	8	9
10	11	12	13	14	15	16
17	18	19	20	21	22	23
24	25	26	27	28		

– el hotel de lujo

– el país – tus actividades

– el tiempo

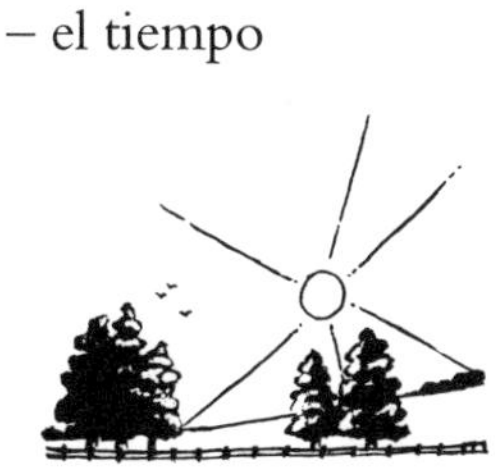

3 El año pasado pasaste tus vacaciones de verano en Málaga. Quieres volver este año. Escribe una carta a la oficina de turismo de Málaga.

Ofrece esta información:
– cuántas personas viajarán
– el tipo de alojamiento que queréis
– las fechas de tu visita
– cómo vas a viajar a Málaga

Describe:
– por qué te gusta Málaga
– por qué no quieres alojarte en el mismo hotel

Pide:
– información sobre excursiones desde Málaga

4 Tu instituto organiza un intercambio con un colegio español. Tienes que preparar una hoja de información describiendo tu colegio y tu región para los estudiantes españoles.

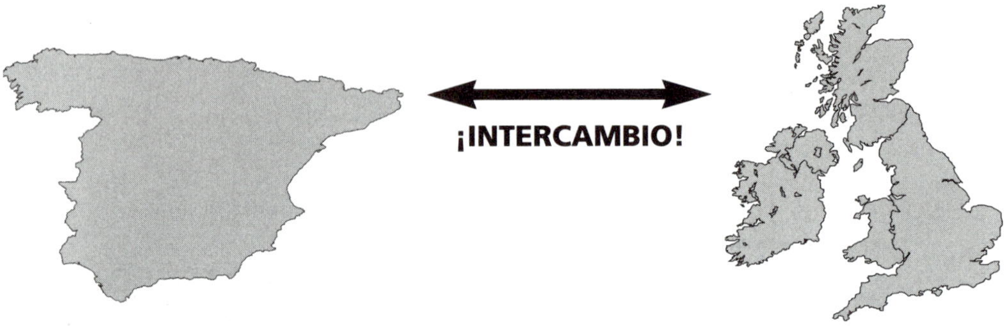

Menciona estos puntos:
– una descripción de tu colegio
– lo que se puede hacer en el tiempo libre
– las ventajas de alojarse con una familia inglesa
– los sitios de interés en los alrededores
– la mejor manera de viajar a tu región desde España

Listening transcripts

Recording 21

Valencia

Valencia está en la costa mediterránea y es importante porque tiene un puerto. Muchísimos barcos usan el puerto todos los días. A muchos ingleses les gusta vivir en Valencia por su clima. Casi nunca nieva en invierno. Hay fiestas magníficas en febrero y muchos turistas visitan Valencia en ese mes.

Recording 22

Estás en un café. Cada cliente pide algo de comer y una bebida ¿Qué piden los cinco clientes?
Cliente 1
Buenos días. Déme mariscos por favor. Y una cerveza.
Cliente 2
Hola. Quiero patatas por favor. Y un vaso de leche.
Cliente 3
Buenos días. Quiero pescado. Y un zumo de naranja.

Cliente 4
Quiero un bocadillo de queso y un vaso de vino.
Cliente 5
Déme un helado. Y un café solo.

Recording 23

De compras

Estás en el Corte Inglés. Quieres comprar una blusa, una maleta, unos plátanos y una corbata.

Planta baja	Joyería, Fotografía, Equipaje
Primera planta	Deportes, Relojería, Ropa de hombres
Segunda planta	Música, Ropa de mujeres, Electrodomésticos
Tercera planta	Comida, Fruta, Legumbres

1 ¿A qué planta vas para la blusa?
2 ¿A qué planta vas para la maleta?
3 ¿A qué planta vas para los plátanos?
4 ¿A qué planta vas para la corbata?

Recording 24

El futuro

José
A mí no me gustan los idiomas. Prefiero las ciencias sobre todo la biología. Me interesa la biología porque el profesor es tan joven e interesante. Un día quiero ser médico y me gustaría trabajar en el extranjero. En mi tiempo libre me gusta patinar. Hay una pista de patinaje cerca de mi casa.

Lolita
No me gusta la historia en absoluto. ¿Sabes por qué? Los libros que usamos están muy pasados de moda. Mi asignatura favorita es el francés. Voy a Francia todos los años de vacaciones. Un día quiero ser profesora de francés. Mi hobby favorito es la lectura. A veces leo tres o cuatro novelas a la semana.

Recording 25

El médico

Tu problema no tiene nada que ver con lo que has comido. No tiene nada que ver con el sol y la playa tampoco. ¡El problema es que te acuestas muy tarde todas las noches! ¡Y bebes demasiado!

Recording 26

El cine Astoria

Estás escuchando un servicio automático para los clientes del cine Astoria. Hoy y mañana solamente ponemos una película histórica llamada *Corazón de acero*. Es una película americana con subtítulos.

Pasado mañana durante siete días ponemos una película de horror llamada *Los muertos*. Se trata de unos fantasmas en una casa antigua en Inglaterra. Finalmente a partir del 23 y hasta el fin del mes ponemos *No me toques* una comedia que ganó una medalla de oro en Italia. Hay tres sesiones para cada una de las tres películas, a las dos, a las siete y a las doce.

Recording 27

El tiempo

Buenas tardes, este es el pronóstico del tiempo para hoy lunes, mañana martes y pasado mañana miércoles.

Hoy lunes habrá un viento glacial con chubascos fuertes. Mañana martes una transformación porque las nubes van a desparecer y se prevé tiempo soleado y estable todo el día. El miércoles se prevé otro cambio porque los vientos y el frío van a volver con lluvia fuerte en todas partes.

Recording 28

Un señor

Me levanto temprano para poder hacer footing antes de ir a mi trabajo. Me gusta mi trabajo y trabajo ocho horas al día. Pero nunca hago horas extraordinarias porque no quiero cansarme. A mediodía voy a la piscina y paso una hora nadando. Nunca bebo alcohol y tengo cuidado con lo que como y cuánto como. No salgo nunca por la tarde y poca gente me visita en casa.

Recording 29

Un empleo

¿Desempleado? ¿Por qué no trabajas para La Compañía Rovi? Buscamos representantes que puedan trabajar en el medio oriente. No pagarás impuestos y el alojamiento será gratis. Llámanos.

Recording 30

Conversación de novios

Conchita
No sé si podemos seguir así. Es la quinta vez que salimos juntos y es la quinta vez que llegas tarde. Llevo todo el día trabajando y luego tengo que esperarte a ti. No puedo más. Es intolerable.

Ramón
Y yo tengo unas cosas que decirte. Sí, tienes razón. Hemos salido y cuatro veces yo he pagado todo. Nunca compartes los gastos, nunca dices que tú vas a pagar algo. Mis amigos se burlan de mí cuando se lo cuento. Esto no puede ser.

Recording 31

Pero ¡qué bonitas son! Pero ¿cómo sabías que los claveles son mis flores favoritas? Yo creía que ibas a olvidar mi cumpleaños. Te voy a dar un beso.

Suggested answers

Listening

Section 1 (Foundation Tier)

Recording 21

(a) Mediterranean coast. **(b)** It is a port. **(c)** The climate. **(d)** February.

Recording 22

1 (e) (a) **2** (f) (d) **3** (d) (b) **4** (a) (e) **5** (c) (c)

Recording 23

1 (b) **2** (d) **3** (a) **4** (c)

Section 2 (Foundation and Higher Tiers)

Recording 24

1 biología **2** ser médico **3** patinar **4** francés **5** ser profesora de francés **6** lectura

Recording 25

(b) (d)

Section 3 (Higher Tier)

Recording 26

El cine Astoria

	verdadero	falso
Ponen *Corazón de acero* durante tres días.		×
Corazón de acero es una película de amor.		×
Corazón de acero es subtitulado.	×	
Los muertos es una película de miedo.	×	
Ponen *Los muertos* durante una semana.	×	
Los muertos tiene lugar en Gran Bretaña.	×	
No me toques no es una película de risa.		×
No me toques no ha ganado un premio.		×
Se pone cada película tres veces al día.	×	
La última sesión es a medianoche.	×	

Recording 27

(b)

Recording 28

(b)

Recording 29

No tienes que pagar impuestos. El alojamiento es gratis.

Recording 30

Conchita (c) Ramón (c)

Recording 31

1 (c) **2** (a)

Speaking

Role-play 1

Teacher Estás en una estación. Yo soy el empleado/la empleada.¿Adónde vas?
You Quiero ir a Oviedo.
Teacher ¿Qué clase?
You Quiero ir en segunda clase.
Teacher ¿Billete de ida?
You Un billete de ida y vuelta, por favor.
Teacher Tres mil pesetas.
You ¿A qué hora sale el tren?
Teacher A las dos y cuarto.
You ¿A qué hora llega a Oviedo?
Teacher A las seis.

Role-play 2

Teacher Buenos días ¿Qué pasa?
You Buenos días. Mi amigo/a tiene dolor de cabeza.
Teacher ¿Por qué no dice nada.

You Mi amigo/a no habla español.
Teacher ¿Qué causó el dolor de cabeza?
You Mi amigo estaba tomando el sol en la playa.
Teacher ¿Cuánto tiempo estuvo en la playa?
You Seis horas.
Teacher Es demasiado. ¿Cuándo volvéis a Inglaterra?
You Volveremos en avión el dos de agosto.
Teacher Muy bien. Toma estas pastillas.

Role-play 3

Teacher ¿Qué vamos a hacer?
You Quiero ir a la playa.
Teacher No me gusta la playa.
You Llevo una semana en España y todavía no he visitado la playa.
Teacher Bueno. Vamos a la playa. ¿A qué hora?
You A las dos y media.
Teacher No puedo. Tengo que comer a las dos y media.
You Entonces vamos a las tres y media.
Teacher Vale.
You ¿Nos encontramos en la estación de autobuses y tomamos el autobús a la playa?
Teacher Perfecto. Hasta luego.

Reading

Section 1

1 **1** **(a)** 975.
(b) Winter clothes.

2 **(a)** Dogs.
(b) Ball games.

3 **(a)** How many years have you played tennis?
(b) Do you play in a team?

4 **(a)** Old furniture.
(b) Old churches.
(c) Basketball.
(d) Dancing.

2 **1** (d)
2 la llave de tu habitación
3 342573
4 cartas
5 una caja fuerte

(5)

3 **1** (e)
2 (d)
3 (b)
4 (c)
5 (a)

Section 2

1 **1** Está en paro
2 (d)
3 (d)
4 (a)
5 (c)

(5)

2

	verdadero	falso	no se sabe
Ejemplo: El folleto habla de transporte barato en tren.	×		
1 La oferta es para el verano.		×	
2 Los adultos también pueden aprovechar la oferta.	×		
3 Se ofrecen billetes a mitad de precio.	×		
4 Hay que tener hijos para aprovechar la oferta.		×	
5 Los niños deben tener la misma dirección que sus padres.	×		
6 No hay descuento para niños de 19 años.	×		
7 La oferta no vale para viajes de ida.	×		
8 Hay que ir a la estación para sacar estos billetes.		×	
9 Esta oferta tuvo lugar el otoño pasado también.			×
10 Los viajes en Talgo son más caros.	×		

(10)

Section 3

1 **1** Pedro **4** José
2 Inocencio **5** Juan Nobles
3 Ramón

(5)

2 **1** (f) **6** (b)
2 (c) **7** (i)
3 (h) **8** (k)
4 (a) **9** (d)
5 (g) **10** (e)

(10)

3 **(a)** (iii).
(b) To be world champion.
(c) To win the British Open.

(3)

4 **(a)** 10pm Tuesday December 8th 1980.
(b) He did not try to escape, he dropped his gun and said 'I've killed a Beatle'.
(c) The Soviet Press informed Eastern countries.
(d) John Lennon refused him his autograph.
(e) The hope of seeing the Beatles re-united.

(7)

Writing (Foundation and Higher Tiers)

1 **1** el supermercado
2 la panadería
3 la zapatería
4 la frutería
5 la lechería

2

Hola Pedro:

Acabo de pasar dos semanas en España – del catorce al veintiocho de junio. Nuestro hotel era excelente: había dos piscinas. Fui a la playa, jugué al tenis y visité las discotecas. Hacía sol todos los días.
Hasta pronto

James

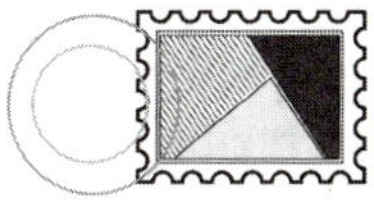

9 The Street
Smalltown
Northshire NT33 6XY
Gran Bretaña

3

Swansea
el 4 de abril

Estimado Señor:

Soy inglés y pasé unas semanas del año pasado en Málaga el año pasado. Quiero volver a Málaga este año. ¿Puede Vd. encontrarme un hotel barato?

Seremos cuatro: mi amigo, mi hermano, mi hermana y yo. Buscamos cuatro habitaciones individuales y preferimos habitaciones con baño. Llegaremos en avión el tres de junio y nos marcharemos el diecisiete de junio.

Me encanta Málaga. Me gustan las playas y las montañas cerca de la ciudad. Sobre todo me gusta el clima. El año pasado me quedé en el Hotel Sol cerca del ayuntamiento. No quiero volver allí porque era demasiado ruidoso, había insectos en la cama y creo que el dueño es un ladrón.

Este año quiero hacer más excursiones para visitar los sitios de interés cerca de la ciudad. Haga el favor de mandarme detalles de excursiones cerca de la ciudad.

Le saluda atentamente
J. Parkinson

4

Mis amigos españoles:

Esperamos vuestra visita con mucha ilusión. Estamos muy orgullosos de nuestro colegio y tendréis que visitarlo y asistir a las clases. Tenemos laboratorios, una piscina, terrenos de deporte, canchas de tenis y muchos otros aspectos interesantes.

Durante vuestra visita, vamos a salir por la tarde a las discotecas por aquí. También hay clubs para jóvenes y un cine con doce pantallas y un teatro. Los jóvenes de aquí esperan vuestra visita con mucha impaciencia.

Estaráis alojados con familias inglesas durante vuestra visita. Es la mejor manera de aprender inglés y nadie tendrá que compartir habitación.

Cerca de aquí hay unas montañas interesantes y vamos a organizar una excursión para que podáis verlas. Además Londres no está tan lejos y podremos ir a visitar los monumentos e ir al teatro.

La mejor manera de viajar aquí es en avión. Se puede tomar un tren y el barco y luego otro tren pero es muy pesado. Nosotros iremos al aeropuerto a recibiros.

Hasta muy pronto.
Jane, John etc

Index

EDUCATIONAL

GCSE Spanish CD/Cassette

If you have purchased a copy of our Study Guide for GCSE Spanish and would like to buy the accompanying CD or cassette, or if you have bought the CD and would like to swap it for a cassette, please tick the relevant box below, complete the order form and return it to:

Letts Educational Ltd
Aldine Place
London W12 8AW
Telephone 020 8740 2266

Forenames (Mr/Ms) ______________________________

Surname ______________________________

Address ______________________________

____

______________________ Postcode ______________

Please swap the enclosed CD for a cassette: ☐

Please send me

		Quantity	Price (incl VAT)	Total
GCSE Spanish CD (ISBN: 1-85758-825-8)	☐	_____	£4.00	_____
GCSE Spanish cassette (ISBN: 1-85758-822-3)	☐	_____	£4.00	_____
Add postage – UK and ROI 75p for each CD/cassette				_____

I enclose a cheque/postal order for £ _____
(made payable to Letts Educational)

Or charge to Access/Visa card No. ☐☐☐☐☐☐☐☐☐☐☐☐☐☐☐☐

Expiry date ______________________________

Signature ______________________________